Ever Closer Union?

By the same author

Passages from Antiquity to Feudalism
Lineages of the Absolutist State

Considerations on Western Marxism
Arguments within English Marxism
In the Tracks of Historical Materialism
The Antinomies of Antonio Gramsci

English Questions
A Zone of Engagement
The Origins of Postmodernity
Spectrum

The New Old World
The Indian Ideology
Brazil Apart

American Foreign Policy and Its Thinkers
The H-Word

Ever Closer Union?

Europe in the West

Perry Anderson

London • New York

First published by Verso 2021

1 3 5 7 9 10 8 6 4 2

Verso
UK: 6 Meard Street, London W1F 0EG
US: 20 Jay Street, Suite 1010, Brooklyn, NY 11201
versobooks.com

Verso is the imprint of New Left Books

ISBN-13: 978-1-83976-441-7
ISBN-13: 978-1-83976-444-8 (US EBK)
ISBN-13: 978-1-83976-443-1 (UK EBK)

British Library Cataloguing in Publication Data
A catalogue record for this book is available from the British Library

Library of Congress Cataloging-in-Publication Data
A catalog record for this book is available from the Library of Congress

Typeset in Minion Pro by MJ & N Gavan, Truro, Cornwall
Printed and bound by CPI Group (UK) Ltd, Croydon, CR0 4YY

CONTENTS

ACKNOWLEDGMENTS

The first version of Chapter 1 appeared in *New Left Review* 119, September–October 2019; Chapters 2, 3 and 4 in the *London Review of Books*, 17 December 2020, 7 January 2021 and 21 January 2021 respectively.

My thanks to William Allen, Daniel Cohen, Anton Jäger, Zep Kalb, Kawai Masahiro, Nicholas Mulder, R. Taggart Murphy, and Merijn Oudenampsen for advice on different aspects of this book.

PREFACE

This book can be regarded as a sequel. In 2009 I published a study of the European Union, *The New Old World*, that brought together an assessment of the nature of continental integration with considerations on the recent history of three leading states of the EU—France, Germany and Italy—and the principal candidate—Turkey—for its extension further east. Composed in the years following the Treaty of Maastricht, *The New Old World* appeared as the hammer blow of the global financial crisis of 2008 started to hit Europe. A decade later, *Ever Closer Union?* was written as the global pandemic of 2020 swept the West, shaking Europe and the United States with comparable severity.

The inter-connexion between the two wings of the Atlantic zone was one of the leitmotifs of the *New Old World*, which traced the determinant role of Washington in the inception and consolidation of the European Community, and—a pattern attracting much less notice—the overwhelming predominance of American scholarship in the most original literature, be it economic, political, sociological, juridical or historical, on European integration. In the altered light of today's conditions, *Ever Closer Union?* returns to these two subjects, the factual and the intellectual weight of the United States in the evolution of the

EU. The book's division corresponds to them. In Part I, attention falls on the pivotal role of America in the onset and outcome—not least in Europe—of the global economic crash of 2008. In Part II, the focus shifts to the EU itself, where an intellectual reversal has occurred, American scholarship on Europe dwindling as the United States, torn by intensifying conflicts, has become increasingly introverted, while once lagging European studies now command the field.

In this division, the impact of two writers stands out as central. Adam Tooze and Luuk van Middelaar are the authors of the most important accounts of, respectively, the global financial crisis and the character of European integration which we possess today, *Crashed* and *The Passage to Europe*. Understandably, each has earned wide public celebration of their work. But to date neither has received sustained intellectual scrutiny of the kind attempted below. That they have much in common is clear. Belonging to the same generation, which grew up in the closing years of the Cold War, one is British by birth, holding a chair in New York, the other Dutch by birth, holding a chair in Leiden while active much of the time in Brussels. Both are historians by profession: the first an authority in economic history, the second in political history. Both are accomplished writers, enjoying a broad readership. Both are polymaths, with a range of theoretical and cultural interests far beyond the ruck of their peers. By conviction, both are liberals, and both outspoken champions of the European Union.

Along with such similarities come several contrasts. Tooze, as he explains in the introduction to *Crashed*, is a liberal of the left, where by reason of philosophical formation and party affiliation van Middelaar is a liberal of the right. The former is proficient with financial and logistical statistics that are in some measure *terra incognita* for the latter, more at home with the history of ideas than of figures. Nor is the corpus of the two symmetrical. In the Anglosphere *The Passage to Europe* (2013) predates *Crashed* (2018) by five years, and by a further four years in Dutch (2009); likewise van Middelaar's second book *Alarums and Excursions* was published in the Netherlands in 2017. *Crashed*, on the other hand, forms the conclusion of a trilogy whose preceding volumes *Wages of Destruction* (2006) and *The Deluge* (2014) cover the First World War, its aftermath and the Second World War, all three viewing Europe in the light of America. Van Middelaar's pair of studies has no such longitude, though its tacit horizon of reference goes further back, to the time of the Congress of Vienna.

In each case, I have sought to take into account the overall arc of their work, rather than simply its best-known expression, and to relate its arguments to alternative explanations of the same history. In the case of Tooze's trilogy, this has meant: first, looking at the way in which its volumes are interconnected by the special position accorded the United States in global developments of the past and the present century, above all those affecting Europe; second, considering the hermeneutic preferences that underlie the set; third, registering accounts of the origins of the financial crisis of 2008, and of the measures taken to repair it, more critical than those offered in *Crashed*; and lastly, reflecting on the experience of the one great centre of advanced capitalism, Japan, which escapes Tooze's attention, and what light it throws on the performance of the self-proclaimed 'Firefighters' of the Federal Reserve and the Treasury in Washington. In the case of van Middelaar's diptych, the same approach has meant looking at the importance of a philosophical mentor in his formation, Frank Ankersmit; distinguishing the status of *Passage*, a work of history composed after seasons as an assistant in Brussels and The Hague, from *Alarums*, a political legitimation of the performance of the EU under a president whom he served as adviser and speechwriter; asking how far van Middelaar's profile finds a precedent in the epoch of the Restoration; and, finally, surveying independent European minds who have studied the evolution of the EU from angles—economic, juridical, political, social or cultural—overlooked by van Middelaar, and reaching rather different verdicts on it. The work of these writers forms the focus of the third chapter of this book.

The concluding fourth chapter considers the special case of Britain and the reasons behind its exit from the Union in 2020. It looks at the arguments advanced for and against preservation of its membership of the EU, the social configuration of the camps locked in struggle over the question, and what the outcome might suggest for the future of Europe in a Union otherwise left intact. In a foreword to *The New Old World*, I remarked that I did not regret the absence of Britain from it, as so little of moment had happened there since the departure of Thatcher. The validity of that judgment lapsed with the fall of New Labour, whose thirteen nondescript years in office, principally devoted to setting Thatcher's legacy in amber, were broken only by its debacle in Iraq. Thereafter, from the austerity imposed by the Cameron regime to meet the global financial crisis, to the shock delivered to the country's bipartisan establishment by the referendum on Europe in 2016 and its aftermath, the line of eventful descent is clear enough. Whether after Brexit the United Kingdom is any more secure in its own borders than was Europe before Brexit remains to be seen. Not raised here, that question is addressed in a separate essay, tracing the fortunes of the British political system since the sixties.[1]

1 'Ukania Perpetua?', *New Left Review* 125, September–October 2020, pp. 35–107.

Where do the US and the EU stand today? As in the past, during Trump's Republican presidency the American economy performed better than the eurozone, posting an average growth rate of 2.5 per cent through 2017–19, as against 1.8 per cent across the Atlantic, with unemployment at 3.8 per cent compared with nearly 8 per cent. Once the pandemic struck, the US economy contracted by some 3.5 per cent, while the eurozone doubled that to some 7 per cent, though the distance between the two in unemployment narrowed significantly—figures concealing greater popular misery in America, given its higher rates of poverty and lack of social protection. Yet as after the crash of 2008, economic recovery once again came quicker in the US than in Europe; no doubt a factor, along with falling unemployment and rising worker incomes in the previous three years, accounting in part for the relative popular resilience of the Republican vote amid defeat in 2020.[2] Politically speaking, however, economic contrasts with the US were no more relevant in Europe during these years than they were under the two preceding administrations. What mattered to official and public opinion was less the domestic record than the foreign policy of the Trump regime.

There, unease between Europe and America was not new. Bush's invasion of Iraq split the governments of the EU and widely antagonized public opinion in the Old World, offended by the brusque style of his administration. Obama was greeted with little short of popular adulation, but chancelleries were soon aware how rarely his mind was engaged by Europe.

2 See Christopher Caldwell's reflection on 'the first egalitarian boom since well back into the twentieth century'—in 2019, 'the share of overall earnings going to the bottom 90 per cent of earners *rose* for the first time in a decade': 'The Biden Popular Front Is Doomed to Unravel', *New Republic*, 25 November 2020.

Imperceptibly, the two sides of the Atlantic had already drifted somewhat apart by 2016. Trump's belligerent proclamation of America First inevitably widened the distance between them. In trade, the protectionism of the new administration, though more noisy threat than action, inevitably ruffled feathers. Conflict brewed over taxation of Silicon giants, without coming as yet to the boil. Tensions were more acute over policies towards the rest of the world. There, the area of maximum friction lay in the Middle East, as Trump rescinded the deal Obama had reached, together with Europe, to force Iran to abandon its nuclear programme, tightening sanctions the deal had never entirely lifted. Though resentful of this unilateral action, the EU signatories to the deal—Germany, France and Britain—were in no position to circumvent it, given US control of the international banking system. Nor, however much they disapproved, could Atlantic etiquette allow them to protest Trump's relocation of the US embassy in Israel to Jerusalem, or say-so for prospective annexations in the West Bank. The traditional solidarity between Europe and America was strained but not ruptured by these initiatives.

Elsewhere, as in the past, it still operated at full bore. In the Sahel, US arms and special forces supported French troops in a common battle against jihadis. In the same cause, French and British bombers supported US air and land power in Syria. In Latin America, the EU closed ranks with the US in recognizing the congressional claimant to the Venezuelan presidency. Along the most important front of all, relations with the two great powers of China and Russia, a more nuanced unity prevailed. Where China was the prime foe for America, against whom Trump declared an all-out economic and political offensive, Russia was treated as a lesser danger. For the EU both were menaces to Western democracy, but the order of battle tended to be the opposite. Viewed from Europe, Russia was not only closer geographically, but perceived as a deadlier threat; whereas China was a more distant power, and notwithstanding its own charge-sheet of repression, might—if held at arm's length—serve as potentially pragmatic partner in questions of commerce and climate. Member states resisting American pressure to cancel the Nordstream gas line from Russia to Germany, and to defer a trade pact with China, the EU has so far pursued its own economic interests, while joining with the US in resonant demands for an ideologically tough-minded defence of the Free World.

If much transatlantic ill-feeling—muffled at summits, violent in assorted media on the European side—marked Trump's tenure of the US presidency, without ever becoming an open rift, diplomatic *politesse* was not the only reason. For all its verbal belligerence, his administration was aware of the electoral risk of foreign adventures, and in practice was in some ways more prudent than its predecessor: overtures to North Korea, no surge in Afghanistan, no threats of war on Iran, no subventions to revolt in Syria, no second Libya, no second Yemen; even imports from the PRC continued to rise. Publicly, the advent of the Biden presidency heralds a grand reconciliation between the EU and the US, as that of Obama did in its time. How far this will extend from ceremony to substance is less clear, if only because of the internal distractions of each, and the limits of Trump's departure from established US norms. But certainly the prospect of a New Cold War would solder the hierarchical unity of the Atlantic order fast once more. As in the past, the inequality of the pact between the two sides, inflected but not so far fundamentally altered this century, rests on the overwhelming military preponderance of the Pentagon and the financial grip of the Treasury on the world's banking and trading system, neither of which Europe is in a position to challenge.

For the moment, nothing perhaps captures the emergent relationship between Europe and America in the West better than the way in which the EU has responded to the crisis of the pandemic—with a 'Next Europe' package that for the first time authorizes the creation of mutual bonds, to the tune of 700 billion euros, to stave off bankruptcies and succour the stricken: just what so many faulted the Union for failing to produce in the global financial crisis. Among them was Adam Tooze, and in greeting the bonds as a historic breakthrough for the Union, he is joined by Luuk van Middelaar. For leading statesmen of the EU, Macron at their head, these offer a momentous step towards a Europe that can hold its own with America and China. Yet how was their promise popularly described, in the press and parliament of the continent alike? At long last, the 'Hamiltonian moment' of the Union. In the European imaginary, America remains the lodestar. The title of this book refers, of course, to the best-known phrase of the preamble to the Treaty of Rome, whose implications for Europe remain still unresolved. But it can be given an ambiguous twist. Tacitly, it lends itself to the West as well.

I. ATLANTIC ORDER

1

THE ARC OF LEADERSHIP?

In his thoughtful consideration of Adam Tooze's *Crashed: How a Decade of Financial Crises Changed the World*, Cédric Durand salutes the magnitude of Tooze's achievement—a 'landmark account' of the mechanisms precipitating the economic disaster that started to engulf the West in 2008 and of the remedies and ruins that followed. Particularly impressive, he remarks, is the way the book illuminates 'the technical workings of financial markets and asset-backed commercial paper without losing sight of the political dynamics at stake':

> As Tooze writes: 'Political choice, ideology and agency are everywhere across the narrative with highly consequential results, not merely as disturbing factors but as vital reactions to the huge volatility and contingency generated by the malfunctioning of the giant "systems" and "machines" and apparatuses of financial engineering.' *Crashed* is, indeed, a highly political book.[1]

1 'In the Crisis Cockpit', *New Left Review* 116/117, March–June 2019, pp. 201–2, 212. *Crashed* was received with virtually unanimous applause in the periodical press—*New York Times, Financial Times, Washington Post, Guardian, New York Review of Books, London Review of Books*, and so forth—but, if only for reasons of space, little or no engagement in depth.

At the same time, Durand observes, its narrative is no simple—or rather in this case, of course, highly complex and intricate—empirical tracking of the crisis and its outcomes. It possesses definite 'conceptual underpinnings', suggested by Tooze himself in acknowledging his debt to Wynne Godley's use of 'stock-flow consistency' to model the financial interactions between public, private and foreign sectors. This in Durand's view supplies 'the unstated backbone' of Tooze's general argument.[2]

Both judgments appear sound. But in Durand's exposition a paradox attaches to each of them, since by the end of his review, somewhat different notes are struck. For Godley, one of the key advantages of the stock-flow consistency approach was that it integrated the financial with the real economy, as alternative models did not. Durand, however, remarks that *Crashed* 'does not discuss the concrete intertwining of the financial and productive sectors in the global economy at all', and so 'fails to set the financial crisis in the context of the structural crisis tendencies within contemporary capitalist economies'. This observation in turn generates another, which might seem to put in question Durand's overall tribute to the book. For eventually he writes of 'Tooze's unwillingness to investigate the relations between the political and the economic', a reluctance that 'ultimately undermines his account of the crisis decade'.[3] Logically, the question then arises: do these two apparent contradictions lie in Tooze's work, or in Durand's review of it? Or can both be coherent in their own terms?

I

Perhaps the best way of approaching this question is to turn to Durand's own work on the metastases of contemporary

2 Ibid., p. 208.
3 Ibid., pp. 209–11.

capitalism. With a reticence that does him honour—all but unheard of in an Anglosphere where even bibliographies so often become mere catalogues of self-promotion—he makes no reference to *Le Capital fictif*, which appeared in France in 2014 (its English edition *Fictitious Capital* in 2017), though its bearing on the concerns of *Crashed* is plain. A succinct, luminous study, in it Durand displays a combination rare in the literature on the economic landscape of the new century: in a bare 150 pages, a driving conceptual energy joined to a controlling empirical grasp of statistical data across all the major capitalist states. Organized around the growth in the object of its title—a term coined by the first Earl of Liverpool, secretary for war in North's administration under George III, received by Ricardo, theorized in differing ways by Marx and Hayek alike, whose history it traces—*Fictitious Capital* sets out to show the character and logic of the financial system that brought the world to crisis in 2008, and has only continued to burgeon since.

What are the leading themes of the book? At the root of the instability that has triggered successive crises in the last forty years, first in the periphery and then in the core of the global capitalist economy, lies the peculiarity that distinguishes financial markets from markets in goods and services.

> Whereas in normal times rising prices weaken demand in the real economy, the opposite is generally true of financial securities: the more prices increase, the more these securities are in demand. The same applies the other way round: during a crisis, the fall in prices engenders fire sales, which translate into the acceleration of the price collapse. This peculiarity of financial products derives from the fact that their purchase—dissociated from any use-value—corresponds to a purely speculative rationale; the objective is to obtain surplus-value by reselling them at a higher price at some later point.

On the way up, 'the self-sustaining price rise fuelled by agents' expectations is further exaggerated by credit. Indebtedness increases prices, and since the securities can serve as the counterpart to fresh loans, their increasing value allows agents to take on more debt.' On the way down, as asset bubbles start to burst, 'economic agents trying to meet the deadlines on their debt repayments are forced to sell at discounted prices', unleashing 'a self-sustaining movement towards depression, which only state intervention can interrupt.'[4]

Since the deregulation of capital flows in the eighties, this general mechanism has been turbo-charged by the huge expansion of financial markets within the global economic system, with not only vastly larger forms and magnitudes of private credit, public bonds and equities—the three forms of fictitious capital designated by Marx—but the development of new kinds of transaction still further removed from processes of production, as shadow banking and financial innovations twist and lengthen the chains of indebtedness. 'Contract swaps, structured products and option contracts are multiplying and combining among themselves. They are limited by nothing other than the imaginations of the financial actors.' High-volume speculation ceases to be an outgrowth of booms: thanks to the flexibility of derivatives, 'it becomes an activity independent of the business cycle.'[5] The result is a radical transformation of the relations between financial and commercial transactions, and a vertiginous rise in the weight of finance in the world economy. By 2007, the total (notional) value of derivatives was some ten times that of global GDP. By 2013 the value of purely financial

---

4 Cédric Durand, *Fictitious Capital*, London–New York 2017, pp. 28–9. Henceforward *FC*.

5 Ibid., pp. 66, 69.

transactions outclassed those of trade and investment combined a hundred to one.[6]

That such an inverted pyramid should in one way or another topple into crises is no surprise, each time requiring central banks to act as unlimited lender of last resort, and governments to sustain demand by letting deficits soar, to save the system—the crash of 2008 being the latest and most spectacular case to date. But as Durand observes, the very success of such rescue operations breeds the conditions for the next crisis. If 'economic policies have undeniably succeeded in their effort to keep the collapse under control: all the post-war financial crises have been contained', the subsequent return of confidence in due course undoes itself, as financial operators become increasingly willing to take new chances in the knowledge that central banks 'will do everything to prevent systemic risk becoming a reality'. Such is the paradox of government intervention. 'As capacities for crisis-management improve and financial actors as well as regulators become more optimistic', financial innovation revives and regulation relaxes, leading to yet more complex and sophisticated products, expanding credit at the cost of the quality of the assets acquired. 'This, in turn, leads to small crises which are rapidly overcome thanks to the improved capacity to handle them. This cumulative dynamic produces a financial super-cycle through which the accumulated risks become increasingly large—that is, the relative weight of speculative finance and Ponzi schemes constantly increases', and with it the scale and cost of state intervention to contain the crisis. According to IMF calculations, between the autumn of 2008 and the beginning of 2009, the total support extended to the financial sector by states and central banks of

6 Ibid., pp. 69–71.

the advanced capitalist countries was equivalent to 50.4 per cent of world GDP.[7]

The swollen size of the financial sector in the economies of the West has meant, as is well known, that its share of total profits has increased too. For Durand, this raises the question which has puzzled others working in a more or less Marxist tradition of where these profits come from. But here, as he notes, there is a larger problem. Since the eighties, the rate of investment in the core zone of capitalism has steadily fallen, and with it rates of growth, decade by decade. Yet in the same period, profits have remained high. Indeed, as David Kotz has shown, in the United States the years between 2010 and 2017 saw a rate of accumulation lower, yet a rate of profit higher, than in any decade since the time of Reagan.[8] So where are these profits in general coming from? Durand's answer is that they represent an updated version of Hobson's vision of the future at the start of the twentieth century: namely the extraction of high levels of profit from investment in production in zones of cheap labour in the periphery of the system, above all in Asia. If this is so, the 'enigma of profits without accumulation' would dissolve, because firms are indeed investing; not in their domestic economies, where growth, employment and wages stagnate, but in overseas locations, where they have secured very high rates of return.

Prima facie there are two difficulties with this argument. The first is where in principle the boundary of 'fictitious' capital —if defined as capital which 'circulates without production having yet been realized, representing a claim on a future real

7 Ibid., pp. 31–2, 39.

8 'End of the Neoliberal Era? Crisis and Restructuring of American Capitalism', *New Left Review* 113, September–October 2018, p. 45.

valorization process'[9]—lies, since formally speaking virtually all investment meets this criterion, as capital laid out in anticipation of profitable returns.[10] The second is how in practice the significance of purely financial payments, as distinct from straightforward profits from productive operations, is to be estimated in the flow of foreign direct investment to cheap labour markets.[11] In taking dividends from foreign assets as a proxy for these—he cites research from the US and France—it is unclear how far Durand is simply re-tabling the first difficulty. That a 'knot between financialization and globalization', as he puts it, exists, is not in doubt. But how analytically it is tied remains elusive.

No such ambiguity attaches to the conclusion of his book. Contrary to received wisdom, though financial instability has 'negative externalities that affect all actors', it does not follow that its absence is therefore a blessing for all. Financial stability is not in itself 'a public good from which everyone benefits'. It is enough to see the payoffs of the operations to restore it in

9 *FC*, p. 55.

10 See on this Costas Lapavitsas, *Profiting without Producing: How Finance Exploits Us All*, London–New York 2013, pp. 28–9, who defines Marx's concept of fictitious capital, distinguishing it from loan or other interest-bearing forms of capital, as 'a technical idea amounting to net present value accounting—that is, to ideal sums of money that result via discounting streams of future payments attached to financial assets. These ideal sums correspond to financial prices that could fluctuate independently of the money capital originally expended to purchase the financial asset in question.' Put in other terms, capital is 'fictitious' if expended not on anticipated future returns from production or physical assets, but on values generated at one or more—today, infinitely many—removes from these, which can diverge very sharply from them.

11 Suggesting a hesitancy in his exposition, Durand speaks both of the financialization of non-financial firms, and of the paradox of profits without accumulation, as 'partly' an illusion or an artifice, without further specification: *FC*, pp. 145, 149.

2008–09. A year later the share of US government bonds held by the richest 1 per cent of the population had climbed to over 40 per cent. Durand's verdict is trenchant.

> The hegemony of finance—the most fetishized form of wealth—is only maintained by the public authorities' unconditional support. Left to itself, fictitious capital would collapse; and yet would pull down the whole of our economies in its wake. In truth, finance is a master blackmailer. Financial hegemony dresses up in the liberal trappings of the market, yet captures the old sovereignty of the state all the better to squeeze the body of society to feed its own profits.[12]

II

Enough has been said to indicate why Durand could, for all his admiration of *Crashed*, conclude that ultimately it falls short of the promise of its postulates. In itself, however, such a limiting judgment offers no specification of what might explain the gap perceived between the two. What kind of method permits bracketing of the real economy in a diagnostic of the vicissitudes of finance? What sort of politics informs the architecture of the ensuing work? Initial clues to these questions can be found in two passages from Tooze's writing. In the first, a review of Geoff Mann's *In the Long Run We Are All Dead: Keynesianism, Political Economy and Revolution* (2017), he defines the distinctive virtue of Keynes's outlook as a 'situational and tactical awareness' of the problems for liberal democracy inherent in the operations of the business cycle in a capitalist economy, requiring pragmatic crisis management in the form of punctual adjustments without

12 Ibid., pp. 155, 100.

illusion of permanency.[13] In the second, from the Introduction to *Crashed*, he puts his political cards on the table. 'The tenth anniversary of 2008', he writes, 'is not a comfortable vantage-point for a left-liberal historian whose personal loyalties are divided among England, Germany, the "island of Manhattan" and the EU.'[14]

To see how these remarks bear on the issues raised by Durand, it is best to consider *Crashed* as the third volume of a trilogy, preceded by Tooze's two previous works, *The Deluge: The Great War and the Remaking of Global Order* (2014) and *The Wages of Destruction: The Making and Breaking of the Nazi Economy* (2006), a set which has arguably made Tooze the outstanding modern economic historian of his cohort.[15] As a public voice, he is more than this, ranging across the pages of the *New York Times*, *Wall Street Journal*, *Die Zeit*, *Der Spiegel*, *Financial Times*, *Guardian* and more, as well as radio and television. The trio of books that now defines his career does not trace a continuous narrative, and its composition does not follow a chronological sequence—the first book deals with the years 1933 to 1945, the second 1916 to 1932, the third 2006 to 2018—nor possess a uniform focus. But that it displays a governing thematic unity is plain.

13 Tooze, 'Tempestuous Seasons', *London Review of Books*, 13 September 2018.

14 *Crashed: How a Decade of Financial Crises Changed the World*, London 2018, p. 21.

15 Niall Ferguson, an obvious alternative candidate, after a trio of impressive works in the nineties, culminating in *The Pity of War* (1998), altered course in the new century, a turn described in a later volume: 'Like four of my five last books, *Civilization* was from its earliest inception a television series as well as a book': *Civilization: The West and the Rest*, London 2011, p. xviii. Tooze, a close contemporary of Ferguson, grew up partly in West Germany—he is bilingual—and has held positions successively at Cambridge, Yale and Columbia.

A massive work of detailed historical scholarship, *Wages of Destruction* unfolds a commanding account of the German economy that Hitler inherited on coming to power in the depths of the Depression, the rapid recovery that the Nazi regime engineered with a high-speed rearmament programme, the resource constraints it had hit by the end of the thirties, its ensuing military conquests to overcome these, their over-reaching in the invasion of the Soviet Union, and the desperate ratcheting up of production, with an intensified resort to slave labour, as defeat loomed in the East and the Allies closed in from the West. If Tooze overstates the comparative backwardness of the German economy, dragged down by its ailing small-peasant and archaic-landlord agriculture, and underrates the rise in popular consumption under the Third Reich so long as it remained at peace,[16] such questions of emphasis scarcely affect the scale of his achievement, above all as his account moves into high gear, plotting the interplay between economic and military decisions in the Second World War itself.

Framing this narrative, however, is a thesis whose connexion with it is disconcertingly forced: a claim essentially supererogatory, tenuously stitched around the story it tells of the 'making and breaking' of the Nazi economy. Contrary to common belief, Tooze argues, in Hitler's mind the supreme enemy against which his mobilization of the Third Reich for continental war took aim lay not in the steppes to the East, but across the ocean to the far West. Not the bacillus of Bolshevism but the might of the United States, headquarters of world Jewry, was the existential threat to Germany that obsessed him, and governed his ambitions of

16 For these criticisms, see Robert Gordon, 'Did Economics Cause World War Two?', National Bureau of Economic Research, Working Paper 14560, December 2008; and Harold James, review of *Wages of Destruction* in *Central European History* 40: 2, June 2007, pp. 366–71.

aggression. The destruction of Communism and conquest of Russia was just a means, not an end, Operation Barbarossa no more than a way-station—the acquisition of a territorial and resource platform capable of rivalling the vast open spaces of the American colossus—in the battle for world domination. Historically, then, 'America should provide the pivot for our understanding of the Third Reich.' Projects of Eastern expansionism, along with rabid anti-communism and anti-Semitism, were generic features of the German right after 1918. What distinguished Hitler, defining 'the peculiarity and motivating dynamic' of his regime, was the centrality of America in his worldview as 'the global hegemon in the making', and 'fulcrum of a world Jewish conspiracy for the ruination of Germany and the rest of Europe.'[17]

On what evidence did Tooze base this construction? Principally, Hitler's so-called 'Second Book', an unfinished and unpublished sequel to *Mein Kampf*, probably composed in 1928; and a scattering of *obiter dicta* during the war. But neither his words nor deeds provide any coherent support for it. Like any European of his time, Hitler knew how large was America's population and domestic market, but in the 900 pages of *Mein Kampf*, where the 'infamous mental terror' of socialism and the Jewish features of the 'grinning, ugly face of Marxism' have pride of place from the start, the United States is accorded not so much as a single page, even paragraph; while the occasional mentions it earns are not especially hostile. In his 'Second Book', Hitler did talk of the future threat to Europe from America, given the size of its population and wealth of its market, its lower production costs and stream of inventions, which could give it predominance over the Old World. But neither the substance

17 *The Wages of Destruction: The Making and Breaking of the Nazi Economy*, New York 2007, pp. xxiv, 657, 284.

nor the salience of the ensuing thoughts corresponds to Tooze's characterization of them.

For Hitler went on to explain that the key advantage of America lay in its ethnic composition. Nordic emigration to the New World had created in the United States a 'new national community of the highest racial quality', a 'young, racially select people', filtering immigration to extract the 'Nordic element' from all the nations of Europe, while barring the door to Japanese and Chinese. Russia might have a comparable land surface, but its population was of such poor quality that it could pose no economic or political threat to the freedom of the world, merely flood it with disease. Pan-European schemes to counter the rise of America, hoping to cobble races of every sort together into some sort of union, were a delusion of Jews and half-breeds. If Germany continued to allow its best bloodlines to emigrate to the US, it was bound to deteriorate into a people of no value. Only a state that could 'raise the racial value of its people into the most practical national form' could compete with America. In the future, conflict between Europe and America might not always be peacefully economic in nature, but the nation that would be most in danger from the US was not Germany but England.[18]

In other words, when Hitler turned his mind to America, in his only real disquisition on the country, it was in admiration rather than denunciation of the US, not merely as economically more advanced, but essentially and explicitly as more Aryan than Germany itself was in danger of becoming. How large did these thoughts loom in 1928? Attention to America lasts for a dozen pages—just 5 per cent of the manuscript of his 'Second Book'. South Tyrol commands double the space. Nor is there evidence of any continuing preoccupation with the US in the

18 *Hitler's Zweites Buch*, Stuttgart 1961, pp. 123–32, 173.

succeeding years. Far from being central to his world view, in the thirties America faded from Hitler's horizon, as he decided that it was not, after all, a stronghold of manly Nordic virtues, but a sink-hole of mongrels and degenerates, in which at best only half—at other times they became a sixth—of the population were of decent stock, and with Jews uppermost: a state of weaklings, wracked with unemployment and enfeebled by neutrality laws, that could be discounted as a force in *Weltpolitik.*[19]

Once entrenched in power, Hitler laid out the international tasks of the Third Reich as he saw them in his 'Four Year Plan' memorandum of August–September 1936. It contains not a line about America. After explaining that 'politics was the leadership and conduct of the historical struggles for life of peoples', whose intensification since the French Revolution had found its most extreme expression in Bolshevism—bent on 'eliminating the traditional elites of humanity and replacing them with worldwide Jewry'—and declaring that no state could withdraw or keep its distance from the ensuing confrontation, he announced in italics: '*Since Marxism has by its victory in Russia converted one of the largest empires in the world into its base of further*

19 'Oscillating between admiration and contempt, Hitler's conceptions of America possessed neither any realistic nor stable content': Detlef Junker, *Kampf um die Weltmacht: Die USA und das Dritte Reich 1933–1945*, Düsseldorf 1988, p. 24, much the best treatment of Hitler's attitudes to the US. Tooze singles out Philipp Gassert's *Amerika im Dritten Reich* for praise as a study superseding all others, but in fact it has little to say about Hitler's strategic relationship to America. Noting that up to the early thirties, 'power-political' considerations played 'virtually no role at all' in his thinking about the US, and even after coming to power, 'gaps in Hitler's image of America' have to be filled by recourse to the 'cultural environment' in which his foreign-policy decisions were taken, rather than any pronouncements by the Führer himself, Gassert's book is actually a 'broad reception history' of German attitudes to America under the Third Reich, rather than a study of Hitler's own intermittent mish-mash of these: *Amerika im Dritten Reich: Ideologie, Propaganda und Volksmeinung*, Stuttgart 1997, pp. 87–8.

operations, this question has become critical. An ideologically founded, closed authoritarian will to aggression has entered the ideologically tattered democratic world.' The democratic states were incapable of waging a successful war against Soviet Russia, leaving Germany—'as always the ignition point of the Western world against Bolshevik attacks'—the duty of securing its own existence against impending catastrophe with every means at its disposal. '*For the victory of Bolshevism over Germany would not end in another Versailles, but the final destruction, in fact extermination of the German people.*' The scale of such a disaster was incalculable. '*In face of the need to defend us against this danger all other considerations recede as completely irrelevant.*' Expanded rearmament, at top speed, was required to ready the German army and nation for war in four years.[20]

Here the abiding phobias of *Mein Kampf*, in its fusion of anti-communism and anti-Semitism, had become state doctrine; the fight against Bolshevism, in Ian Kershaw's words, 'the lodestar of Hitler's thinking on foreign policy'.[21] The future of German expansion lay in the East, not in the West. When in 1939 his invasion of Poland led, contrary to his expectations, to British and French declarations of war with Germany, and he defeated France in short order, he expected Britain to come to terms with him, as a long-time admirer of its empire, which he had no wish to break up. Baffled by its refusal to do so, and unable to invade it by sea, as early as July 1940 he decided instead to invade Russia—in defiance of any rational strategic calculus, recreating the war on two fronts he had always maintained was the overriding reason for German defeat in 1914–18. Military common sense would have directed the Wehrmacht south rather than

20 'Denkschrift Hitlers über die Aufgaben eines Vierjahresplans', *Vierteljahrshefte für Zeitgeschichte*, April 1955, pp. 204–5, 210. Italics in original.

21 Ian Kershaw, *Hitler 1936–1945: Nemesis*, London 2000, p. 12.

east, forcing Spain—where Franco's regime, little more than a year in the saddle, was in no position to resist an ultimatum to fall into line—into war with Britain and, with control of both sides of the Straits of Gibraltar, closing the Mediterranean, seizing Egypt and the Iraqi oilfields: a saunter compared with Operation Barbarossa.[22] But the ideological premium lay where it had always been: wiping out Bolshevism and colonizing the East, in a war of extermination without counterpart in the West. Nor, in the expected aftermath of its success, was there any talk of a conquered Russia providing a platform for taking on America. Hitler's Directive No. 32, 'Preparations for the Period after Barbarossa', drafted eleven days before the Russian campaign began, was free of any thought of Washington, projecting instead a sweep of the Wehrmacht around the Mediterranean, closing in on the Suez Canal—just what he had fatally foregone.

Where America did feature in Hitler's outlook was in the Far East, where he hoped Japan would pin down the US, preventing it from helping Britain in Europe, and incited Tokyo to launch an attack on it already in April 1941, before Japan was either resolved or ready to do so. In itself a rational enough calculation, Hitler rendered it lunatic by promising that Germany would declare war on America as soon as Japan did, and being as good as his word in December, bringing down on him the world's greatest power without having any possibility of so much as reaching it by land, sea or air.[23] Tooze correctly observes

22 It is sometimes argued that Hitler did not proceed because of the conflict between French possession of Morocco and Spanish designs on it, not wishing to antagonize Petain's regime by granting expansion to Franco's, both ideologically aligned with his own. This can scarcely have an insuperable problem: in a similar conflict, he had little difficulty imposing the Second Vienna Award, dividing Transylvania between Romania and Hungary, with a view to brigading both states for what became Barbarossa.

23 In January 1942 Oshima, the Japanese ambassador in Berlin, reported to Tokyo: 'The Führer is of the view that England can be destroyed. How

that this 'sealed the fate of Germany',[24] without registering how fatal it also is to his construction of the centrality of America to Hitler's worldview. For what the Führer's gratuitous gift to Roosevelt (who would have had great difficulty in declaring war on Germany in the wake of Pearl Harbor, when national outrage and demand for retribution were focused on Japan) revealed was Hitler's staggering level of inconsequence and ignorance where anything to do with the United States was actually concerned.

In a respectful but wide-ranging critique of *Wages of Destruction*, the most substantial engagement with it to date, Dylan Riley cites Adorno's cool verdict: 'The German ruling clique drove towards war because they were excluded from a position of imperial power. But in their exclusion lay the reason for the blind and clumsy provincialism that made Hitler's and Ribbentrop's policies uncompetitive and their war a gamble.'[25] From 1942 onwards Hitler would, in his rambling monologues to intimates, have more to say about the US, increasingly vituperated in Nazi pronouncements as—an inherently mobile location—the headquarters of world Jewry, but never rising above know-nothing bluster and dilettantism. His worldview comprised a limited number of *idées fixes*—anti-communism, anti-Semitism, a racialized social Darwinism—to which passing moods or fancies could add a wide variety of temporary hobby horses and inconsistent opinions, vague and self-contradictory ideas about America among them.

---

the USA can be defeated, he doesn't yet know'; see Junker, *Kampf um die Weltmacht*, who makes short work of the notion that Hitler ever had a serious plan for the conquest of America: pp. 25, 31–2.

24 *Wages of Destruction*, p. 668.

25 Dylan Riley, 'The Third Reich as Rogue Regime: Adam Tooze's *Wages of Destruction*', *Historical Materialism*, 22: 3–4, 2014, p. 346. The quotation is from Adorno, *Minima Moralia*, London–New York 2005, p. 106.

In framing *Wages of Destruction* by Hitler's relationship to America, however, Tooze was not making an arbitrary decision. For the starting point of his narrative is not the backdrop that might be expected of a study of the Nazi economy, the Great Depression. More devastating in its effects in Germany than in any other industrial society, the slump is taken as a given, without causal explanation. What holds centre stage is the tragic failure of the German elites to hold fast to the wisdom of Stresemann, the leading statesman of the twenties, in seeing that the path to recovery after defeat in the First World War lay not in futile rebellion against the settlement at Versailles but in signalling Germany's willingness to pay reparations, and thereby opening the door to 'a special relationship with the United States' as the 'dominant force in world affairs, both economically and as a future superpower', with the aim of positioning Germany as a key ally of Washington in a transatlantic partnership.[26] But after the Dawes and Young Plans, hopeful steps in the right direction, Stresemann died and Wall Street crashed. The result was 'the collapse of American hegemony in Europe', leaving the continent 'orphaned as it had not been since World War I', and Germany at the mercy of Hitler's demonic ambitions. Happily, with the defeat of the Third Reich, Adenauer could realize Stresemann's vision, at last sheltering a German parliamentary democracy in the safe harbour of America, orphanage over.[27]

III

Published eight years later, *The Deluge* supplies the prequel to *Wages*. Its theme is the emergence out of the Great War of 1914–18 of a new world order, led by America, which outlasted

26 *Wages of Destruction*, pp. 5, 25, 33.
27 Ibid., pp. 657–8.

the demise of its architect and gave way only under the strain of the Great Depression. The narrative opens with the military deadlock in Europe in 1916, and Wilson's decision to enter the war in support of the Entente in the spring of 1917, making of the struggle 'something far more morally and politically charged' than a mere great-power conflict—'a crusading victory', an American president in the lead, 'fought and won to uphold the rule of international law and to put down autocracy and militarism'. With the defeat of Germany and the dissolution of Austria–Hungary, the US—already a super-state towering above all others in economic might—became the master power of the succeeding peace. Its post-war hegemony, however, would be no mere replacement of what had once been the Pax Britannica. It was a paradigm shift in international relations, a deliberate attempt to construct a global economic and political order as conceived by Wilson—a system of a new kind: 'by common agreement, the new order had three major facets—moral authority backed by military power and economic supremacy.'[28]

True, though the agreement was common, it was not quite universal. By the time Wilson had taken America into the war, the February Revolution had broken out in Russia. 'First and foremost a patriotic event', this spelt no defection from the ranks of the Entente, whose leaders were justifiably confident that 'Russia's democratic revolution would re-energize the war effort, not end it'. 'Kerensky, Tsereteli and their colleagues set themselves frantically to rebuilding the army as a fighting force', and in the early summer of 1917 troops 'under the dynamic command of the young war hero, Lavr Kornilov' were making headway against the Habsburg forces in front of them.[29] But to

28 *The Deluge: The Great War and the Remaking of Global Order*, London 2014, pp. 8, 14–15.

29 Ibid., pp. 70, 81–2.

the North, Bolshevik subversion led to mutiny, and the Russian front collapsed. As peasant soldiers 'abandoned the cause en masse', and radicalized units around Petrograd marched on the city, the Provisional Government—'despite its profound commitment to democratic freedom'—'had no option but to order the mass arrest of the Bolshevik leadership', but made the fatal mistake of failing 'to decapitate it' as the circumstances required, a taboo on the death penalty inhibiting the necessary executions. Three months later, Red Guards stormed the Winter Palace and nascent Russian democracy was extinguished. In power, the Bolshevik dictatorship repudiated Russia's foreign debts—an action amounting to a rejection of 'the very foundations of international law', severing any possibility of an understanding with the Entente—and, signing the Treaty of Brest-Litovsk with the Central Powers, exited the war. The Allied interventions in Russia which followed this capitulation were not motivated by any counter-revolutionary intent, but simply the aim of ousting a regime that had become, objectively speaking, a ward of German militarism. Lenin was only saved from the political bankruptcy of his collusion with Berlin by the collapse of the Second Reich in the autumn, which took the wind out of the need for these.[30]

The self-exclusion of Russia from the new world order in the making in 1919 did not materially affect its birth at Versailles. Treatment of Wilson and Lenin as if they were equivalent figures, ranged against each other, is a retrospective illusion, so dramatic was the implosion of Russian power at the end of the war, and so pitifully weak was the emergent Bolshevik regime. The year 1919, Tooze observes, had nothing in common with 1945, when the United States and the Soviet Union squared off against each other in a bi-polar international system. Rather, it 'resembled the unipolar moment of 1989', when 'the idea of

30 Ibid., pp. 82–3, 129, 156–7, 170.

reordering the world around a single power bloc and a common set of liberal, "Western" values seemed like a radical historical departure', but in fact was a reprise of the dramatic outcome of the First World War.[31] Much arguing and bargaining marked the negotiations at Versailles, but the victors stuck together in a moderate settlement, the fruit of compromise, that allowed for the eventual reintegration of Germany into the comity of leading powers under the aegis of Wilson's brain-child—a League of Nations whose covenant was signed by all in advance of negotiations over the Treaty itself.

Tragically, however, Wilson was unable on his return to the US to secure ratification of American membership of the League from the Senate, a 'heartbreaking fiasco' that was certainly in part due to his personal rigidity, and by then physical frailty.[32] But the deeper roots of this disaster lay in the paradox that America, the advance guard of economic and cultural modernity in the world at large, had yet to modernize its political order at home. Despite the Progressivist vision of leaders such as the first Roosevelt and Wilson, the US state remained crabbed and confined within its eighteenth-century constitutional matrix. The archaic prerogatives of the Senate, requiring a two-thirds vote for approval of any international treaty—without equivalent anywhere else in the world—were one expression of this lag, the most direct obstruction to Wilson's hopes. The fiscal underdevelopment of the Federal state, still essentially dependent on customs-and-excise revenues, was another. The war had been financed largely by monetary loosening, bank credits that doubled prices. In lieu of an income tax, this was in effect an inflation tax, which when abruptly reversed by the Treasury in 1920 plunged the country into deflation and mass

31 Ibid., p. 10.
32 Ibid., pp. 18, 336, 338.

unemployment, putting a Republican back into the White House with the largest electoral majority of the century.

For Tooze, underlying the rhetoric of Wilson and his domestic opponents alike, and culprit for the failure of the US to rise to the challenges of the hour, was the quite recent ideology of American exceptionalism, essentially a higher form of nationalism at odds with the internationalist requirements of global leadership. Yet he detects a kernel of Burkean wisdom in this outlook, a sense of the need to preserve the continuity of the country's history after the trauma of the Civil War. Nor did it in practice mean any decisive retreat from the tasks of building a new world order. Contrary to legend, Harding's administration presided over a demonstration of it more successful than Versailles: the Washington Conference of 1921–22, which saw Wilson's defeated Republican rival of 1916, Charles Evans Hughes, pull off a triumph of internationalist diplomacy in persuading Britain and Japan to cede naval ascent gracefully to the United States, in the manner of Gorbachev yielding to Bush seventy years later. Thereafter, successive presidents and their envoys, public or private, laboured to stabilize Europe in the wake of the tensions left by the reparations clauses of Versailles, with constructive proposals for easing financial difficulties in Germany such as the Dawes and Young Plans, and eventually even a moratorium offered by Hoover on the war debts of France and Britain to the US itself. Nor were these efforts at pacification of international relations without admirable European, and for that matter Asian, counterparts. In England Austen Chamberlain, in France Aristide Briand, in Germany Gustav Stresemann—every one a Nobelist—were all convinced Atlanticists, looking to the US as their indispensable partner in the pursuit of peace; so too a resolute Ramsay MacDonald and the courageous Taisho reformers in Japan.

Why then was the progressive liberal project of these forward-looking statesmen in the end derailed? Its flaw lay in the limitation of the American hegemony that it required and embodied. For common to Wilson and his successors was a refusal, not of enlightened engagement with the affairs of the rest of the world, but of the ultimate responsibility of leading an international coalition of powers to preserve free trade and collective security. Instead, their basic impulse was 'to use America's position of privileged detachment, and the dependence on it of the other major powers, to frame a transformation of world affairs', the 'better to uphold their ideal of America's destiny'[33]—a radical vision abroad, tied to a conservative attachment at home. For a decade, the combination yielded impressive achievements. But when the tragic test of the Great Depression came, it was not enough. International cooperation collapsed, and revolt against the once-hopeful moderation of the twenties erupted in the fanaticisms of the thirties, anticipated in their different ways by Hitler and Trotsky. But the very extremity of such reactions was evidence of the strength of the emergent order they sought to overthrow.

> The spectacular escalation of violence unleashed in the 1930s and 1940s was a testament to the kind of force that the insurgents believed themselves to be up against. It was precisely the looming potential, the future dominance of American capitalist democracy, that was the common factor impelling Hitler, Stalin, the Italian fascists and their Japanese counterparts to such radical action.[34]

---

33 *Deluge*, p. 516.

34 'Once the extremists were given their chance, it was precisely the sense that they faced mighty opponents that animated the violence and lethal energy of their assault on the post-war order': ibid., pp. 7, 18.

Yet the visions of statesmen like Briand were not in vain. For the 'restless search for a new way of securing order and peace was the expression not of a deluded idealism, but of a higher form of realism', which understood that only international coalition and cooperation could secure peace and prosperity on earth. 'These were the calculations of a new type of liberalism, a Realpolitik of progress.'[35] That came to fruition under the second Roosevelt. It is still much needed. Striking without hesitation a contemporary note, Tooze asked: 'Why does "the West" not play its winning hands better? Where is the capacity for management and leadership? Given the rise of China, these questions have an obvious force.'[36]

Clearer answers to the two questions raised by Durand—what method is implied in Tooze's work, and what politics inform it?—start to come into view once *The Deluge* and *Wages of Destruction* are read together as installments of a common project. In each, a 'situational and tactical' approach to the subject in hand determines entry to it *in medias res*, dispensing with a structural explanation of its origins: in *Wages*, the Depression; in *Deluge*, the First World War. In both, the overarching theme is the dynamism of American power as skeleton key to the twentieth century. In both, the political standpoint is, as self-described, that of a left-liberalism. Each of the terms around the hyphen is liable, however, to a range of meanings, and the compound has often, perhaps typically, proved unstable, one or other of its elements acquiring greater valence. *Wages*, as a study of the Nazi economy, offers less scope for considering the balance between them. Viewed in historical context, its central claim that Hitler's real antagonist, the enemy that mattered, was America, not

35 Ibid., pp. 517–18.
36 Ibid., p. 19.

Russia, of course fitted well with axiomatic assumptions of the Cold War. If the Nazi war machine was ultimately directed against the United States, the binary struggle between democracy and totalitarianism was preserved—the Soviet Union, rather than being the principal target of Hitler's regime and the overwhelming agent of its downfall, as in historical fact it was, becoming the even greater totalitarian danger further east, to be dealt with in due course. But gratifying though such a deduction might be to American and West German audiences, Tooze never suggests it, and the salience of the Red Army in the narrative of *Wages* discounts it.[37]

---

37 See by contrast Brendan Simms, *Hitler: Only the World Was Enough*, London 2019, a mammoth inflation of the claim that a battle with 'Anglo-America'—above all the United States—was Hitler's overriding obsession. Simms, an Irish neo-conservative, founder of the Henry Jackson Society, depicts a Führer consumed less by anti-Semitism or anti-communism than by a rabid anti-capitalism. His hostility to Anglo-Saxon capitalism was 'crucially, anterior' to his anti-Semitism, and 'dwarfed his fear of Communism'—in his eyes simply an inferior 'instrument of international capitalism'. 'Hitler's principal preoccupation throughout his career was Anglo-America and global capitalism, rather than the Soviet Union or Bolshevism': (pp. 22, 87–8, 53, xviii). Geopolitically, it was 'the immense American industrial potential', which had been 'a staple of his thinking in the 1920s, and had dominated his strategy since the late 1930s', that motivated his invasion of Russia in 1941. Operation Barbarossa was 'ultimately directed against the Western Allies', and 'the push on Stalingrad, like the entire war, was primarily driven by the contest against Anglo-America': (pp. 457, 408, 471). Mining his sources single-mindedly in pursuit of this case, Simms not only ignores evidence making a mockery of it—he can cite Hitler's Four Year Plan without letting drop it ever mentions the USSR (pp. 260–1)—but himself contradicts it with admissions that demolish it. Far from planning any world-historical showdown with America, as promised by the book's subtitle (*Only the World* ...), in 1933 'Hitler envisaged a future peaceful relationship between the new Reich and the United States, based on a common set of so-called racial values'; in 1938 'would have greatly preferred to remain at peace' with the British Empire and United States; in 1941 'sought not world domination, but world power status' and 'had no strategy for defeating the United States, because there obviously wasn't one': (pp. 164, 328–9, 450). The upshot is a construction not much less

The Deluge, composed after Tooze's move from Cambridge to Yale, is politically more outspoken, a full-throated endorsement of the victors' self-understanding of the First World War and the abiding vision that, for all their differences, inspired their efforts to build a progressive peace after it. Historiographically it can be described, with apologies to Elie Kedourie, as a distinctive exercise in the Chatham House version of the period. By starting his narrative in 1916, Tooze avoids any reckoning with the question of what determined the outbreak of hostilities in 1914, and so of the nature of the war itself, simply asserting without further ado that American entry, provoked by German aggression, converted it into a battle for democracy and international law.

Imperialism, in this accounting, was a very recent phenomenon, global competition just a few decades old—the Seven Years' War and conquest of India might never have happened—and once the war had come to a successful end, the world was confronted with the problem of how it was to be peacefully ordered 'after imperialism'.[38] The narrative is constructed, in other words, by taking for granted the Entente apologetics in contemporary usage, a literature now so abundant that Tooze may have felt it unnecessary to spell out its truths once again, although they have little or nothing to do with a serious understanding of the conflict. 'The structural reality', as Alexander Zevin has written, 'is that the First World War took place over empires, for empires and between empires.'[39] For the extent of

incoherent than Hitler's own confusions of the time. But the ideological purpose of a consecration *a contrario* is transparent enough: if what Hitler really hated above all else was global capitalism and its stronghold in America, how could these be other than quintessentially good? That he never laid a significant finger on capitalism within the Third Reich hardly matters.

38 *Deluge*, p. 20.

39 Alexander Zevin, 'The Snuffer of Lamps', *New Left Review* 94, July–August 2015, p. 139.

this bedrock fact it is enough to consult the survey of the combatants in a recent comprehensive account, *Empires at War*, which covers all of them, down to the Portuguese wing of the East African theatre of hostilities, where the British imperial death toll exceeded the total of American dead in Europe.[40] It was the uneven distribution of planetary spoils that precipitated the Great War: in a system where every state took for granted the connexion between power and possessions, Germany, the largest and most rapidly expanding industrial economy, surrounded by the three largest territorial powers of the continent, had no commensurate share of the plunder, while Britain had such a hugely disproportionate empire, compared with any other, that no stable international equilibrium was possible, as Lenin saw at the time and more critical historians have pointed out since.[41]

The sponge that palaeo-Entente justifications pass over the First World War, taken as read by Tooze, permits an enormity to follow. The inter-imperialist slaughter that cost some 10 million lives on the battlefield, and 40 million casualties of one kind or another, is exonerated from any responsibility for the violence that followed it, attributed instead to an extremist rebellion against the pacific strength of the post-war settlement—Hitler and Trotsky twinned for the purpose. No word even refers to the scale of the killing unleashed by the liberal civilization of the Belle Epoque, let alone to its socio-psychological consequences in hardening the world to more of the same, with scarcely a break after 1918. In treating of the Russian Revolution, Tooze

40 See Robert Gerwarth and Erez Manela (eds), *Empires at War 1911–1923*, Oxford 2014, p. 143. To prevail in the struggle, Britain mobilized some two and a half million, France half a million troops from their respective empires.

41 See inter alia David Calleo, *The German Question Reconsidered*, Cambridge 1978, pp. 4–5, 24–5, 83–4, 158–9.

even regrets there was not more of it during the war: had only a few more tens of thousands of peasant soldiers been able to hold on under commanders like Kornilov, without Bolshevik sedition sapping their patriotism, the solidarity of the Entente would have been saved, and the Central Powers held at bay in the East, instead of acquiring Lenin, foolishly spared the firing-squad by the Provisional Government, as their pawn. In Ireland, where 'extreme Irish nationalists launched a suicidal assault on British power' in 1916, damaging the responsible backing of Redmond and his party for the war effort, and the guerrilla war for independence of 1919–21 took 'a terrible toll', compounded by a civil war provoked by Sinn Fein's 'apocalyptic radicalism', the upshot of this mayhem 'stored up violence for the rest of the century'.[42] Some 1,400 lives were lost in the war for Irish independence; perhaps 2,000 in the civil war. Whereas 30,000 Irishmen died in the trenches of France, the Balkans and the Middle East. Non-violently? Missing in *Deluge* is any sense of Henry James's reaction to the war:

> The intense unthinkability of anything so blank and infamous in an age we have been living in and taking for our own as if it were a high refinement of civilization—in spite of all conscious incongruities; finding it after all carrying this abomination in its blood, finding this to have been what it *meant* all the while, is like suddenly having to recognize in one's family circle or group of best friends a band of murderers, swindlers and villains—it's just such a similar shock.[43]

---

42 *Deluge*, pp. 180, 376–7.

43 Letter to Claude Phillips, first Keeper of the Wallace Collection, three days before the outbreak of the war. Though soon an adoptive English patriot, James confessed a 'terrible sense that the people of this country' might with 'brutal justice' now have to pay for their 'grossness and folly and blatancy', exhibited from 'so far back': Percy Lubbock (ed.), *The Letters of Henry James*, London 1920, Vol II, p. 389–90.

If the war ended as a victory for democracy and the rule of law, what of the peace that followed it? Did it embody these? Tooze finds no special fault with the Treaty of Versailles, giving credit to Wilson, Lloyd George and Clemenceau—with particular sympathy for the last—for their understandably differing concerns and willingness to compromise between them to impose a satisfactory common settlement on the country they had defeated. Since Germany was the aggressor, the war-guilt clause of the Treaty, the formal ground for extracting open-ended reparations from it, could be taken as given. What mattered was that Germans, however much they detested it, should—in their own interests—take their medicine. Keynes's philippic against the Treaty, rhetorical tour de force though it may have been, was an irresponsible piece of mischief-making, not only encouraging reckless German resistance to paying up, but poisoning relations between London and Paris, and handing a propaganda gift to Lenin and Trotsky into the bargain. 'No single individual did more to undermine the political legitimacy of the Versailles peace'; and no danger of the time exercises Tooze more than the possibility that the new-born German Republic would have the nerve to reject the Allied ultimatum that it must sign the Treaty on the dotted line.

Thankfully, the madness of ultras like Max Weber, who called for guerrilla resistance to it, and even such a moderate social-democrat as then premier Philipp Scheidemann—who advocated a stance all too reminiscent of Trotsky's 'Neither Peace Nor War' at Brest-Litovsk—was at the last minute overcome, and the Treaty accepted by Germany. There was still much recidivism in Weimar, whose Rapallo Pact with the pariah Soviet state reached by Rathenau three years later—'a self-indulgent nationalist fantasy'—was not in keeping with the spirit of Versailles; and another high-risk crisis the next year, when France occupied the Rhineland to ensure its portion of reparations was coughed up. But Stresemann, unlike Rathenau, had understood all along that Germany must look to America to improve its situation, and in 1924 the Dawes Plan, supplying funds from Wall Street to ease reparation payments, rescued German democracy by taking the sting from Versailles.

Such judgments follow naturally from the premise that the Great War saw a triumph of relative good over evil. Retribution was required, and to rejoin the ranks of respectability the offender must for its own good accept the measure of punishment, by no means excessive, meted out to it. That no stable peace could be built on such a self-serving historical fiction, rejected as dishonest and unjust by the virtual entirety of the nation forced to accept it, is a consideration that cannot occur within this mental framework. So too the thought that Germany might have avoided the rise of Hitler had it taken the course advocated by Weber or Scheidemann, refused the diktat of the Allies and let them see what benefit occupation of the country would bring them, in face of all the inevitable resistance, and how long their own populations would have put up with it.[44] In the Germany of 1919, such resistance would have united most of the politically active country. By their capitulation, the centrist politicians who feature as the heroes of the hour in Tooze ensured that the banner of a rejection which they themselves knew was perfectly justified, and was bound in due course to prevail, would pass to the radical right alone. The foundations

44 Tooze dismisses this prospect, which the French high command was ready to jump at, contending that the Allies would instead simply have lopped off big chunks of Germany and waited for the starving residue to come to its senses, in a kind of Morgenthau Plan *ante diem*, no less fanciful or more likely to have been adopted than the treasury secretary's ruminations in 1944: *Deluge*, p. 315.

of the edifice erected at Versailles were rotten from the start, foreordained to collapse.

The fate of Germany—so hopeful as long as Stresemann was at the helm—forms the central thread of Tooze's narrative of the new world order that emerged after 1918. But the panoramic scope is wide, a notable strength of the book, encompassing China, Japan, India, Egypt, South Africa, even a slide inserted from Patagonia. What balance sheet of American hegemony, as postulated by Tooze, emerges from it? If the conceptual setting of *Deluge* situates it at a point along the political spectrum where liberalism ceases to have any particular implication with the left—its account of the Russian Revolution is of pure-bred Cold War stock[45]—the subsequent story it tells is much more ambiguous. Tooze does not venture full-scale portraits of any of his protagonists, but much of what he reports of Wilson is plainly incompatible with the role initially assigned him of prophet and principal architect of a world made safe for peace and democracy. 'Thrilled' by America's victorious war with Spain and acquisition of her Caribbean and Pacific colonies, 'more aggressive than any of his predecessors' in dispatching troops to the Caribbean and Mexico, devoted to the preservation of—in his own words—'white supremacy on this planet', Wilson made no mention of self-determination in his Fourteen Points, vetoed discussion of Ireland at Versailles, and had no truck with Japan's call for a commitment to racial equality in the Covenant of the League, enthroning instead the Monroe Doctrine as one of its founding principles.[46]

---

45 Coinciding with his move to Yale, Tooze could report that he now enjoyed 'entrée to a new world of American policy debate' at confabulations with the National Intelligence Council: *Deluge*, p. xxiii.

46 Ibid., pp. 44, 60, 120, 193, 326, 269.

In 1919, having cut off financial aid to Italy to oblige it to scrap the treaty with Britain and France which awarded its entry into the war on their side with gains in Tyrol and the Adriatic, within days Wilson was telling China it must abide by the treaty extorted from it assigning Japan gains in Shandong and Manchuria, because 'the sacredness of treaties' was one of the principles for which the war had been fought.[47] At home, the world champion of democracy presided over the greatest single wave of political repression in modern American history, replete with a pogrom against immigrants of the wrong ethnic background. All this can be found in *Deluge*. But it is never aggregated, and the mass arrests of 1919 are tacitly deflected to Wilson's attorney-general.

Beyond the person, the larger question is whether Tooze's picture of global American dominance already in the interwar period—over allies, effectual up to the Depression; in the imaginary of opponents, throughout—is accurate. Certainly, the signal merit of *Deluge* is its demonstration of the continuing leverage enjoyed by the US over the leading European states by the loop between the war debts to it of Britain, France and Italy, and the reparations owed France and Britain by Germany, leaving Washington in a position to adjust the two as suited its interests. The gist of Tooze's exposition of this financial chokehold is that it was generally, though not invariably, put to benign purpose, seeking to temper the sharp edge of the arrangements at Versailles and restore Germany to what today would be called 'the international community'. Underplayed, however, are two features of the transatlantic relationship: the implacability of the avarice of the American state—entitled, one might argue, to the later sobriquet of vulture capitalism—in extracting

47 To credit Wilson with a gift for hypocrisy in cases like these is unnecessary: vanity and self-deception sufficed.

compensation for its support of the Entente regardless of the relative burdens of the war; and the unsleeping fear of revolution that led it to back forms of political reaction wherever required to crush any threat of it, nurturing excellent relations with Mussolini from the start.[48]

To the financial arsenal of US power, the Washington Conference added naval gains. But how far did these two assets—money and warships—permit an American *hegemony*, the term persistently used by Tooze to describe the US role in the world from 1919 to 1932? This was a period when the size of the American army, under 200,000, was smaller than that of Portugal; when the US Foreign Service, dating only from 1924, was still pupal;[49] when it had no embassy in Moscow; when its presence in China could not compare with that of Britain, effectively in charge of the country's fiscal system; when in Europe it was a bystander to the sequel to Versailles at Locarno. What was the initiative for which it was best known? The Kellogg-Briand 'Peace Pact'

48 While it set the tone for hyperbolic narratives of 'US pre-eminence' permeating interbellum Europe with 'an impressive display of economic, political and moral power' (even many contemporaries would have been surprised to learn, 'from Switzerland to the Soviet Union, Europeans acknowledged America's cultural leadership'), Frank Costigliola's study *Awkward Dominion* (1984), the first of several precursors to *Deluge*, was less euphoric in outlook. Conceding that US determination to 'preserve the economic benefits of the international gold standard, the war debt settlements, the foreign investments, and the trade surplus' for itself 'assigned most of the adjustment burdens to Europe', Washington consistently 'favoured reactionaries' where necessary, State Department analysts optimistically comparing the Nazis in 1933 to 'the Italians Fascists with whom the United States had worked so closely': *Awkward Dominion: American Political, Economic and Cultural Relations with Europe, 1919–1933,* Ithaca (NY) 1984, pp. 263, 217, 178, 164, 139, 260.

49 Martin Weil opens his study of the narrow composition of the service: 'This is the story of a small group of Christian gentlemen who founded the profession of diplomacy on a permanent basis in America': *A Pretty Good Club: The Founding Fathers of the US Foreign Service*, New York 1978, p. 9.

of 1928, a wish-list of feel-good futility, leaving scarcely a trace in the history of the thirties.

All this followed from the reality to which Tooze himself draws attention in describing the fiasco of Wilson's project when he got back to America in 1919: the stunted, only half-modern character of the Federal state machine itself. But after arguing and illustrating that with force, he fails to remember it when otherwise writing throughout of American hegemony—even of European orphanage once it faded, as if kindly parental guidance by Washington had alone kept the Old World safe till the slump. The claim is jumping the gun. The world of 1919 was in no sense unipolar. US hegemony would, of course, come in due course. But backdating it to the time of Harding and Coolidge is an anachronism, answering to an authorial hobby-horse rather than to the historical record.

IV

With *Crashed*, Tooze's problematic finally enters into its own. Durand has provided so full an account of the very great achievement of the book that there is little need to recapitulate it here. It is enough to recall its main case. The financial crisis that broke out in 2008 was the product of a sudden paralysis of the interlocking matrix of corporate balance sheets, as the interbank lending on which it depended seized up in the US and EU in the wake of the Lehman default; its global fallout a dramatic demonstration that the central axis of world finance was not, as often imagined, American–Asian, but American–European. As the danger of a second Great Depression loomed, it was the United States alone that averted it, with emergency measures taken by the Fed and the Treasury in a set of bold innovations—central bank swaps, quantitative easing, macroprudential regulation—stabilizing the system. European response, by contrast, was not only laggard but counterproductive, until Draghi repositioned the European Central Bank four years later. Out of the crisis, US hegemony was reasserted, and the dollar emerged more dominant than ever in the global financial system. But a pragmatic managerialism that bailed out bankers and stockholders left society as unequal and even more divided than before, detonating populist revolts that have destabilized both America and Europe in a mutation of the crisis that has yet to end. In spatial sweep, narrative brio and striking detail, no other work on the crash comes near Tooze's account of it.

Where does his conclusion of the trilogy leave Durand's two queries, of politics and method? In keeping with its predecessors, *Crashed* takes the hypertrophy of finance that is the heuristic object of Durand's study as a situational given, without structural explanation. In that sense, it too starts *in medias res*. The conditions that generated the crisis of 2008 are reduced to the demise of Bretton Woods—attributed to pressure from 'the struggle for income shares in an increasingly affluent society' and 'the liberalization of offshore dollar trading in London', as if the war in Vietnam was a cost irrelevant to Nixon's decision to cut the painter to gold—and the ensuing need for neo-liberal discipline to halt inflation: three trifling sentences in a work of six hundred pages. It is as if the decade-by-decade decline in growth of the real economy, across advanced capitalism—the long downturn that arrived in the seventies—had occurred on another planet.

If that structural framework, determining a system-wide displacement of productive capital into bloated global finance, is missing, the American response to the crisis suffers in this telling from a similar blankness of background, if more paradoxically. For at the outset, after stating that the US alone proved able to master the challenge posed by the crisis, Tooze writes: 'that capacity is an effect of structure—the United States is the only state that can generate dollars', then immediately adding 'but it is also a matter of action, of policy choices—positive in the American case, disastrously negative in the European case'. The work that follows, however, brackets the structural capacity completely—it is not mentioned once thereafter—delivering instead an encomium of the policy choices taken by the Fed and the Treasury under Bernanke and Geithner as saving the world from disaster, albeit at the cost of some unhappy side effects. What this edifying story omits is the simple, central fact of the unique leeway the US enjoyed in the prerogatives of the dollar, as the world's premier reserve currency and store of value.

A historical comparison is enough to show why the Obama administration could avert an economic depression as the Hoover administration could not. When the Kreditanstalt collapsed in Austria in 1931—the real trigger, rather than the Wall Street crash of 1929, for the onset of the slump—Hoover, less rigid than his legend, passed the most expansionary budget of the decade, with a deficit of over half Federal expenditure. So strong, however, was domestic and foreign disapproval of such licence that he back-tracked with tax increases the following year. For so long as the US was tethered to the gold standard, it could not afford significant fiscal or monetary loosening without risking a run on the dollar, which its authorities were not prepared to incur.[50] Eight decades later, by contrast, the US

50 Hoover 'shared with many contemporary economists the view that fiscal and monetary policies must be directed to support gold rather than directly to promote domestic economic expansion or bank stability': Nicholas Crafts and Peter Fearon, 'Lessons from the 1930s Great Depression', *Oxford Review of Economic Policy* 26: 3, 2010, pp. 285–317, which also disposes of the opposite legend that the New Deal was based in large measure on fiscal stimulus. For the classic demonstration that failure to loosen monetary policy—for Friedman and Schwartz, the principal cause

could run a huge trade deficit and print money as it wished without fearing retribution from foreign bondholders or investors, typically all the keener on T-bills and Wall Street stocks the more anxious economic conditions at large became. So the Obama administration could run up the biggest peacetime fiscal deficit in US history—it jumped from 2.7 per cent of GDP in 2007 to 13 per cent in 2009—with impunity. No eurozone country could do anything like this. There, the Stability and Growth Pact of 1997–99 in principle banned any deficit above 3 per cent, a rule cemented by the Fiscal Compact of 2013, even written into the constitutions of Italy and Spain. This enormous structural difference disappears in *Crashed*, where the institutional framework of the Treaty of Maastricht and the monetary union it created do not rate so much as an entry in the index. The divergent responses to the crisis of America and Europe were not just a question of policy options: they were the product of two radically contrasted—one enabling, the other inhibiting—structures.

Those who enjoyed the imperial latitude of the dollar have boasted not just of the success of the actions they took, but of their valour in taking them. The ghost-assisted memoirs of Bernanke and Geithner, entitled respectively *The Courage to Act* and *Stress Test*, present their time in office as a nerve-racking ordeal, bravely confronted and boldly surmounted, saving the nation with measures of unprecedented novelty as it teetered on the edge of an abyss. *Crashed* criticizes the implication that they themselves had no responsibility for the dangers they battled with, and that the upshot of their efforts was of undivided

---

of the Depression—was essentially determined by a rational fear under the gold standard of an exchange-rate crisis and devaluation of the dollar, see Barry Eichengreen, *Golden Fetters: The Gold Standard and the Great Depression, 1919–1939*, New York 1992, pp. 295 ff.

benefit to all. But it doesn't seriously question the self-serving pathos of power heroically exercised.[51]

V

That is in part because there is a missing piece in the jigsaw puzzle of global finance that Tooze otherwise puts together with such skill. Japan, the third-largest economy in the world, is not to be found in *Crashed*. That is certainly not due to any lack of competence or interest on Tooze's part; *Deluge* pays due attention to the country and its economy in the inter-war period. Rather, its omission is a requirement of the narrative, on which its inclusion would have cast a different light. For virtually all of the daring innovations with which Tooze credits the US authorities for stopping the crisis of 2008—and more—had been pioneered by their Japanese counterparts, most of them well beforehand, starting in the nineties, and in wider and ampler measure, without resort to chest-thumping. Not only QE—central bank purchase

51 'The terror of those days ... the overwhelming burden of responsibility combined with the paralyzing fear of catastrophic failure ... the loneliness and the numbness'—Geithner's ghost-writer, on loan from *Time*, in top gear: *Stress Test*, p. 200. Tooze: 'There is no reason to doubt the sincerity of these professions. It was a fearful situation': *Crashed*, p. 164. Since then, in a lecture for the *London Review of Books*, he has gone further, recounting an interview—'the conversation went extremely well'—with the former treasury secretary, now banker for Warburg Pincus, in which he describes the 'formidable charisma and energy that Geithner exudes to an extraordinary extent—he is truly a Napoleonic figure', and repeats a phrase of Geithner's that above all impressed him: 'Since the nineties, we've been defying gravity.' Tooze continues: 'That really shocked me.' Why? Because 'for somebody of my disposition, America isn't subject to gravity; America *is* gravity: America is the gravitational force that organizes global power in the twentieth century.' There was no occasion to be surprised. The same trope was already on display in *Stress Test*, p. 105. At work is a not-so-subliminal image of the US from the popcorn culture of the speaker, to be read in the opposite register: America cruising aloft, Superman in his cape.

of bonds to inject cash into the financial system—and forward guidance, but PKO—'price-keeping operations' (ironically so-named after the UN euphemism—to support stock values, and QQE—central bank purchase of corporate bonds and equity. Not only ZIRP—zero interest rate policy—but the first use of negative interest rates, and of yield-curve control. All this on a scale making American use of heterodox tools look modest. The excess reserves created by the Bank of Japan's use of QE have been larger than those created by the Fed, in an economy a quarter the size of that of the US.[52] As a percentage of GDP, the BOJ's balance sheet is nearly four times bigger than the Fed's.

This enormous injection of liquidity into the economy was possible not only because, unlike the United States, Japan has posted a trade surplus for most of the past forty years, but also because 95 per cent of its public debt, denominated in its own currency, is held by domestic institutions and households, making it virtually as proof against loss of foreign confidence as the supremacy of the dollar renders America's, if not more so, even though the debt is double in size. So too, finally the most important innovation of all in 'the completely new range of policy tools', as Durand summarizes Tooze, 'macroprudential supervision' of the financial system. In 1998–99 the Japanese Ministry of Finance's resolution of eleven 'city banks' into just three 'mega-banks' and a domestic-operations-only fourth, not to speak of the Bank of Japan's grip on a stock market where it is owner of 75 per cent of the exchange-traded fund market and a top ten shareholder in 40 per cent of Japanese companies,[53] puts Geithner's squeamish tinkering with Citigroup and the rest, and

52 Fed: $2.1 trillion; BOJ: $2.87 trillion (¥305 trillion): see Richard Koo, *The Other Half of Macroeconomics and the Fate of Globalization*, Chichester 2018, p. 131.

53 *Financial Times*, 27–8 July 2019.

its enfeebled issue in Dodd–Frank, in the shade. More radical in all these ways than the Treasury, so too was the Ministry of Finance in the more traditional area of fiscal policy, unleashing 'the largest single peace-time government expenditure in history',[54] amid successive stimulus packages in the nineties totalling some $1.3 trillion—nearly twice the size of Obama's American Recovery and Reinvestment Act.[55] In doing so, it could draw on historical precedent. Pre-war Japan led the world in recovering from the Depression with its coordination of monetary expansion and full-throttle fiscal stimulus—something never attempted by the New Deal—under Finance Minister Takahashi Korekiyo.[56]

When the crisis of 2008 broke, manufacturing was hard hit: Japanese exports plunged and the country suffered a fall in GDP, something it had never known since the mid-seventies, even when the property bubble burst in 1989. But the financial system was little shaken by the Lehman shock:[57] tribute to the

---

54 See R. Taggart Murphy, *Japan and the Shackles of the Past*, New York 2014, p. 190, whose analysis of the institutions and vicissitudes of the post-war Japanese economy is in a class by itself. The bailout package of October 1998 came to ¥72 trillion. (In absolute size, the PRC package of 2009 was double that of Japan's in 1998, though on a per capita basis five times lesser.)

55 Sean Ross, 'The Diminishing Effect of Japan's Quantitative Easing', *Investopedia*, 25 June 2019. Taking alarm at the potential cost of the ensuing deficits should interest rates rise, the Ministry of Finance would periodically lame expansion by increasing the sales tax, each time to negative effect, as emphasized by Murphy: 'Privilege Preserved: Crisis and Recovery in Japan', *New Left Review* 121, January–February 2020, pp. 21–52.

56 See inter alia Barry Eichengreen, *Hall of Mirrors: The Great Depression, the Great Recession and the Uses—and Misuses—of History*, Oxford 2015, pp. 256–7: 'This, then, was an aggressively reflationary monetary policy made credible by fiscal expansion. In other words, it was precisely the policy claimed, erroneously, to have been followed in the United States under FDR. But in Japan, unlike the United States, the fiscal expansion was real.'

57 See Mitsuhiko Nakano, *Financial Crisis and Bank Management in Japan (1997 to 2016)*, London 2016, p. 94. The plight of the manufacturing sector, of course, affected banks as creditors to firms that fell into difficulty, a

fact that Japanese banks, unlike European, were not entangled in such a fatal nexus with their American counterparts. If the BOJ drew on dollar swaps from the Fed to lend to them, it was never obliged to do so, since the foreign exchange reserves in Tokyo were more than seven times larger than such loans, 'so it could be said that Japan had no need of its swap line',[58] and so it has no place in Tooze's narrative of the crash. Yet few stock images of the period are so familiar as the awful fate of Japan, dutifully conjured up for White House consumption by Geithner: years of persistent stagnation since its property bubble burst in 1989, compared with buoyant American growth before 2008 and rebound since. Don't they make its recent history an object lesson in what to avoid? Certainly, the Japanese variant has not escaped the common blights of advanced capitalism in this era—increased poverty, precarity, inequality; declining unions, arrested wages, rising profits. Yet its growth rate per capita has been not that much worse than America's, as even Bernanke concedes;[59] unemployment has never risen as high, there is

---

conventional pressure altogether distinct from a freeze-up of interbank lending.

58 William Allen, *International Liquidity and Financial Crisis*, Cambridge 2013, p. 136; peak use of swaps by the BOJ was $127.6 billion; foreign exchange reserves stood at $971.6 billion: p. 129. Why did the BOJ have recourse to swaps at all? Formally speaking, Japan's reserves—held in a Foreign Exchange Special Account—are controlled by the Ministry of Finance. But though since 1998 the BOJ has been technically independent of the MOF, and in outlook the two are not always at one, the MOF is a 'sovereign' administration, as the BOJ—55 per cent state-owned—is not, and can dispose of its reserves as it wishes; so this was scarcely an insurmountable difficulty. See Akio Mikuni and R. Taggart Murphy, *Japan's Policy Trap: Dollars, Deflation and the Crisis of Japanese Finance*, Washington DC, 2002, pp. 48–9, 115. The Fed, however, was anxious that dollar holdings held by foreign treasuries not be cashed out, for fear of causing panic, and probably the Japanese authorities complied to appease it, the BOJ applying for swap lines in a spirit of solidarity—also status as a member of the club of major central banks—rather than necessity.

59 Ben Bernanke, 'Some Reflections on Japanese Monetary Policy', Brookings

little polarization of opulence and misery, the health, education, safety and life expectancy of its citizens are all superior. Behind a veil of Rawlsian ignorance, who would prefer existence in the Land of the Free?

More largely, if the underlying nature of the Great Recession, and what it might portend for the future, is never really addressed by Tooze, it is in part because here too the exclusion of Japan from his compass exacts a significant cost. In the nearly 2,000 footnote references of *Crashed*, there is none to the remarkable Taiwanese economist at Nomura Research, Richard Koo, one of the most original minds in the field,[60] whose *Balance-Sheet Recession* of 2003 first explained the reasons why, after the collapse of Japanese asset prices in the nineties, ultra-low interest rates and massive injections of liquidity into the economy by the BOJ failed to overcome stagnation: essentially because companies had switched from the normal imperatives of profit maximization to debt minimization, ceasing to borrow—and invest—no matter how cheap or abundant the funds available to them.

But why then was there insufficient demand to induce firms to invest? Fifteen years later, in *The Other Half of Macroeconomics*

2017, p. 4. Bernanke has consistently preened himself on his foresight in criticizing shortcomings of Japan's management of its economic affairs, and failure to exhibit 'Rooseveltian resolve' of the sort he would embody: see his 'Japanese Monetary Policy: A Case of Self-Induced Paralysis?', 1999, and subsequent purring ('much of what I wrote about Japan in the decade before the global financial crisis has held up reasonably well'). In *The Courage to Act*, he informs the reader with Pooteresque self-satisfaction that 'the Bank of Japan adopted my suggestions fourteen years later'; even better, the Tokyo press now expected incoming BOJ governor Kuroda to 'adopt more "Bernanke-like tactics"': pp. 41, 552.

60 Son of a leading opponent of the Guomindang takeover of the island who after 1947 went into exile in Japan, where Koo was born and grew up; later working for a time under Volcker at the New York Fed, before moving back to Tokyo.

and the Fate of Globalization, Koo went on to offer an answer. Historically, paths of growth could be divided into three periods: an era before the Lewis turning point (LTP) when an abundant supply of surplus labour from the countryside allowed industrialization based on cheap wages and widening inequality to take off; a 'golden age' when the LTP was reached, as urbanization became standard, labour markets tightened, employers had to raise wages and productivity, and inequality contracted, powering mass consumption and much faster growth; finally a 'pursued' stage, post-LTP, when competitors enjoying pre-LTP wage-levels yet modern technologies invade the markets of those who are henceforward chased, shrinking their opportunities for domestic investment, and driving firms to export capital to cheap-wage locations abroad, depressing growth rates and increasing inequality at home. Workers, 'exploited' in the first phase, 'pacified' in the second, are 'on their own' in the third, deserted by employers and left on their uppers. The United States was the first to suffer from pursuit, by Japan and Germany in the sixties and seventies; Japan in turn was pursued by South Korea and Taiwan in the eighties, and now China was the pursuer of all these. Characteristic of the contemporary period, Koo argues, is the quickening arrival and shortening life of the golden ages enjoyed by newcomers, as more and more countries join the global bandwagon.[61]

It can immediately be seen how the upshot of this comparative historical schema converges with Durand's hypothesis of the vent of financialization in the 'pursued' economies; as too with Robert Brenner's explanation of the long downturn that set in across them from the seventies onwards.[62] Without taking

61 Koo, *The Other Half of Macroeconomics and the Fate of Globalization*, pp. 54–77.

62 Brenner, *The Economics of Global Turbulence*, London–New York 2006, passim.

note of Koo's work, Lawrence Summers has recently offered a scenario that fits it in striking fashion from another angle. What if the standard recipes of the hour for avoiding another crisis—monetary flexibility, fiscal expansion, macroprudential regulation—became inadequate? Then extreme measures might prove necessary. 'Think of what Japanese macroeconomic policy has had to resort to in order to sustain demand and maintain 1 per cent annual growth over the last twenty years: interest rates, both short and long, close to zero, large fiscal deficits leading to a very large increase in public debt, massive central bank purchases, and recourse to external demand in the form of a current account surplus'—the last, crucially, 'an option that would not be available to other countries if the same weakness were to affect all of them. Were Japan to be a template of things to come for the rest of the advanced countries, what would be needed would indeed be a macroeconomic policy revolution.' Was this a realistic prospect? 'If the United States or Europe were to go into recession in the next couple of years, in all likelihood their situation would look much like that of Japan, with zero rates, large fiscal deficits, below-target inflation, and inadequate growth. We may be one cyclical downturn away from the need for a revolution.'[63] Cutting the temerities of the Fed drily down to size, this from the embodiment of neo-liberal swagger at Clinton's side in the confident nineties.

---

63 Without even so much as a need to mention the $17 trillion worth of negative yielding debt—up from $8.3 trillion just nine months previously—weighing on the global economy. Olivier Blanchard and Lawrence Summers, 'Introduction: Rethinking Stabilization Policy: Evolution or Revolution?', in (eds) *Evolution or Revolution? Rethinking Macroeconomic Policy after the Great Recession*, Cambridge (Mass.), 2019, pp. xxxviii–xxxix; a volume containing contributions from the *crème de la crème* of the central banking world and the areopagus of scholarly reflection: Bernanke, Draghi, Haldane, Coeuré, Rubin, Gopinath, Rodrik, Rajan, Eichengreen, Reinhart and so on.

VI

In the crisis, one monetary innovation which the Fed did claim as its own was its swap lines supplying dollar liquidity to European banks, on which Tooze lays legitimate emphasis as an unadvertised transgression of its domestic mandate.[64] Yet the very interlocking American and European financial systems that form the central theme of his book make it clear that, once embarked on bailing out US banks and insurance companies, the Fed had no option but to follow suit with European counterparts, so intertwined were the two—the latter indeed dominating the market in the riskiest layer of securitized mortgages in America. There is no call to make heroism out of such necessity. On the other side of the swaps, it seems fairly clear that European central banks, rather than being startled and overwhelmed by the generosity of US largesse, counted on it in advance. As one of Tooze's anonymous central bankers—perhaps Mervyn King—told him: 'Given our long history of relations with the Fed, we didn't expect to have any difficulty getting hold of dollars.' Why this should be described as 'an astonishingly audacious assumption', rather than its comfortable opposite, is obscure.[65]

Nevertheless, Tooze's mastery of the North Atlantic nexus within the landscape of global finance yields a striking picture

---

64 In their joint self-congratulation for popular consumption, Bernanke, Geithner and Paulson allocate just four discreet sentences to swaps: *Firefighting: The Financial Crisis and Its Lessons*, New York 2019, pp. 42–3. In historical reality, as distinct from current legend, central bank swaps were not a brainwave of 2008. They date from the sixties, when the Fed chairman of that period, William McChesney Martin, instituted them to defend the dollar from speculative attack and halt the drain of gold from US reserves during the Vietnam War. For particulars, see 'The Fed's Novel Idea', in Daniel McDowell, *Brother, Can You Spare a Billion? The United States, the IMF and the International Lender of Last Resort*, New York 2017, pp. 54–63.

65 *Crashed*, p. 90.

of its European wing, puncturing complacent self-images of the Old World. The notion that 'social Europe' differed in any significant way from the logic of financial capitalism in America he exposes as an illusion. In reality, Europe was far more heavily over-banked than the US. In size of assets, the three biggest banks in the world in 2007 were European, while the liabilities of the banking system in every member state of the eurozone, measured against their GDP, were at least three times larger than those of America.[66] It was no accident that the first tremors of the earthquake to come originated not in the US but in the EU, with the crisis of BNP Paribas and collapse of Northern Rock in August–September 2007. Entanglement with America to the West; predation in Europe itself to the East, where Tooze shows the extent of the financial appropriation of local assets in the former Communist countries by Dutch, Austrian and Scandinavian capital. Nor, of course, has he anything but scorn for the role of the ECB and the turn to austerity once the crisis broke.

There, in one of the many gripping set-pieces of the book, Tooze delivers a damning verdict on the treatment of Greece by the Commission, the ECB and the IMF, and subsequently the European Council, which presided over its fate from 2010 onwards. The crushing of Syriza's attempt to negotiate less draconian terms for its society and economy is not only vividly portrayed, but set in the wider context of the thwarting of governments of the left in these years by the external imposition of 'political and financial discipline' on them. No one could doubt on which side Tooze's sympathies lie in this exercise of brute power. But just where did discipline come from, and how far did it extend? At this crux, his account takes leave of absence. At its centre lies the nature of the European Union, and the position of Germany within it. Evasive on the first and inconsistent on the

66 Ibid., p. 110.

second, *Crashed* offers no coherent relationship between them, for it is too protective of each.

Decisive in this regard is its abstraction of the decisions taken by policymakers from the structures in which they were working. What was the matrix of the monetary union created at Maastricht? In *Crashed*, Tooze vouchsafes not a word on the Treaty, though elsewhere he has spoken of its aims as creating a 'European society by stealth', and 'binding Germany to Europe'.[67] Ignored is the carefully crafted ordoliberal design of a single currency managed by a supranational bank, elevated clear of any democratic electorate, insulating market forces from a popular will inherently destructive of them—advocated by Hayek already before the war, and realized by his Freiburg disciples after it; the intellectual world of Quinn Slobodian's *Globalists*. The sole mandate of the ECB would be price-stability, to which a fiscal straitjacket was added in the nineties. The authors of each were German: Karl-Otto Pöhl and Theo Waigel. The provisions of the latter were soon flouted by Germany itself, penalties unenforced; of the former with more difficulty, since they prohibited the Central Bank from purchase of government bonds. But in due course that rule too was circumvented when need arose.[68] QE started under Trichet at the ECB, if far too meagerly for Tooze.

Dismissing the idea that any inescapable conflict between markets and peoples, capitalism and democracy had much to do with pressures on Greece and weaker members of the eurozone in the crisis, Tooze blames instead the refusal of the ECB to buy

67 Tooze, 'A General Logic of Crisis', *London Review of Books*, 5 January 2017. Of its economic intent, he merely remarks antiseptically that it sought 'to install a permanent disinflationary regime'.

68 See the revealing candour with which this operation wvould later be depicted by the head of research at the ECB in Trichet's time, Lucrezia Reichlin, in the *Financial Times* of 8 February 2012.

bonds in the required quantity. Once it did so under Draghi, however, the squeeze on Greece did not abate, but continued, as he himself notes.[69] His account of the role of Germany in these years contradicts itself no less freely. On the one hand, he insists that its history forbade any 'strategies of domination or even overly assertive leadership', acquitting its political class of any such temptation. On the other, he is obliged to report that when Papandreou and Berlusconi were ousted as premiers of Greece and Italy in 2011, senior officials in Berlin could be heard boasting: 'We do regime change better than the Americans'; and to admit that the Fiscal Compact of 2013 was a straightforward imposition of the German 'debt brake' on the rest of the eurozone. Even Habermas could speak with dismay of Germany openly claiming hegemony in Europe.[70]

The reality is that the European Union, as it came to be constructed at Maastricht, half-way between confederal and federal principles, was an institutionally complex, *sui generis* structure whose logic, as its membership expanded, virtually required a leading state or bloc of states to give it direction. By reason not only of the size of its economy and population, but also the local ideology and experience of its political class, Germany was the natural candidate for this role, as itself at once a federal union, architect of the Central Bank that would guide the monetary union of Europe, and source of the legal culture behind it. Perceptive German minds, contrary to Tooze, had no difficulty explaining their country's role as the hegemonic power within the EU of the new century, as necessary to its coherence as Prussia had been to the Second Reich, another federal structure, under Bismarck.[71] At inter-state level, of course, as Hayek

69 Compare *Crashed*, pp. 397 and 532.

70 Compare *Crashed*, pp. 113–14 with pp. 412, 417–18, 534.

71 For two leading cases, see *The H-Word*, London–New York 2017, pp.

had shown, popular sovereignty was excluded. At national level it remained, if now properly qualified. Regrettably, however, direct expression of the popular will, unacceptable in the Federal Republic, persisted in not a few member states. A referendum in France had nearly undone Maastricht itself, one in Denmark had excluded it from the single currency, another in Ireland had threatened the same to the Treaty of Nice, and worst of all—truly dismaying—a European Constitution laying down the free market as a core value of the Union was overwhelmingly rejected, not only by the famously fickle French but even the staunch Dutch in the referendums of 2005. What was to be done? Germany lost no time. Merkel swiftly confected a facsimile of the charter as a treaty for signature by governments, who could be relied on to do their duty, as opposed to voters who could not, and at Lisbon the requisite document was adopted *nem. con.*

How do these events feature in *Crashed*? 'Left-wing hostility to the pro-market character of the EU and nationalist hostility to Brussels' united to deliver a profound shock to Europe's elite. 'Whatever the rights and wrongs of the constitution, popular democracy had asserted itself.' For the space of a sentence, one might say. Imperturbably, Tooze continues:

> Given the reality of increasingly close economic and financial integration and the extension of the EU to Eastern Europe, the project of reorganizing Europe could not be simply abandoned. A substitute had to be found. If a true constitution was no longer a viable proposition, Europe would have to proceed by the tried-and-tested formula of intergovernmental treaty. This gave a key role to Germany and from November 2005 that meant Chancellor Angela Merkel.[72]

169–76.

72 *Crashed*, p. 113.

In other words, the vital task of 'reorganizing Europe' had nothing to do with democracy—quite the contrary—and the appointed leader in neutering it was—not a word of explanation is even required: who else?—the chancellor of Germany. Its 'key role' was simply 'given'.

Not that the nested structures of an ordoliberal confederation and hegemony of Berlin within it have ever been a complete fit, or that the operationalization of the first invariably requires the second. Elsewhere, Tooze can be blunter about the activities of the ECB, German-designed but whose head has never so far been a German, describing the demand by Trichet and Draghi that the Spanish and Italian governments cut spending and increase taxes—in Italy, if necessary by invoking emergency Cold War powers, on pain of being denied purchase of local bonds—as a 'blatant attempt to shift the balance of social and political power by means of monetary policy'.[73] But neither episodes like this, nor the subsequent imposition of the Fiscal Compact—not by coincidence, grotesquely rammed into the constitutions of Spain and Italy—nor even the racking of Greece, not to speak of the still harsher fate of Cyprus (punished with a ruthless expropriation of local depositors, while EU financial institutions lost not a cent), which is passed over in silence, ever yield a critical overall reflection on the Union responsible for them. Of its own accord, a situational-tactical narrative excludes this.

Behind it, however, in this instance plainly lies a *parti pris*. The single currency is the ark of a covenant that is not to be questioned. Tooze does not enter into the particulars of its untouchability, depositing allusion to these into a footnote supported by a handful of technical say-sos declaring doubts irreceivable. But an extreme susceptibility on the issue is plain from treatment of arguments at variance with this core value

73 Ibid., pp. 398–9.

as little better than regression to tropes of national socialism.[74] Evidence of the economic benefits of the euro, hard to come by, is not required.[75] Explaining his pledge to do whatever it took to save it, Draghi did not waste time trying to demonstrate these. He simply told his listeners, in words Tooze might echo, that they should not underestimate 'the amount of political capital that is being invested in the euro'. Political capital: what is that? The investment of the political class in its own immunity from popular jurisdiction within the *zone franche* of the single currency.

Yet though it is taken for granted in *Crashed* that the Union of Maastricht is a public good, its performance after 2008 offers Tooze few grounds for satisfaction. If at the end of the day the eurozone remained intact, it was not of its own doing. So utterly inadequate was its response to the crisis that by 2010, 'European affairs could no longer be safely left to the Europeans'.[76] Only

74 Insinuation in 'A General Logic of Crisis' that Wolfgang Streeck, a leading critic of the EU since Maastricht, must be infected with anti-Semitism belongs in the *sottisier* of a Euro-dovecote prone to be flustered into such flights of imagination, alongside Habermas's warning to French voters that if they rejected the European Constitution of 2005 they would be inviting a second Auschwitz. In Tooze's case, it should be said, this was a rare lapse: in debate he has usually been even-tempered and generous.

75 Writing on the eve of the crisis in 2008, Andrea Boltho and Barry Eichengreen, both supporters of European integration, concluded that the Common Market may have increased GDP by 3–4 per cent from the late fifties to the mid-seventies; that the impact of the European Monetary System was negligible; that the Single European Act may have added perhaps another 1 per cent; and that it was unlikely that the Monetary Union had had 'more than a very small effect on the area's growth rate or even level of output'. For these judgments, see 'The Economic Impact of European Integration', Discussion Paper No. 6820, Centre for Economic Policy Research, May 2008. None of the writers—Martin Sandbu, Waltraud Schelkle, Erik Jones—cited by Tooze as concurring with his attachment to the euro (*Crashed*, p. 619) offer a single figure in support of the notion that it has promoted growth.

76 *Crashed*, p. 398.

American leadership and example, once the ECB had learnt to follow the Fed, could extricate it from floundering—'the eurozone was saved by its belated Americanization.' But that was in keeping with the origins of European integration, and the early, heady vision of its future that could now be envisaged once again: 'America had reasserted a new version of liberal hegemony. Europe resumed the forward march to a United States of Europe it had begun under American guidance in 1947.'[77]

What then of the United States itself? There, paradoxically, Trump's victory in 2016, a more drastic reversal than any development in Europe, leads to a verdict on Obama's record more caustic and consolidated than can be found in Tooze's treatment of either the institutions or leading states of the EU. Due homage is paid to those who averted Armageddon. But they did so with technocratic fixes and 'spectacularly lopsided bailouts' that made American capitalism even more concentrated and oligopolistic than before, yielding a 'dismal recovery'—one so inequitable that 95 per cent of what growth it generated was annexed by the top 1 per cent of Americans, the remainder seeing virtually no improvement in their income after the crisis. Obama's much touted healthcare reform, the Affordable Care Act, even if it had created its own constituency, was by any larger measure 'deeply disappointing.' Little or no support was forthcoming to distressed mortgage-holders: unlike the bankers and fund managers among whom Bernanke and Geithner would slide into luxurious berths after departing government service, 'they were the powerless ones.' Centrist liberalism might seem

77 Ibid., p. 444. After attributing this prospect to unnamed academic optimists, Tooze ratifies it as 'a reasonable assessment', even if the stabilization of 2012, and 'the important phase of state building' it involved, would come at a steep political price.

to have triumphed, but its complacency was unwarranted. In 2014 the Democratic electoral rout should have been warning enough. Trump a few months away, Obama was telling people to ignore dark talk about society, and just 'take a walk in the sun, watch their kids playing and hear the birds chirping', to remind themselves what normal American life was like.[78]

Abroad, his administration had rescued Europe from financial breakdown and institutionalized the swap lines between the six principal central banks of the OECD. Even as the political scene was deteriorating at home, 'the global dollar system was being given a new and unprecedentedly expansive foundation'.[79] Yet however technically effective, this was an extension of the reach of American power without public authorization, comparable in its way to the electronic surveillance system of the NSA—each in their fashion offering a security blanket for the US and its allies. This pairing, unsettling for any patriot, is followed by the least conventional chapter of the book, a spirited critique of Western policy towards Russia and intervention in the Ukraine, in which the US and EU share the odium of arrogance and blundering.

Already unexpectedly laudatory of Putin's response to the financial crisis of 2008, 'one of the largest in the world', a package of measures 'dwarfing those undertaken by West European governments',[80] Tooze leaves no doubt of his view about where primary blame lay in the descent of Ukraine into civil war five years later. When the arrival of a client regime mentored by US proconsuls in Kiev met retaliation from Moscow with a Russian takeover of the Crimea, the Obama administration reached for its weapon of choice with states recalcitrant to the American

78 Ibid., pp. 454–60; 581, 321; 565.
79 Ibid., p. 483.
80 Ibid., p. 225.

will, and imposed sanctions—their first and only appearance in *Crashed*, though from the beginning of its story they were the inseparable, geopolitical face of the global dollar system whose expansion it records. Steadily ratcheted up by Washington, complemented with follow-my-leader steps from Brussels, and compounded by a steep fall in oil prices, the result was a worse economic crisis in Russia than in 2009, hitting the population much harder. The Treasury's war, as an exultant practitioner has termed it, had racked up another benchmark as Obama exited: a new Cold War with Russia.[81]

Crashed ends with a chapter, 'The Shape of Things to Come', on China. Is that where the epic of American leadership of the world, in the trilogy Tooze has devoted to it, finally encounters its limits, terrain beyond its inspiration or control? By no means was the PRC immune to the crisis of 2008, exports tumbling and unemployment rising. The CCP's response was a 'gigantic surge in stimulus spending', amounting to over 19 per cent of GDP, that commands Tooze's unstinting admiration. This was the largest Keynesian operation in history, a mobilization of resources on a scale Western economies had only ever achieved under the pressure of war. Its global impact was decisive. 'In 2009, for the first time in the modern era, it was the movement of the Chinese economy that carried the entire world economy.' Relieved at the outcome though Washington might be, could it be altogether reassuring? For what it now faced, 'for the first time since the rise of Nazi Germany', was 'a power that was, at one and the same time, a potential geopolitical competitor,

81 See Juan Zarate, *Treasury's War: The Unleashing of a New Era of Financial Warfare*, New York 2013; the author, an official of Cuban background, worked for the Bush administration. For a gratified follow-up from the Obama regime in the shape of a manual of how to apply the lessons of successfully bringing Iran to its knees, see Richard Nephew, *The Art of Sanctions*, New York 2018.

a hostile regime type and a capitalist economy success story'. Integrated into the global economy though the PRC might be, 'deeply shared economic interests of the kind that legitimated the Fed's swap lines to Europe' would 'be far harder to develop'. Not that all was necessarily lost. The descent of the Shanghai stock market and flight of wealth overseas in 2015 revealed not only the inexperience of the Chinese authorities in handling capital markets, but their dependence in managing the crisis on a helpful decision by the Fed not to raise interest rates. There solidarity of financial purpose held good. But the Obama administration was not letting down its guard: its campaign for TPP was clearly designed to contain the PRC. For the fact remains that 'the victory of the West in the Cold War was far from complete. China's triumph is a triumph for the Communist Party. This is still the fundamental reason for doubting the possibility of truly deep cooperation with China in global economic governance. Unlike South Korea, Japan or Europe, China is not a subordinate part of the American global network.' The concluding anxious concatenation says everything. What is 'truly deep cooperation'? Subordination. What is 'global economic governance'? One more cloying euphemism for US control. Tooze neither assumes the syllogisms as his own, nor repudiates them.

VII

Enough has been said to bring home the virtues of Tooze's trilogy, an enterprise of formidable energy, ambition and imagination, vaulting in scope, absorbing in detail. What light then does a reading of it cast on the paradox of Durand's judgment of its concluding volume? Methodologically, Tooze's 'situational and tactical approach' plunges the reader immediately into the stream of events; structural features emerge only from the point of view of actors attempting to deal with them. Thus, the inter-imperialist war, the Great Depression, and the hypertrophy of finance are taken as givens as are in different ways the world views of Wilson, Hitler or Geithner. The method makes for compelling historical narrative, but it is premised on repressing structural explanation. Politics and economics are indeed interrelated, as Durand observes, but restrictively: treating the latter simply as the pragmatic field within which the heroes and villains of the story make their political decisions.

Thematically, the trilogy is unified by a single, highly individual optic: it is star-struck by America. Not uncritical of it; but, as it were, mesmerized. Tooze's background in the Bonn Republic, where a long-lasting strand in post-war culture mingled wide-eyed excitement with studious reverence for the US—a cross, one might say, between the fandom of a Wenders and the pupillage of a Habermas—clearly accounts for much of this. 'Perhaps particularly as one who grew up in West Germany in the seventies and eighties, as I did,' Tooze explained to his *LRB* audience, 'America *is* gravity.' That belief is the kink in the arc of his work. It is not an ideological vow, like Habermas's 'unconditional orientation to the West', but something closer to a personal—or, as he would have it, generational—quirk. Some political consequences, of course, ensue. Domestically, Tooze has no difficulty finding fault with institutions, policies or persons in the US. Internationally, on the other hand, the US always looms too large in the balance of things—extravagantly in *Wages*, conspicuously in *Deluge*, still perceptibly in *Crashed*; and—not invariably, but too often—from Wilson and Dawes to Bernanke and Geithner, in the role of *salvator mundi*. The stripe of a particular exaggeration runs through the work.

The politics of a left-liberalism require no special reference to America, and if this is set aside, need to be considered in their own right. The compound, as noted, tends to be unstable. Tooze's version is no exception, swerving from a marked inflexion to the right in *Deluge* to a critical turn to the left in *Crashed.* If a single token were to be picked of the change, it would be the disappearance in the latter of the Manichean establishment binary, dividing the world into 'moderates' and 'extremists', pervasive in the former. A radicalization is unmistakable. But it is uneven. Certain of its limits can be seen if *Crashed* is compared with two earlier works covering the crisis of 2008–09 and its resolution, Simon Johnson and James Kwak's *13 Bankers* (2011) and Martin Wolf's *The Shifts and the Shocks* (2014).[82] Neither Johnson, former chief economist at the IMF, nor Wolf, columnist and leader-writer for the *Financial Times*, would think of themselves as connected to a left, however liberal. Yet their treatment of Bernanke and Geithner is more stringent, and their conclusions harder hitting, than anything to be found in *Crashed.*

Opening his book with Bernanke's vainglorious speech of 2004 on the Great Moderation—hymning 'a world of outstanding stability and superlative monetary policy'—Wolf terms it, with polite contempt, 'quaint'.[83] It was the Panglossian confidence of economists like these that, absent exogenous shocks, crises were impossible, which four years later generated the crisis. For Johnson:

> Paulson, Bernanke, Geithner and Summers chose the blank cheque option, over and over again. They did the opposite of what the United States had pressed upon emerging market governments

---

82 Subtitled, respectively: *The Wall Street Takeover and the Next Financial Meltdown* and *What We've Learned—and Have Still to Learn—from the Financial Crisis.*

83 Martin Wolf, *The Shifts and the Shocks*, London 2014, p. 2.

of the 1990s. They did not take harsh measures to shut down or clean up sick banks. They did not cut major financial institutions off from the public dole. They did not touch the channels of political influence that the banks had used so adeptly to secure decades of deregulatory policies. They did not force out a single CEO of a major commercial or investment bank ... The cost of all those blank cheques is virtually incalculable.[84]

The difference is palpable, too, when it comes to prescription. What, post-crisis, is to be done? Johnson, after a blistering attack on the 'American Oligarchy' of half a dozen mega-banks, says the only remedy is to break them up, confining any financial institution to a hard cap of 4 per cent of GDP, and investment banks to 2 per cent. Wolf is willing to go much further, urging renewed consideration of Irving Fisher's plan to abolish the ability of private banks to create money altogether, by obliging them to hold 100 per cent reserves against their deposits, and giving the state the exclusive right to issue money. No comparable proposals of any kind can be found in *Crashed*. Tooze can legitimately reply they would be out of place in the work of a historian. But as a prolific topical commentator in a wide variety of publications,

84 *13 Bankers*, p. 173. Reviewing *Crashed*, Johnson noted that Tooze 'treads gently' where US deregulation is concerned: 'The people who get off lightest are senior officials at the Federal Reserve, including Timothy Geithner, president of the New York Fed during the go-go years', whose self-serving claims Tooze accepts with unwarranted credulity: *Washington Post*, 11 October 2018. For Geithner's cramming of his Treasury staff with Wall Street operatives—his chief of staff was a former top lobbyist for Goldman Sachs, others came from Citigroup, Blackstone, Merrill Lynch—and constant communing—over eighty times in his first seven months in office—with the heads of Goldman, JP Morgan and Citigroup, see *13 Bankers*, pp. 186–7. A major theme of Johnson's book, scarcely broached at all in *Crashed*, is the political corruption of Washington by the country's financial institutions.

the same does not apply. There too, however, abstention would seem to be the rule.

Liberalism has always contained different shades, and its dominant version has varied across countries and periods. In the capitalist world, going back to the eighties, the line of division separating a liberal politics from a politics of the left is their respective attitudes to the existing order of things: does it require structural change or situational adjustment?[85] The degree envisaged of each defines relative locations on either side of the dividing-line. To see where Tooze's position might lie requires a sense of the dominant liberalism of the period.[86] That comes in two interrelated packages. Between states, the 'liberal international order' has for thirty years been the touchstone of geopolitical reason: free markets, free trade, free movement of capital and other human rights, policed by the most powerful nation on earth with help from its allies, in accordance with its rules and its sanctions, its rewards and its retributions. Within states, 'neo-liberalism': privatization of goods and services, deregulation of industries and of finance, fiscal retrenchment, de-unionization, weakening of labour, strengthening of capital—compensated by recognition of gender and multicultural claims.

The first has reigned far more unchallenged than the second. Very few liberals have seriously contested the principles of free trade, the primacy of the United States, or the rule of international law as enshrined in a United Nations whose decisions

85 Matters differed in the communist world: there, of course, liberalism did mean commitment to structural change, and in an exceptional figure like Dmitri Furman could produce a liberalism of the left of a purity and power unlike anything to be found in the West in the same period: for a description, see *London Review of Books*, 30 July and 27 August 2015.

86 For discussion of the dominant, see Alexander Zevin, *Liberalism at Large: The World According to the Economist*, London–New York 2019, pp. 395–6 ff.

the US has for the most part been able to determine at will. The liberal international order remains a precious icon. Many, on the other hand, have questioned or resisted the full application of neo-liberal measures within their own societies, nowhere implemented in their entirety. The extent to which the first shapes the intellectual universe of contemporary liberalism can be judged by the adaptation of leading minds once on liberalism's left to its requirements: thinkers like Rawls, Habermas and Bobbio all furnishing apologetic glosses on US wars of intervention against states declared outlaws by Washington, with or without the affidavit of the Security Council.[87] Tooze has never compromised himself in this way. But the language of 'global economic governance', cleansed of any reference to its most prominent innovation, the proliferation of sanctions to strangle or bludgeon recalcitrant countries into line—'war by other means', as Ambassador Blackwill candidly describes it—offers a route to much the same.[88]

What of the national plane of politics? Tooze has written with all due trenchancy: 'Under modern conditions, neoliberalism is, de facto, an anti-democratic politics, which resolves the tension between capitalism and democracy either by limiting the range of democratic discretion or by interfering directly in the democratic process.'[89] He has attacked the escalation of economic

87 See 'Arms and Rights', *New Left Review* 31, January–February 2005, pp. 5–40.

88 Robert Blackwill and Jennifer Harris, *War by Other Means: Geoeconomics and Statecraft*, Cambridge (Mass.) 2016. The liberal consensus around sanctions exceeds even that in favour of its cousin, humanitarian intervention. In Congress, there were just five votes in the House and the Senate against CAATSA—Countering America's Adversaries Through Sanctions Act. Four were Republican, the fifth was Bernie Sanders, who—unlike the others—explained that he was, of course, in favour of sanctions against Russia. Every single Democrat in the two chambers voted for the bill.

89 'Tempestuous Seasons'.

inequalities under the neo-liberal regimen with no less vigour, and criticized Pollyanna solutions to it. Piketty's well-meaning proposal of a global wealth tax, he writes in *Crashed*, 'wasn't wrong':

> It just sidestepped the reason it was needed in the first place, the brutal struggle for privilege and power, which for decades had enabled those at the top to accumulate huge wealth, untroubled by any serious effort at redistribution. The answer, if there was one, was clearly not technical. It was political in the most comprehensive sense. Power had to be met with power.[90]

When writing in this vein, Tooze has certainly earned his place on the left of liberalism. But the compound is labile. Elsewhere in *Crashed*, he can write without demur of Obama's failure to deliver 'a concerted drive to unify American society around a sustained programme of investment-driven growth and comprehensive modernization.'[91] Unify American society or—power against power—cleave it?

If there is no clear-cut resolution of these tensions in *Crashed*, it is in part because so much rhetorical emphasis falls on the technical complexity of the 'giant "systems" and "machines" of financial engineering', and the vital role of a pragmatic managerialism in keeping them running. Central banks, Tooze has insisted, far from being stoppers of democracy, have often been flywheels of progress. After all, without the good sense of the Bank of England and the Federal Reserve, could the Entente have won the First World War, or the Allies the Second? Without helpful counteractions by Carney and Draghi, could the fallout of unfortunate developments like the victory of Brexit in

90 *Crashed*, p. 462.

91 Ibid., p. 454.

one referendum, or the defeat of Renzi in another, have been contained? 'It would be a grave theoretical error and missed practical opportunity if technocratic structures were held to be a diminution of politics.' They can enhance them. Think of the 'astounding flair for the situation'—magic term!—of someone like Mario Draghi.[92]

When he writes in this mode, rather than looking to possible avenues of democratic control over them, Tooze explains that 'there are good reasons to defend technocratic government against the unreasoning passions of mass democracy. It is all too obvious today how important it is to be able to identify matters of potential technical agreement beyond politics.' Sanity and lunacy so distributed, how can irrational masses be brought to accept rational decisions taken by the Bernankes and the Draghis? There, vital is it that 'coalitions be assembled for unpopular but essential actions'—not just as a conjunctural, but as a permanent necessity: 'building such ad hoc and lopsided political coalitions is what the governance of capitalism under democratic conditions entails'.[93]

Unpopular but essential actions: Tooze's indictment of the EU brutalization of Greece is searing enough. But does he have anything to say about Tsipras's shredding of a referendum to comply with it? Nothing. A silent sigh of relief can be deduced. For wasn't such surrender the responsible course of action, as Stresemann showed? It is enough to compare Durand's verdict in *Fictitious Capital* on the overall tale Tooze's book tells to see the difference between them: 'Finance is a master blackmailer. Financial hegemony dresses up in the trappings of the market,

92 'Für eine Politik der Geldpolitik: Habermas, Streeck und Draghi', co-authored with Danilo Scholz, *Merkur*, May 2017, pp. 19–21, which extends Tooze's criticisms of Streeck, and takes Habermas's conversion to the president of the ECB as a measure of his wisdom.

93 'Tempestuous Seasons'; *Crashed*, pp. 615, 613.

yet captures the old sovereignty of the state all the better to squeeze the body of society to feed its own profits.' That note is missing in *Crashed*. There, blackmail—not called as such—is regrettable, but acceptable.

Ad hoc and lopsided coalitions: to date, the most specific illustration Tooze has offered comes in a recent piece on Germany, his European land of reference, in the *London Review of Books*. In it, he argues for the creation of a Red–Red–Green alliance of the SPD, Die Linke and the Greens, in place of the current Black–Red coalition of the CDU–CSU–SPD that has ruled the country since 2013, as previously from 2005 to 2009. Within the alternative bloc of his hopes, his preference plainly goes to the SPD, hailed as 'no ordinary political party', but one that for 150 years, from the time of Bismarck to that of Merkel, has 'stood for a vision of a better, more democratic and socially just Germany'—as if these were adjectives that could encompass the vote for war credits in 1914, the use of the Freikorps to dispatch Luxemburg and Liebknecht, the McCarthyism of the *Radikalenerlass* in the seventies, and the practice of renditions in this century: not the whole record, but an indelible part of it. Today, obstructing the prospect of a Red–Red–Green alliance is 'Die Linke's ingrained hostility to NATO'.[94] The good sense of the SPD's *Kaisertreu* fealty to it goes without saying.

Such questions aside, what should be the programme of a future Red–Red–Green government? Formally speaking, Tooze's article is a review of four recent books on Germany, to which he adds three others as he proceeds, though, as often in the *LRB* reference to them is cursory, none is accorded the dignity of an actual review. Much of the substance of the piece is devoted to the social consequences of Hartz IV, Schröder's

---

94 Tooze, 'Which Is Worse?', *London Review of Books*, 18 July 2019.

'tough new system of welfare and labour-market regulation', imposed in 2005. Though Tooze prefers a more to a less lenient view of its neo-liberal agenda, and complains that the SPD gets no credit for 'earnest efforts to rebalance' its consequences—a minimum-wage law has since belatedly ended a situation in which Germany was one of the last countries in Europe without one[95]—he leaves no doubt that the condition of the country is far from ideal: inequality has soared, precarity has spread, and with it social and political unrest. To remedy such ills, what agenda of social repair does he outline for a Red–Red–Green coalition? Answer: Germany needs 'a more pro-European government', one capable of responding to the 'bold vision of Europe's future' offered by a 'charismatic' Emmanuel Macron[96]—a leader famously capable of constructing a transverse, if lopsided, coalition and taking unpopular but essential decisions. Nothing else. 'Europe can ill afford further delay.' That empty signifier is all.

It would be wrong to make too much of this. Tooze spreads himself widely, and his accents and formulations vary from place to place. That's often the price of a growing reputation—*la primadonna è mobile*—and shouldn't be taken too seriously. To criticisms of inconsistency, he can in any case reply quite reasonably that nothing he has written falls outside the parameters of a basic commitment to liberalism as it has developed in the West, from the time of Wilson and Lloyd George to that of Geithner and Macron, and no one can accuse *Crashed* of lacking a social sensibility in keeping with this tradition. Yet in today's world, the question can be asked: how far does that differ from

95 A minimum wage was repeatedly proposed to the SPD by Die Linke and declined by it, at a time when the two parties had sufficient votes to pass one in the Bundestag.

96 'Which Is Worse?', pp. 19, 22; for 'bold vision' and Macron, see *Crashed*, pp. 595, 562.

running with the hare and hunting with the hounds—indignant sympathy for the hare, awed admiration for the hounds? 'Power must be met with power.' Truly?

II. EUROPEAN ORDER

2

THE SPECIAL ADVISER

By repute, literature on the European Union and its pre-history is notoriously intractable—dull, technical, infested with jargon: matter for specialists, not general readers. From the beginning, however, beneath an unattractive surface it developed considerable intellectual energy, even ingenuity, as contrasting interpretations and standpoints confronted each other. But for some sixty years after the Schuman Plan was unveiled in 1950, there was a striking displacement in this body of writing. Virtually without exception, the most original and influential work was produced not by Europeans, but by Americans. Whether the angle of attack was political science, economics, law, sociology, philosophy or history, the major contributions—Haas, Moravcsik, Schmitter, Eichengreen, Weiler, Fligstein, Siedentop, Gillingham—came from the United States, with a singleton from England before it acceded to the Common Market, in the pioneering reconstruction of Alan Milward.

This has finally changed. In the past decade, Europe has generated a set of thinkers about its integration who command the field, while the US, now increasingly absorbed in itself, has largely vacated it. Among these, one stands out. By reason both of the reception and the quality of his work, the Dutch philosopher-historian Luuk van Middelaar can be termed, in Gramsci's vocabulary, as the first organic intellectual of the EU. Though related, applause and achievement are not the same. *The Passage to Europe: How a Continent Became a Union*, which catapulted van Middelaar to fame and the precincts of power, is a remarkable work. The tones in which it has been widely received are of another order. 'There are books before which', a Belgian reviewer declared, 'a chronicler is reduced to a single form of commentary: an advertisement.' As once of *The Name of the Rose* there was now simply a 'before and after of its appearance'.[1] The author himself posts some forty encomia of his book on his website, in seven or eight languages, tributes ransacking the lexicon of admiration: 'supremely erudite', 'brilliant', 'beautifully written', 'a gripping narrative that reads like a Bildungsroman', 'all the fields of human knowledge and culture are convoked in abounding richness', 'succeeds as no one else has done in understanding the essence of what it is to be European', 'near-Voltairean', 'like all great novels, tells us something about our European condition', 'a Treitschke with the tongue of Foucault'. Even the austere *European Journal of International Law* found it 'thrilling'.

I

Signal amid this enthusiasm has been a general lack of curiosity about the author himself. That could be expected in the columns of newspapers and magazines, less so in academic journals. But in the depoliticized ether of professional Euro-studies, enquiry into the background of a scholar is not *comme il faut*; while

1 Jacques De Decker, 'Hourrah pour l'Europe!', *Espace-Livres*, 30 January 2012; the author held a chair in the Royal Academy of French Language and Literature in Belgium.

the Netherlands is in any case among the countries of Western Europe whose culture and politics are least familiar outside its borders. To understand *The Passage to Europe*, however, a sense of where the author comes from is required. Van Middelaar, born in 1973 in Eindhoven, the company town of Philips in Brabant, took history and philosophy at the University of Groningen in the early nineties. There he studied under the philosopher of history Frank Ankersmit, a *sui generis* thinker whose ideas left a lasting mark on him.[2] Good political thought, for Ankersmit, was never of the sort personified by Rawls: an abstract system of principles detached from any concrete reality. It was always a response to urgent historical problems, produced by thinkers —Bodin, Hobbes, Locke, Burke or Tocqueville—immersed in the great conflicts of their time: religious strife, civil war, revolution, democracy. The first and most original of this line was Machiavelli, confronting the crisis of Italy's division at the turn of the sixteenth century. It was he who founded the novel idea of *raison d'état* that would become a central tradition in European political thought, and one formative of modern writing about history, as Meinecke had shown in his studies of historicism.[3]

For Machiavelli, statecraft was the art of mastering the contingency of fortune with a virtuoso existential decision capable of giving shape to a political order that, while not fearing conflict, would prove as stable as any such order could hope to be. In this, he prefigured a problematic that would in different ways haunt Western thought down to our own time. For what, after

2 For a careful, balanced introduction to Ankersmit's work, see Herman Paul and Adriaan van Veldhuizen, 'A Retrieval of Historicism: Frank Ankersmit's Philosophy of History and Politics', *History and Theory* 57, March 2018, pp. 33–55.

3 F.R. Ankersmit, *Aesthetic Politics: Political Philosophy beyond Fact and Value*, Stanford 1996, pp. 2–4, 15–16; *Political Representation*, Stanford 2002, pp. 28–32.

all, Ankersmit asked, is the appropriate definition of representation? Is it a resemblance to what is represented, or a substitute for it? Rousseau mistakenly believed it was the first; Burke showed it was the second. In politics as in painting, representation is not a biometric likeness of what is represented, but an act of basically aesthetic nature—the creation of something new, which was never imagined or existed before.[4] It was an effect of *style*, beyond fact or value. The creative politician perceived a possibility, glimpsed by no one else, of founding a new conception of things capable of winning the assent of citizens as so many connoisseurs viewing a painting or a building.[5] The supreme act of such an aesthetic politics was the construction of a compromise between conflicting parties, which was at once the condition and core of any modern democracy. 'The politician formulating the most satisfying and lasting compromise is the political "artist" par excellence.'[6] Contrary to received opinion, the origins of such an aesthetic politics did not lie in the Enlightenment, but in Romanticism. Its first glimmering came in the German *Frühromantik*, where Schlegel extolled the manifold of opposites in a clouded language that Carl Schmitt would later attack for its vagueness, yet which just for that reason was propitious for compromise. But it was the French *doctrinaires* of the Restoration, above all Guizot, who gave full expression to this breakthrough, as they laboured to reconcile what had been irreconcilable—the nostalgia of ultras for the *Ancien Régime* and the cult by radicals of the French Revolution or of Napoleon—in a politics of the *juste milieu*.[7]

Such was the true formula for the parliamentary democracy

4 *Political Representation*, pp. 107–15.
5 *Aesthetic Politics*, pp. 156–62.
6 *Political Representation*, p. 198.
7 *Aesthetic Politics*, pp. 125–41; *Political Representation*, pp. 93–9.

emergent in the nineteenth and perfected in the twentieth century: the antithesis of the direct democracy preached by Rousseau, which had dishonoured representation by extraditing it to the boundless impulses of a collective political libido.[8] After the Second World War, the genius of compromise on which Western democracy rested would reconcile the conflict between capital and labour with the invention of the welfare state which brought peace between them, while preserving capitalism intact.[9] Today, however, division in society no longer sets one camp against another. Instead, the unprecedented issues of crime, environment, ageing, juridification of every relationship, split human beings inwardly, leaving a conflict within themselves. Such problems could only be resolved by a strong—though certainly lean—state, as the necessary locus of power. Ignored in a Rawlsian matrix concerned only with rights rather than interests, such a state was the indispensable lever of an aesthetic politics capable of restoring the boundaries between public and private realms in the century.[10]

Ankersmit terms himself a conservative liberal. Distinctive in the heady brew he offered is the combination of a meta-politics generally associated with the radical right—Mussolini had vaunted a politics of style, and Benjamin concluded that the aestheticization of politics was a trademark of fascism—with a politics of the moderate centre: the *juste milieu* of the French liberals of the Restoration as the last word of democratic maturity. Meinecke, whose historicism is perhaps the most important single influence on Ankersmit, could be described as another conservative liberal displaying something of the same mixture:

8 Ibid., pp. 346–7.

9 *Political Representation*, pp. 209–10. See, for a commendable example from the Netherlands, pp. 211, 261.

10 *Aesthetic Politics*, pp. xv–xvi, 354–60.

in 1918 a founder of the liberal German Democratic Party; in 1939 an enthusiast for Hitler's invasion of Poland. In Ankersmit, *les contraires se touchent* in a more theoretically articulated fashion, capable of another kind of imprint on listeners receptive to it. Under his guidance, van Middelaar set off for Paris in 1993 to write a Master's thesis on French political thought since the war. There he would find a local mentor in Marcel Gauchet, a leading light of the anti-totalitarian galaxy of the eighties who by that time had become a critic of the promotion of human rights to a central position in democratic thought. In 1999 van Middelaar published the result of his labours in the Netherlands, *Politicide. De moord op de politiek en de Franse filosofie*—'Politicide: The Murder of Politics in French Philosophy'. Perhaps advised that this penny-dreadful note might not go down well in France, the book did not appear in the country it was about.

Its lurid title, however, captured the crudity of the work, much of it warmed-over Cold War pabulum. Touted in the preface as the first treatment of all three generations of misbegotten French political thought since 1945—the Marxism of (the early) Merleau-Ponty and Sartre, the Nietzscheanism of Foucault and Deleuze, and the Kantianism of Ferry and Renaut—it glossed Vincent Descombes's critique of the first two as vicious derivations of Kojève, and the rejection by Gauchet and others of the third as pious reversions to the thought-world of the Categorical Imperative. Overall, this was a body of thought that 'invariably led to a defense of terrorism or a declaration of impotence',[11] the two united in a common moralism—active in the Marxists and Nietzscheans, passive in the Kantians—whose effect was to put politics to death. Redemption was to be found in the wisdom of Gauchet's teacher Claude Lefort, whose great work on Machiavelli, taking its cue from the Florentine's masterly analysis of the

11 *Politicide. De moord op de politiek*, Amsterdam 1999, p. 9.

relations between ruler and ruled, had restored democracy to its proper dignity by redefining it as the empty space of liberty in which contention between different voices and forces could of necessity never end.

Little of this was new in the Paris of Aron and Furet, Rosanvallon and Descombes, though it could hardly fail to please. In the more provincial context of the Netherlands, on the other hand, it was greeted as a revelation. Garlanded with prizes, its author was declared a philosophical prodigy, and returned to Paris for further research in 1999. There, meanwhile, the country had been shaken four years earlier by the massive wave of strikes against the package of pension and welfare cuts introduced by Chirac's prime minister Alain Juppé to comply with budgetary requirements of the Treaty of Maastricht. Confronted with the largest social movement since 1968, the country's intelligentsia split. Bourdieu led widespread support for the uprising. Lefort was among those who supported the government, pronouncing the movement against it infected by 'rancor and resentment', 'populism', 'archaeo-marxism, maoism and sartrism'.[12] Unhappily, public opinion did not heed the resuscitator of politics, but expressed overwhelming solidarity with the protests, which ended with a humiliating defeat for the government.

Perhaps with a view to seeing how such setbacks could be avoided, van Middelaar started to study pension systems in the EU at the École des hautes études en sciences sociales. But worse was to follow. Cycling past the Place de la Bastille a few months after 9/11, he was appalled to see a rag-tag crowd of youth waving red banners against the American invasion of Afghanistan, and sat down to pen a blistering attack on such idiocy. After a few more imprecations against Sartre and the other advocates of terror who had fostered it, he pointed out

12 'Les dogmes sont finis', *Le Monde*, 4 January 1996.

that even if Bin Laden was not being hidden by the Taliban, who in their right mind could be against a war on the regime in Kabul? The West stood for the values of civilization, and was bringing modernity to Afghans and others across the world who craved it. Yet:

> We Westerners, weighed down by the past, hardly even dare to understand this any longer. The White Man's Burden, that heroic civilizing mission depicted by Rudyard Kipling in his proud poem of 1899 as the destiny of the white race, has turned against us and become a true burden, a depressing sense of guilt about colonization, slavery and economic exploitation of the developing world. Which now prevents us from understanding that colonization did—indeed!—mean something good for the colonized. Colonization brought schools, hospitals, science, emancipation of women. Colonization brought modern reason and freedom within reach of individuals hitherto unable even to be individuals. Sure, colonial crimes occurred—rape, torture, institutional racism—and yet, what a beautiful body of work!

Today, the main political question had become:

> Can human rights spread globally without the action of a Napoleon? The answer is no. Anyone who thinks that it can has a moralistic view of reality. Anyone who thinks that good may impose itself on the world without struggle or the use of power is mistaken. Anyone with a basic understanding of politics knows that what is good does not come automatically. That may require an army. A Napoleon. Or a George W. Bush. A price must be paid if we want human rights to spread. We should not blame Napoleon for using violence, but for not going far enough. Napoleon's mistake was that he employed freedom and equality as symbols to help his army win battles rather

> than incorporating these concepts in sturdy institutions in the constitutions which he scattered across Europe. To continue the analogy: our hope must be that Bush finishes his job thoroughly, dragging Afghanistan into modernity with bombs and abundance.

Van Middelaar ended his peroration:

> And we, meanwhile, are patiently waiting for a modern-day Kipling who realizes that not white but modern people have a world-historical mission: to sing proudly and unabashedly in praise of the Modern Man's Burden.[13]

By this time, he had become bored with pensions, and wrote to a conservative contact working with the Dutch commissioner in Brussels asking if he could find him an internship where he might study power close up. An interview was arranged. Van Middelaar has a highly developed sense of self-presentation, which he likes to dramatize. Introducing his *Politicide* a decade later, he would write: 'My book did not pass unnoticed. It was a surprise that an unknown 26-year-old should unexpectedly dare to challenge consecrated French thinkers. Without knowing it, I was putting into practice an aphorism of Stendhal: entry into society should be conducted as if it were a duel. And what opponents I had chosen!'[14] It took some nerve to pass off this plagiarism from Nietzsche as his own discovery. Van Middelaar's

---

13 'Et voilà: de moderniteit. Het ontzeggen van onze wereld aan mensen die ernaar hunkeren, is en moedloos makende traditie', *Trouw*, 3 December 2001.

14 *Politicide: De moord op de politiek*, Groningen 2011, p. 5. The passage was lifted from Nietzsche's reflections on David Strauss in his last work *Ecce Homo*, London 1911, p. 79. Invocations of Stendhal would shortly become a standard trope in advertisements for a heroic young self. Ironic reflections on the fashion and its political significance can be found in Régis Debray, *Du génie français*, Paris 2019, p. 34.

account of his ascent to Brussels is another little piece of theatre. More original and no less theatrical:

> In another era, on Tuesday March 27 2001, I took the train from Paris, where I was living at the time, to Brussels. I was nervous. A student in political philosophy living in a garret of no more than 18 sq meters, I arduously put on a suit that morning. Approaching the metro, I asked a surprised, well-dressed passer-by whether he could help me fix the knot in my tie. I was on my way to the European quarters in Brussels, where I was to have lunch with the Dutch European commissioner and his personal assistant.[15]

The commissioner with whom he landed the post that he wanted was Frits Bolkestein. In the Dutch political landscape Bolkestein cut an unusual figure. Son of a president of the Court of Amsterdam, after a polymathic education—degrees successively in mathematics, philosophy, Greek, economics (at the LSE) and law—he joined Shell, serving it for sixteen years as an overseas executive in East Africa, Central America, London, Indonesia and Paris. In 1976 prompted, as he would later explain, by his experience in handling trade-unions in El Salvador, where he was posted during one of its various death-squad regimes, he became interested in politics, and quit Shell to run for parliament on the ticket of the VVD, the Dutch variant of a liberal party. By this time the original 'pillar' system of post-war Dutch politics, in which the electorate was divided into four columns—Catholic, Protestant, Labour and Liberal—had been simplified by the merger of Catholic and Protestant forces into a Christian Democratic party along bi-confessional German lines, and voting had become more fluid. The Liberal sector of the system, upper-class and

15 *De passage naar Europa: geschiedenis van een begin*, University of Amsterdam 2009, p. 5.

originally anti-clerical, rooted in business and the bureaucracy, was politically the weakest. Though the party was a standard, if not invariable, fixture of the coalitions on which all governments were based, there had never been a Liberal prime minister since the time of the First World War.

The hallmarks of Dutch political culture, as first criticized by the political scientist Hans Daalder, and later celebrated by the American Arend Lijphart, were an imperative of consensus, a requirement of secrecy for reaching it, and a cult of practicality. Consensus demanded a permanent disposition to accommodation between parties. That was best reached behind closed doors. Business-like deals negotiated discreetly precluded a battle of ideas. The supreme national virtue of *Zakelijkheid*—down-to-earth, no-nonsense practicality, with a self-righteous timbre distinct from its more neutral cousin, the German *Sachlichkeit*—had no time for intellectualism of any sort. In the memorable dictum of the country's current premier, VVD leader Mark Rutte: 'vision is like an elephant that obstructs one's sight'. For Lijphart the system was an admirably 'consociational' democracy. For Daalder, it was a legacy of the 'regent mentality' of the country's pre-democratic patriciate, a merchant class facing neither a powerful nobility nor a fractious plebs, settling affairs of state comfortably among themselves without need of concepts or credos, confident of the passivity of the masses. The political elite of post-war Netherlands was their complacent descendant.[16]

16 Daalder's address of 1964, 'Leiding en lijdelijkheid in de Nederlandse politik', can be found in his *Van oude en nieuwe regenten: Politiek in Nederland*, Amsterdam 1995, which contains two subsequent lectures toning down its arguments, and a concluding address of 1984, reaffirming 'the strength of collegial and corporate traditions' in the elite, from which regent traditions and values had by no means disappeared, in a political culture to which Daalder paid ambivalent respects. For the background to all this, see the outstanding study of Merijn Oudenampsen, *The*

Into this scene Bolkestein burst like a bazooka. He had plenty of ideas; and, a fluent writer and eloquent speaker, no inhibitions in aggressively expressing them. He soon made his mark. In the eighties, the dominant figure in Dutch politics was Ruud Lubbers, a Christian Democrat who led the country for a dozen years (1982–94), and was for a time regarded by Thatcher as the nearest thing to a soulmate she had in Europe. But to her disappointment he domesticated rather than crushed the trade-unions, and mindful of the golden rule of consensus, administered only moderate doses of privatization and welfare reduction. Bolkestein, by contrast, had read his Hayek and was contemptuous of such paltering. What the economy and society of the country needed was a true neo-liberal makeover, breaking the clammy grip of corporatism and welfare dependence to release the creativity of the free market. Nor were these tares the only threats to a modern liberalism. Culturally speaking, the Dutch elites had surrendered to a local New Left, floating harebrained schemes and upending moral restraints in the sixties, and were now failing to stem an inrush of Muslim immigration whose religious beliefs and customs were incompatible with Western values. There, Huntington and Kristol were needed to fortify Friedman and Hayek. With this combination of neoliberal and neo-conservative ammunition, Bolkestein did battle within the VVD too, and as he did so he caught the tide of a New Right that swelled a season later than in the Anglosphere, generating Pim Fortuyn and Gert Wilders as successive tribunes of a libertarian economics and Islamophobic politics. Both were formed in the VVD, Wilders serving for a time as Bolkestein's chief of staff.[17]

Conservative Embrace of Progressive Values: On the Intellectual Origins of the Swing to the Right in Dutch Politics, Tilburg University 2018, pp. 57–69.

17 *The Conservative Embrace of Progressive Values*, pp. 113–50.

Though by 1990 Bolkestein led his party in parliament —a position which did not automatically make him its candidate for premier—he remained in a minority within it. The party, moreover, was now in a coalition headed not even by the Christian Democrats but by Labour, in a cabinet of which Bolkestein declined to become a minister. Invigorated by him, the VVD increased its vote in 1994, and in 1998 achieved its highest score ever. But it was still in second place behind Labour, and believing that the Labour leader Kok would refuse him the Foreign Ministry, Bolkestein quit parliament. In his hardline combination of free market economics with anti-immigrant sentiment, he had been the Dutch version of Enoch Powell.[18] Both proved lastingly influential, yet also remained outsiders and personal failures. Though Bolkestein was well read and, compared with norms of the Dutch elite, at home with ideas, he was not—he confessed—really an intellectual, more of 'a politician and pamphleteer'. By background a businessman, and less of a dedicated ideologue than Powell, he lacked the latter's scholarly and poetaster side, and above all was not a temperamental isolate. Blunt but convivial, Bolkestein never lacked companions and collaborators, and was not a political failure. Though he never became premier, it was he who paved the way for the triumph of the VVD under Mark Rutte, now ruler of the Netherlands for a decade.

By way of compensation for frustration in The Hague, the job Bolkestein took in 1999 at Brussels was and is, after its president, one of the most powerful in the European Commission, the Internal Market portfolio. German ordoliberals had

18 He once told Ian Buruma: 'One must never underestimate the hatred Dutch people feel for Moroccan and Turkish immigrants. My political success is based on the fact that I was prepared to listen to such people'—a remark straight out of Powell's play-book: *Murder in Amsterdam: The Death of Theo van Gogh and the Limits of Tolerance*, London 2006, p. 64.

once worked to ensure that European integration conformed to the principles of a free market, keeping any truck with dirigisme at bay. Bolkestein was a natural successor, and tutoring van Middelaar in the ways of the Commission, evidently found him a good learner, since he extended the younger man's internship in Brussels. There van Middelaar could observe close up, perhaps even have a speech-writing hand in, the final episode of Bolkestein's public career, the Directive on Services he promulgated in the spring of 2004, which decreed that firms could in future employ workers at pay and conditions in a firm's country of origin rather than of their work—in effect, the lower wages prevailing in the newly incorporated states of Eastern Europe where immigrants came from, rather than at rates customary or obligatory in Western Europe. No decision of the Commission before or since has caused such an uproar. Deputies agitated, trade-unions mobilized, port workers stormed the European Parliament, protesters 100,000 strong descended on Brussels. Uniquely, too, the Directive had to be first watered down, and eventually converted into something not unlike its opposite. By that time, his term of office over, Bolkestein was safely at home in a bespoke chair at the University of Leiden. It may have been another kind of lesson for van Middelaar. Europe was not necessarily always best served by the Commission.

II

Van Middelaar's own career proceeded smoothly upwards. After service in Brussels, he became political secretary to Jozias van Aartsen, Bolkestein's successor as leader of the VVD in The Hague. There, the muffled world of the Binnenhof, where the Dutch elite transacted discreet business between consenting parties, was revealed to him—an eye-opening opportunity, he explained to a friend, to dwell for a time at the centre of power. Van Aartsen, averse to Bolkestein's *tranchant*, came from the temporizing moderate wing of the party to which van Middelaar readily adapted, rising high in his chief's confidence. When a commission including Ankersmit was formed to produce a new manifesto for the party in 2005, van Middelaar wrote the final eighty-page document *For Freedom*, a carefully weighed composite of (classical, social and neo-) liberal themes. Ingredients included calls for a flat tax and clearing beggars off the streets, a directly elected prime minister and curbing of quangocrats, private pensions and strict compliance with the EU's Stability Pact, help for the neediest but no truck with a basic income.

> The primary responsibility for material well-being lies with the individual himself. Private initiative, self-reliance, entrepreneurial spirit and willingness to roll up one's sleeves are completely normal and in principle accessible to everyone. It is pre-eminently the hard-working middle class who embodies these liberal virtues.[19]

The VVD could be proud that 'when immigration and integration were still taboo topics', it was the first to see that 'the unregulated influx of asylum seekers and the uncritical embrace of multiculturalism would cause major problems'.[20] It did not countenance Islamophobia, but warned Muslims what could be coming to them if they sought to introduce fundamentalism into the country: 'In 1535 a group of Anabaptists rebelled in Amsterdam, seeking to build a religious theocracy. The city

19 *Om de Vrijheid: Liberaal Manifest*, The Hague 2005, p. 48.
20 Ibid., p. 10.

council crushed this radical uprising, to the great satisfaction of most citizens.'[21] This was a century to which people should look back for inspiration.

The Dutch were now doing well. On average, they were satisfied or very satisfied with their lives. But they should always remember that 'the desire for freedom is the foundation of our nation', as was not the case with their neighbours:

> The origin of our country does not lie in an elusive distant past, as in the case of England or France. Nor was the country forged from above by a strong will, like Germany or Italy. No, our country was born at the end of the sixteenth century from the tough, concerted effort to wrest freedom from the authority of a tyrannical Spanish king. Freedom and tolerance ignited the light of our Golden Age. These two enabled the miracle of a country inhabited by barely two million people that left every other European country far behind in entrepreneurial spirit, culture, science and political-philosophical wisdom.[22]

Every country has its own brand of smugness. But patriotic uplift and pledge of regressive taxation were of little avail to the VVD, which under van Aartsen's stewardship was steadily sinking in the polls. Six months later, after telling just two intimates—Rutte and van Middelaar—that he would resign if the party fell below 14 per cent in upcoming municipal elections, van Aartsen quit when it failed to do so. Rutte became leader, the manifesto was forgotten and van Middelaar was out of a job. He retired to his study, and over the next two years wrote the book that would make him famous. Published in 2009 (the English-language edition appeared in 2013), it showed how much he had learnt

21 Ibid., p. 63.
22 Ibid., pp. 9–10.

since his time in Paris. *The Passage to Europe* is not the masterpiece of the extravagant bouquets that have covered it. But it is a work of impressive scholarship and historical imagination, whose range of intellectual reference and polish of style make it unlike anything written about the EU before or since. Van Middelaar took great pains with its literary surface, if not always to its advantage. The title of his book, he once explained, contained a fourfold allusion: to anthropological rites of passage, to Forster's *A Passage to India*, to Benjamin's *Passagenwerk*, and to a romance by … Giscard d'Estaing.[23] In this mixture, epigraphs strewn from Tolstoy to Monty Python by way of Bismarck and Bagehot, Foucault and Arendt, are less than value-added. Such pretensions aside, however, van Middelaar produced something rare in the literature on European integration, an attractively readable account of it. The account, moreover, is powerful and original, fruit of the distinctive blend of philosophy and history taught him by Ankersmit.

It opens by remarking that discourses about Europe have revolved around either offices, states or citizens, with corresponding theories of how it is best conceived—respectively, in the academic literature, in terms of functionalism, intergovernmentalism or constitutionalism: the first oriented to a static present, the second to a familiar past, the third to a longed-for future. Yet none of these pass the critical test of genuine historicity, that flux of unpredictable events which makes of government—van Middelaar cites Pocock—'a series of devices for dealing with contingent time'.[24] To do so requires, instead, that three different spheres in which integration has unfolded be

23 'Telling Another Story of Europe: A Reply in Favour of Politics', *Bijdragen en mededelingen betreffende de geschiedenis der Nederlanden*, January 2010, p. 85.

24 *The Passage to Europe: How a Continent Became a Union*, London 2013, p. 10.

distinguished: an outer sphere comprising Europe understood as a continent—including states not part of the Community—in the world of powers at large, where borders and wars obtain; an inner sphere, comprising the Commission, the Court of Justice and Parliament of today's EU; and an intermediate sphere composed of its member states as they deliberate in the Council of Ministers and its apex, where heads of government assemble, the European Council.

For the founders of modern political thought—Hobbes, Locke, Rousseau—the primordial question was how the state could arise from a condition of nature composed of an anarchy of individuals, pre-existing it: how, in particular, the unanimity required for a pact of civil union to bring a state into being, could lead to majority decisions once it was constituted? The same puzzle, van Middelaar argues, is posed by the emergence of a unitary European polity out of an anarchic order, not of individuals, but of states themselves. To answer it, he reconstructs the path from sectoral agreements between the original Six—France, Germany, Italy, Belgium, the Netherlands and Luxembourg—derived from the Schuman Plan of 1950, which set up the European Coal and Steel Community, to the broader European Economic Community—the 'Common Market'—created by the same Six with the Treaty of Rome seven years later. Under the Treaty, a permanent Commission situated in Brussels, its personnel appointed by the member states, would submit proposals implementing the articles of the Treaty to a Council of Ministers representing their governments, in which decisions required their unanimous consent, with the provision that after eight years, voting by majority could occur. Once set up, the Commission rapidly started to expand its activities. Its first president, the bumptious German diplomat Walter Hallstein, openly spoke of it as the 'executive'—that is, government—of Europe, and in 1962 sought to bounce the Council into according it a substantial tax base, and the hitherto powerless Parliament created by the Treaty, regarded by the Commission as an ally, rights over the Community budget. Germany, Italy and the Netherlands backed him. By this time, however, de Gaulle ruled in Paris and killed the scheme by calmly withdrawing France from the proceedings of the Community, paralysing it. The ensuing 'crisis of the empty chair' was resolved by the so-called Luxembourg compromise of 1966, which in effect accepted that a decision could not be taken by a majority in the Council if 'very important interests' of a member state were at issue, giving it a veto. 'Supranationality has gone', de Gaulle would declare. 'France will remain sovereign.'

The horse, however, had already bolted, through a door that had passed unnoticed by him. Three years earlier, the European Court of Justice ruled that national legislation must comply with Community regulations, and where the two conflicted, courts in the country concerned must enforce the latter. Nothing in the Treaty of Rome authorized this. The Court simply invoked the 'spirit' of the Treaty, rather than its letter. Van Middelaar makes no bones about this, celebrating it as 'a masterful move'. True, 'the Court was bluffing', since 'who can know the spirit of a pact?' But it was to be congratulated for doing so: 'The Court staged a coup on 5 February 1963 in the name of a new, autonomous legal order, while claiming that—although no one had been aware of it—this order was as old as the treaty itself. So its infringement of the status quo was concealed.' Better still, in a second 'handsomely constructed self-affirmation', the Court ruled a year later that since Community law overrode national legislation, citizens could appeal to it against the states to which they belonged. It was, in juridical language, of 'direct effect'.[25]

25 Ibid., pp. 51–3.

In the vocabulary of *The Passage to Europe*, the intermediate sphere where the General had checked the ambitions of the Commission was silently trumped by the strongest actor in the inner sphere.

Nor, in the event, was the outcome in the intermediate sphere an impassable obstacle to further European unity. Though the veto remains 'an invisible weapon in negotiations' between member states, van Middelaar argues that its effect is to foster not conflict but agreement. 'It is the psychological certainty of being able to block a resolution if you truly oppose it that makes consensus possible.' Indeed, even when the principle of majority decisions was formally enshrined in certain areas of the Single European Act of 1987, it was rarely exercised in practice, consensus typically now being reached 'not in the shadow of the veto, but in the shadow of the vote'. Should a member state resist a majority decision, it cannot be enforced, short of foreign occupation, but pressure can be put on it to conform by 'other means'.[26] The alchemy of the Union is to achieve unanimity through the threat of majority, rather than to pass from unanimity to majority as imagined in classical theory.

Such was the rule. There was one decisive exception, however. In 1985 the European Council met in Milan to discuss whether—in order to facilitate the proposed Single European Act, essentially intended to extend the Common Market from goods to services—the Treaty of Rome should be amended to convert the Community into a Union, which required an inter-governmental conference to do so. Led by France and Germany, which had been secretly planning revisions beforehand, seven out of the ten member states of the time were in favour. Three—Britain, Denmark and Greece—were opposed.

---

26 Ibid., pp. 72, 76, 41.

By the convention established at Luxembourg, which rarely even needed to be invoked, that was more than enough to block the move. Overnight, however, Italy—host and chair of the meeting—suddenly announced, in the person of its premier Bettino Craxi, that since convening an inter-conference was a procedural rather than substantive issue, he was putting it to the vote. Thatcher, along with her allies Papandreou and Schlüter, was outraged. Craxi was not deterred, and the motion passed seven to three. Thatcher was furious, but—she lived to regret this—did not use her veto because she regarded the SEA as in some degree her own liberalizing handiwork, as it was. Van Middelaar can scarcely contain his enthusiasm at the outcome. Taking 'the opportunity to capitalize on the flow of time', the 'brilliance of Craxi's bluff' had delivered a 'magnificent moment of passage', opening 'the way to Europe's permanent renewal' and endowing 'the Community with a robust supreme authority'. How was it done? '*Secret*: a coup disguised as a procedural decision.'[27]

After Milan, the 'gate was unbarred' to successive Treaty revisions—1986 (Luxembourg–The Hague), 1992 (Maastricht), 1997 (Amsterdam), 2001 (Nice), Lisbon (2007): each one approved by a unanimous decision of the heads of government, each a step further towards a compact European Union, with juridical authority over its member states. The only national court daring to question this constitutional supremacy, the German *Bundesverfassungsgericht*, after emitting a few grumbles at the Treaty of Lisbon, sensibly set legal niceties aside, since these would have caused 'an acute political crisis', and took no action.[28] Lisbon now empowers the European Council, via the

27 Ibid., pp. 107, 109.
28 Ibid., p. 115.

discreet device of a *passerelle*, to make ongoing Treaty alterations without any need of special conferences or ratifications, merely the Italianate blessing of a 'unanimous non-refusal' by national parliaments, which would prove so useful during the euro crisis.

If these were the critical episodes that brought the Union as we know it today into being, what of the capacity of Europe to act as a single political body in the face of the outside world? There, van Middelaar explains in a resonant exordium invoking Machiavelli's famous image of fortune as a raging river that can either flood a landscape with disastrous consequences or be diked and channelled with practical foresight, the Community must contend with aleatory, unpredictable events—for 'history has no plan, no logic'—and be tested by them.[29] It had to 'step into the river of time' and see how far it might master the current, as Machiavelli had taught his contemporaries that heroes of virtue could. In the second part of *The Passage to Europe*, van Middelaar looks at how the Community fared when it did so. His story unfolds in three stages. In the first, 1950 to 1957, all six member states relied on an American umbrella for their security; only Paris—typically playing a double game—pretending otherwise. Still, in these years it was France, possessed of political tenacity, bureaucratic discipline, diplomatic skills and an eye for the long term its partners could not match, which made the running. Determined to recover control of its destiny after 1945, it brought the Community into existence with the Schuman Plan and later gave shape to the intermediate sphere. Germany, needing both America and France for its political redemption after the Third Reich, preferred to operate in the inner sphere. Britain merely wanted

29 Ibid., pp. 129 ff.

not to be excluded, without being willing to participate. Critical to the birth of the Common Market was the shock of Suez in the outer sphere, when the US forced Britain out of the attack on Egypt. Abandoned by its ally on the battlefield, France turned to Europe with the Treaty of Rome, founded on an understanding between Adenauer and Mollet.

A long second phase, lasting from 1958 to 1989, began with the Franco-German deal exchanging agricultural subsidies Paris wanted for competition policies patronized by Bonn; and after repeated setbacks, saw eventual British entry into the Community, once France realized that the UK could be a counterweight to the growing economic prowess of Germany. Then came the oil shock of 1973, when 'Arab aggressors' in the Middle East imposed an embargo on Europe, and the Bretton Woods system finally collapsed. In this dual crisis, 'the member states did not transfer their political voice to the institutions of the inner sphere as a way of becoming better able to respond to the demands of the outside world'. Rather, 'the heads of state staged a coup, uninvited', when at French initiative—Giscard's incalculable contribution to the unity of the continent—they started regular summits and 'as a result the in-between world of the member-states took shape',[30] evolving into the European Council, the commanding instance of the Union to come.

The third stage of Europe's encounter with the torrent of time came when East Germany collapsed in 1989–90. The ensuing crisis led to the deal struck between Kohl and Mitterrand at Strasbourg: France would accept the reunification of Germany, making the Federal Republic the preponderant power in Europe, in exchange for German acceptance of a single currency, dethroning the Deutschmark. Two years later the Treaty of

30 Ibid., p. 133.

Maastricht that sealed this bargain went further, encompassing the Community within the grander structure of a Union equipped with its own foreign policy, as well as agencies for justice and internal security. Thereafter, the end of the Cold War assured the entry of the former neutrals Austria, Finland and Sweden into the Union, and then its progressive enlargement into Eastern Europe, more than doubling the number of signatories to Maastricht. An important side effect was to qualify the juridical fiction that all member states were equal by introducing weighted voting in the Council of Ministers, to ensure that newcomers from the East did not by mere number rise above their real station in the Union.

Enlargement was a great achievement. But when 'fortune wreaked havoc' as Yugoslavia descended into a series of civil wars, the new-found Union proved powerless to dam the waters of disaster. America, though reluctant to become involved, alone put a stop to genocide in the Balkans. But when another genocide loomed in Kosovo, Europe 'drew a line in the sand', as Joschka Fischer put it, or as van Middelaar would have it, 'NATO bombed Serbia. Europe had finally shouldered its regional responsibility', as it would do again in Libya.[31] But divisions and uncertainties still lay ahead. Europe was irrelevant when 9/11 struck, and split over the war in Iraq. Nevertheless, in 2003 a Franco-German agreement moved the Union forward once more, introducing two vital innovations: the election of the *Spitzenkandidat* of whichever bloc of parties won the most votes in the European Parliament as Commission president; and, more consequentially, the creation of a no longer rotating, but permanent president of the European Council, appointed by its members for a five-year term, and holding—an institutional

31 Ibid., p. 199.

'revolution'—no national office. With this innovation, Europe acquired a figure who could speak for it at the highest international level, where previously it had none. 'That void had now been filled.'[32] Already strengthened, the Union could dispatch crisis missions, military or civilian, across the world, from Kosovo to Iraq, Mali to Afghanistan, and in the war between Russia and Georgia of 2008 stopped the Kremlin from seizing Tbilisi, Sarkozy flying to Moscow and extracting a ceasefire from it, in the name of 'the ancient French state and the power bloc of Europe'. The upshot, van Middelaar concludes, is that 'under pressure from inevitable appearances by fortune, the Union is clambering up into the outer ranges of high politics. In the light of the past, this is remarkable.'[33]

In the third and last part of his book, van Middelaar moves to the problem of locating or constructing, as he puts it, a 'European "we"' that represents it, and so accepts the decisions of the Union as its own. In the eighteenth century, the unworkable fiction of a state of nature out of which by common decision a civil society could arise, gave way to the workable idea of a nation that in fortunate circumstances, as in the thirteen colonies of America, could generate a state enjoying *ex post facto* acceptance of the sleight of hand that circumvented the need for unanimity among them; even if in less fortunate cases—Germany in 1848—this manoeuvre misfired. What these differing experiences made clear, however, was that in all cases 'the initiative arises with the representatives', who must precede the represented and call them into existence as a collective body. For the summons to be effective, more than power from above and habit below are required,

32 Ibid., p. 207.
33 Ibid., p. 210.

since if a 'we' is to come into being, laws and institutions—and their agents: judges, civil servants, police—must be accepted as in some sense 'ours', in the fashion of Hart's citizens who abide by primary rules (do not steal) because they accept the secondary rules behind them (their legitimacy). Over many years, politicians have striven to create that identity for Europe, for politicians can no more do without a public than a football match without spectators, who may applaud or boo the players but do not question the rules of the game. To date, the efforts of such politicians have been of limited effect. But the geopolitical context has now changed, in a direction more favourable to these. For with the end of the Cold War, the division of the planet into First, Second and Third Worlds has disappeared, and big powers—America, China, India, perhaps tomorrow Latin America—detached from what was once the Old World have emerged, demarcating Europeans from others in a new way.

In seeking to attach Europeans to a Union they can call their own, the projectors of the EU have employed three basic strategies that by historical association may be termed respectively German, Roman and Greek. The German strategy, pursued above all by the Commission in the inner sphere of the EU, has sought, in line with the tradition of Fichte and other nineteenth-century pioneers of German nationalism, to foster a sense of common identity among Europeans by a work of symbolic animation. Faced with low voter turnout to the Parliament in Strasbourg, the blue and gold flag was purloined from the (unrelated) Council of Europe of 1947, with its near fifty members, and ceremonially displayed whenever and wherever bureaucratically possible; Beethoven's music to Schiller's 'Ode to Joy' adopted as an official anthem; a pantheon of founders created to baptize squares, buildings, chairs. Euro coins with appropriate symbols were minted; European values declaimed;

European 'criteria' for accession codified. All attempts to give a cultural and historical grounding to the political construct of the Union, however, remain inevitably somewhat arbitrary so long as it still does not actually encompass geographical Europe. Only when all its states are safely gathered under the roof of the Union could the German strategy come to a natural fruition.

By contrast, the Roman strategy relies, as once the empire founded by Augustus, on material benefits—in classical times, order and provision: protection from barbarians and distribution of grain supplies. Protection is no longer an issue. It is provision that can inspire citizens with loyalty to the Union. Unimpeded travel across borders; inexpensive phone calls; access to hospitals anywhere—these are familiar, everyday advantages conferred by the EU, available to anyone. Rights to live and work anywhere in the Union, though universal too, are more ambiguous: a boon for elites, less so for the masses. Benefits that involve redistribution—so winners and losers—are inevitably more divisive than symbols. CAP recalls the corrupting clientelism of ancient Rome, Cohesion Funds are a source of geographical dispute, 'compulsory solidarity' reawakens national animosities. 'Europe is always a benefactor to some at the expense of others'—typically taxpayers in the better-off countries, creating little sense of fellowship.[34] Only the UK ever regarded European integration as legitimated simply by economic gains. The Eurobarometer readings of the Commission can measure only Roman-style acclamation.

The Greek strategy banks not on the creation of a sense of Europe as 'our people', along German lines, or 'to our advantage' along Roman lines, but as a matter of 'our concern'. For in Ancient Greece the public was at once 'spectator and participant': not 'as a player', but like the chorus in Greek tragedy,

34 Ibid., p. 269.

whose part lay in its 'voice', which Nietzsche held more original and important than the action itself. So, what a political body in search of a Greek-style public can give it is a voice, that is, a 'say in decision-making', or a 'drama' that captivates it. Europe, van Middelaar assures his readers, has made 'a huge effort' to grant its population a say in decision-making.[35] But can there be Greek legitimacy without German identity—a European democracy with no *demos*? Commission and Parliament have befriended each other in their quest to become the executive and legislature of the Union. Yet though the Parliament has acquired more and more powers since 1979, it has not won the favour of voters, who have shown less and less interest in it. Bestowal of a 'European citizenship' on them which confers no new rights is little more than a marketing gimmick. The Parliament is not a tribune of the people; it acts like a court musician.

The truth, van Middelaar confesses, is that European politics fail to excite—the public is bored by them. To become engaged, it needs conflict and drama, where the Union proceeds by consensus. In the past, de-dramatization of the European project was a great merit of the Commission—Monnet's 'flight from history into bureaucracy' was far-sighted, allowing Brussels to operate out of sight on low issues of the economy after more ambitious schemes like the European Defence Community had collapsed.[36] Meetings of the Council are somewhat more visible, but in these too disagreements are muffled. So, the public still has its doubts about the project. But it is necessary to be realistic. In an existing democracy, citizens come first, electing representatives who come into being at their decision. But the foundation of a democracy reverses this order: first come the representatives, who speak before they are appointed to be such,

35 Ibid., p. 274.
36 Ibid., p. 303.

then come those whom they will represent in the polity they found—or, as van Middelaar more expressively puts it: 'first the players, then (if necessary) the chorus'. The parenthesis is a tribute to his candour. The upshot? 'We could come straight out with it and call this second version the "coup sequence". Every royal or imperial dynasty starts with a power grab; every founder is a usurper.' Much energy is then invested in smooth inheritance and cultivation of public good will, 'but—as Lady Macbeth's hands remind us—the founding act can never be completely expunged'. Still, van Middelaar continues imperturbably, 'the legitimacy of power is not necessarily adversely affected by the fact that the public appears only afterwards—if it appears.'[37] What might best conjure it into being? 'The European political body', he concludes, 'exists on condition that, in word and deed, it can thrill its manifold public for a moment.' How might that occur? 'Great events and crises sunder the closed horizon of waiting, sweeping away the boredom.'[38]

III

The Passage to Europe is, unquestionably, in its fashion a tour de force. It unites an intricate conceptual structure with a set of provocative historical claims, and wide command of the literature on the origins and vicissitudes of the Union, unfolded in an engaging register that moves fluently from the philosophical to the conversational. It is not difficult to see why it has met with such universal acclaim. Nor, given the pattern of European studies that have accreted round the institutions of the EU, why its tale of triumphant, if still incomplete, progress towards the unity of the continent should have elicited so little critical scrutiny. One

37 Ibid., pp. 305–36.
38 Ibid., pp. 309, 311.

absence in it is so striking that it has occasionally been noticed. The book says virtually nothing about the economic record of European integration. The early rulings of the European Court, the Single European Act, the advent of monetary union, enter the narrative as juridical milestones on the road to union, but their economic outcomes receive no attention. The simple fact that what the Treaty of Rome created was a European *Economic* Community is whited out of the story; the acronym EEC is nowhere to be found. This is not an oversight on van Middelaar's part. It is a function of his insistence that the objectives of European integration—not a term he favours; he prefers 'European project'—were always *political*. Economic steps were a means to a political goal, not ends in themselves. In this he is certainly right. But, of course, since the overwhelming bulk of the activities and enactments of the Community that became a Union have always been, as they remain, economic in nature and in impact, there is no way that the politics of integration can realistically be isolated from them.

That said, the primacy of principle accorded to politics by van Middelaar is in itself an incontestable merit of his book. What becomes of politics in his hands is another matter. For a second striking feature of *The Passage to Europe* is the absence, not just of any substantive economic history, but of virtually any sense of the actual political landscape of Europe in the period it covers. A veil of abstraction falls over partisan identities and conflicts. To all intents and purposes, political parties join economic statistics in the oubliette of van Middelaar's retrospect. In 300 pages, a single brief paragraph adverts to Christian and Social Democrats getting together at the beginnings of the story, before swiftly segueing to the more congenial topic of Charlemagne. The only time an election ever warrants mention is when de Gaulle is thankfully frustrated of a first-round victory by French farmers in 1962, preventing him from going too far in hostility to Brussels, though even then the identity of the party which forced him to a second round remains an anonym. If despite the book's profession of their primacy, it is devoid of politics in its most commonly used sense, one of the reasons is certainly that at Euro-level—that is, in Strasbourg–Brussels—'parties' are wraiths without substance: labels for legislators conglomerated out of disparate national outlooks and conditions, which have no reality outside the chamber in which they sit, where a kind of permanent grand coalition—in effect, an institutional cartel—effaces even the formal distinctions between them, a residuum of pariahs aside.

Since the European Parliament lacks any of the ordinary character of a legislature, van Middelaar is realistic in terming it essentially a court musician to the powers of the Union. But this does not, of course, mean that the political careers and affiliations of the actors at the instances around which his narrative revolves can be bracketed as of no bearing on it. The effect of doing so is blandly apologetic. The background of the judges in Luxembourg, whose decisions made European history, is left a complete blank. As for statesmen, what innocent reader could guess that the hero of the drama at Milan on which van Middelaar dwells with such relish, Bettino Craxi, leader of the Italian Socialist Party, was the single most corrupt Italian politician of his time, a figure so odious to his compatriots that he was pelted by the public with coins of contempt and had to flee the police to Tunisia—living out the end of his days in gilded exile on the proceeds of his extortion of corporate funds and theft of taxpayer money? Other than extolling his 'brilliant bluff' in the European Council, van Middelaar breathes not a word about him. In the world of princes, lowly though a court musician may be, the part of a courtier can be more demeaning.

Where politics does intermittently kick into the story, it is as diplomacy, the relation between states as distinct from electoral fronts or social forces. There, *The Passage to Europe* takes transactions between France and Germany as its guiding thread, justly treating them as the decisive powers shaping the course of integration, and the Council devised by France as the controlling institution in the complex machinery of the Union. Though adding little to a familiar picture, van Middelaar depicts the skein of Franco-German relations well, without neglecting those moments when lesser contributors—principally Benelux—left a mark on events. What the dominance of Paris and Bonn/Berlin has meant for the nature of the Union, not episodically but structurally, he leaves aside. The great merit of his account—its central value—is that more clearly and emphatically than any previous writer, he puts the Council where it belongs, as not just the formal apex, but the overmastering instance of the EU—the last but one part of its architecture to come into being, but the most salient of all. In this he can legitimately claim a realism in the tradition of the *raison d'état* transmitted, as Ankersmit would have it, from Machiavelli through Meinecke. In keeping with it, van Middelaar leaves little doubt of the much lower regard in which he holds the Commission, a useful but humdrum factory of rules, and the Parliament, a windy cavern of words. The Council, by contrast, is the seat of authoritative decisions. The former are given to utopian temptations of European federalism, for which he barely hides his scorn. The latter is the vehicle of the true sense in which Europe has moved—and is continuing to move—towards ever great union, as a club of states bound together by a common project that does not extinguish their identities as nations, but joins them in a common destiny, a new form of *Schicksalsgemeinschaft* under way.

How then does the Council reach its decisions? Behind closed doors, in deliberations of which no minutes are kept, that issue in announcements to the world under the seal of consensus. Van Middelaar supplies a graphic, if tactful, description of the psychological and political mechanisms that generate such consensus. That it is reached far beyond any popular say in the matters so decided, in conclaves where no public gaze is admitted, is not cause for any particular complaint or criticism. For what his admiration for the Council in effect delivers is a transposition of the 'regent mentality' etched by Daalder from a Dutch onto a European plane: the quiet settling of affairs between elites *in camera*, above the heads of an inert populace below. Here van Middelaar departs in one critical respect from Ankersmit, for whom too the future of the Union had lain in the sober statecraft of Council, not the idle fancies of the Commission or Parliament, but who insisted on the difference between the principles of compromise, which he championed, and the vapours of consensus preached by Rawls. In a compromise, the parties reach an agreement without concealing or suppressing the differences between them. In a consensus, on the other hand, the differences are erased: the authority of the Council is monotone. In this, its pendant is the Court of Justice which too deliberates in secret, forbids publication of any dissenting judgment, delivering its rulings as unanimous edicts.

Logically, then, these are the two theatres of van Middelaar's exposition, and encomium, of the ultimate secret of the construction of Europe, the key to understanding its success. That lies in the term which recurs with compulsive insistence at the turning points of his story: the 'coup'. The Court's decisions of 1963 and 1964 establishing the supremacy of the Community over national legislation, without any warrant in the Treaty of

Rome, were successive brilliant coups; the confection of the European Council was a coup; the imposition of a path to revising the Treaty at the Council in Milan was a magnificent coup; the foundation of the Union itself was a coup. In each case, the definition of a coup is an action taken suddenly, by stealth, catching its victims unawares, and confronting them with a fait accompli that cannot be reversed. It is not a term associated with any form of democratic politics—just the opposite—and so finds no place, let alone celebration, in the polite vocabulary of liberal politics or jurisprudence. But its central role in van Middelaar's thought is not a caprice. It can be traced to a significant passage in Ankersmit's *Political Representation*, in which he observes of the notion of *arcana imperii* in early modern thought that illumination of it can be found in the 'truly amazing book' of Gabriel Naudé (1600–53), *Considérations politiques sur les coups d'état*, to which his attention had probably first been drawn by Meinecke's *Idee der Staatsraison*, where it features as the most important sequel to Machiavelli's work in the seventeenth century.[39]

Linking the two thinkers was the belief that political action could not be judged by ordinary moral standards, since in Naudé's words it required 'bold and extraordinary deeds' that 'exceeded common law' in the interests of 'the public good'—or, as Machiavelli had put it, a ruler should do good 'where he could', but 'enter into evil, where he had to'.[40] Heightening the contrast between them, Naudé radicalized the tension between the two codes, of ethical and political conduct. But the more significant ways in which he differed from Machiavelli were

39 *Political Representation*, pp. 27–8, where Ankersmit cites with understandable admiration Peter Donaldson's chapter on Naudé in his *Machiavelli and Mystery of State*, Cambridge 1988, pp. 141–85, at that date the best treatment of his thinking in any language.

40 *Considérations politiques sur les coups d'état*, Paris 2004, p. 101; *The Prince*, Chapter 18.

historical and individual. Writing a century later, Naudé was living in a world from which the city-states of Renaissance Italy had—with the exception of Venice—vanished, overtaken by far more powerful absolutist monarchies whose invasions had made short work of Machiavelli's dreams of a united peninsula; a world, too, now wracked by the wars of religion unleashed by the Reformation and Counter-Reformation, forces beyond Machiavelli's imagination. In person, Naudé was not a diplomat or an office-holder, but a scholar in command of a classical erudition and historical criticism that generated acerbic demolitions of every kind of contemporary superstition—magic, astrology, prophecy. His philosophy was a stoic naturalism. We owe to him and his friends perhaps the first version of our notion of what it is to demystify: in his vocabulary, *déniaiser*.

In Anna Lisa Schino's recent study—*Batailles libertines. La vie et l'oeuvre de Gabriel Naudé*, just off the presses in France—we possess an outstanding study of the milieu and cursus of this thinker. Born in Paris to a modest family, Naudé was distinguished early on not just by exceptional intellectual gifts, but by a keen and lifelong interest in politics, publishing his first polemical pamphlet on them at the age of twenty, followed by another scalding text on the Rosicrucians when he was twenty-two. He spent a brief season at the University of Padua where he befriended the philosopher Cesare Cremonini—the colleague of Galileo who had warned him against leaving the city, which belonged to the Republic of Venice, to return to the temptations of ducal Florence.[41] Back in Paris, still in his

41 For Naudé's time in Padua, see the vivid description in *Batailles libertines*, pp. 18–26, whose original version, *Battaglie libertine*, published in Florence in 2014, has now been updated and modified for French readers. See too the lively account of his subsequent milieu in Rome: *Batailles libertines*, pp. 32–60 ff. Schino's book is sparser on his years and relations in France,

twenties, he published a remarkable manifesto for a library that would include everything in print or in manuscript and be open to all who wished to come to it, announcing what would become the principal passion of his life.[42] Departing from Paris again in 1631, this time as assistant to Cardinal di Bagno, papal nuncio to France reassigned to duties in Italy, Naudé was soon active in Gallic and Francophile circles in Rome, an acquaintance of Poussin, correspondent with Mersenne, Grotius, Selden and Peiresc, in due course an intimate with Campanella. A firm if unspoken atheist, apprehensive of the power of the Inquisition, he watched with concern the tribulations of Galileo, to whom he paid homage when he was blind, and studied the early Hobbes with a mixture of admiration and disquiet at the daring of his theological heterodoxy. An unrelenting foe of religious—and every other sort of—imposture, he was a champion of intellectual and practical progress, of which he thought the seventeenth century a particularly favourable period.

Machiavelli composed *The Prince* outside Florence as a handbook of power in the hope of winning favour with its Medici rulers. Circulated only in manuscript during his life, once published posthumously it rapidly went through multiple editions. Naudé wrote *Considérations* in Rome as librarian for a cardinal who had been the Vatican's envoy in Paris. They begin—a

---

where an earlier American study by J.A. Clarke, *Gabriel Naudé 1600–1653*, Hamden (Conn.) 1970, is fuller.

42 *Advis pour dresser une bibliothèque, presenté a Monseigneur le Président de Mesmes*, Paris 1627, a text that has inspired an arresting work by Robert Damien, *Bibliothèque et état. Naissance d'une raison politique dans la France du XVIIe siècle*, Paris 1995. For James Rice, writing on the eve of the Second World War, the guiding principle of Naudé's writing was set out in this period: to reject everything we read as false 'unless we recognize that it is just and reasonable by means of diligent research and exact control', anticipating by over a decade the later famous precept of *Discours de la methode* by Descartes: *Gabriel Naude 1600–1653*, Baltimore 1939, p. 63.

literary unicum, Sainte-Beuve thought—with the word 'but'.[43] An identification with Lucretius follows on the opening page. Machiavelli had 'broken the ice' in treating mysteries of state, but made the mistake, he thought, of revealing them to the world at large.[44] Naudé had his work printed—ostensibly, perhaps really—in just twelve copies, as too explosive for public consumption and falsely as if produced in Rome, in fact probably in the safety of Leiden. Many of Machiavelli's maxims are familiar worldwide, but his governing concepts—'virtue' and 'fortune'—have lost currency. Naudé's much more restricted focus gave the world a term that has lasted. His usage of it was wider than its current meaning, a coup d'état denoting not just the sudden overthrow of a regime, but any comparably unexpected action undertaken to found, preserve, alter or aggrandize a state. What defined such a stroke—here Naudé departed from Machiavelli—was always *stealth*. Just ruthless, violent actions to seize or defend power—many celebrated in *The Prince*—did not qualify as such, since they might often be announced in advance, and conducted in broad daylight. Prior declaration or intimation of any kind was incompatible with a coup d'état, whose essence was not just suddenness, but secrecy. It must come as a complete surprise.

Two further features follow, neither to be found in Machiavelli. The first and most conspicuous form taken by what the eighteenth-century English translation of Naudé called 'masterstrokes of state' was spectacularity. Where princes are forced to take extraordinary measures in 'difficult and desperate circumstances', there could be no 'reasons, manifestos, declarations and all that might legitimate an action, precede its effects and operations'. For

43 Charles Sainte-Beuve, *Portraits littéraires*, Vol II, Paris 1863, p. 497.
44 *Considérations*, Paris 2004, pp. 92–3.

> in coup d'états one sees the thunderbolt before one hears it growling in the clouds, it strikes before it flames forth, matins are said before the bells are rung, the execution precedes the sentence, everything is done à la judaique—he receives the stroke who thought to give it, dies who thought himself quite safe, suffers who never dreamt of pain; all is done at night, in obscurity, in fog and darkness ...[45]

Such political bolts of lightning—the Sicilian Vespers, the massacre of St Bartholomew's day, the foundation of Islam—were comparable to those prodigies of nature that

> do not show themselves every day—comets appear once a century, monsters, floods, eruptions of Vesuvius, earthquakes occur only rarely, and this rarity gives lustre and colour to many things that would lose them if used too frequently.[46]

Terrifying, awesome, overpowering: such coups were a baroque version of classical *kataplēxis*. But coups could also take an opposite form: hidden too, but so inconspicuous as to be—at first—near invisible. The greatest enterprises or empires could be 'brought to birth, or to ruin, by means that are of almost no consideration', like 'those great rivers that flow impetuously nearly from one end of the earth to the other, and are ordinarily so small at their source that a child can easily step across them.'[47] Nature could produce from a tiny atom of semen an elephant or a whale. 'It is the same in politics: a small neglected flicker often starts a great blaze.' What else was that upheaval of the world, 'the extraordinary changes and revolutions in government and politics' caused by 'the spite of two monks armed only with

---

45 Ibid., pp. 104–5.

46 Ibid., p. 113.

47 Ibid., p. 151.

their tongues and a pen'? Had Charles V acted in time, buying off or disposing of Luther, the spark could have been stamped out before it spread.[48]

Savanarola, another monk, had sought to bring a revolution to Florence, but in Machiavelli's judgment a 'prophet without arms' was fated to be destroyed. For Naudé, it was true that Campanella had failed to found a new faith in Calabria for want of arms, but the Reformation had shown that ideology could be a power stronger and more destructive than force:

> I hold discourse so powerful that till now I have found nothing that is exempt from its empire; for it is that which persuades and instills belief in the most fantastical religions, incites the most iniquitous wars, lends wings and colour to the blackest actions, calms and appeases the most violent seditions, excites rage and fury in the most peaceable souls, plants and cuts down heresies, instigates revolt in England, conversion in Japan.

If a prince had a dozen preachers of eloquence at his disposition, 'he would be better obeyed in his kingdom than if he had two powerful armies'.[49] Naudé's respect for ideology was founded on contempt for those swayed by it—the 'populace'. Machiavelli had valued the plebs in Rome, seeing in its conflict with the patricians the source of the dynamism of the city, and attempted to reproduce an armed citizenry in Florence as the basis for its republic, if to no avail. For Naudé, society was divided intellectually, not politically. There were *esprits forts*, of whose number he was, an enlightened elite of free thinkers able to look steadily at the realities of the natural and social world without the delusions of religion or superstition (for him practically the same); and there

48 Ibid., pp. 151, 153.
49 Ibid., pp. 166–7.

were ignorant, credulous, brutal, excitable masses, dregs lower than beasts—who at least act by natural instinct—in their misuse of reason. Statecraft required that they be controlled by the very stigmata of their gullibility: use of the deceptions of superstition to domesticate and bemuse them, as practised by rulers of the ancient world proclaiming themselves gods, or the genius of Mohammed transcribing the words of god, or the sectaries of the present. 'Since it is natural that most princes treat religion as charlatans and use it as a drug', why should a clear mind be blamed for doing the same?[50] That was why the thunderbolt of the coup d'état should resemble a supernatural event, a wonder petrifying those who witnessed it. Where for Machiavelli fortune was a river that might lead to inundation, but with prudence could be canalized to advantage, for Naudé the populace was a treacherous ocean—a recurrent image—swept by high winds and deadly tempests: it had simply to be navigated.[51]

Behind this difference of outlook was a distinctive philosophical vision and a determinate historical context. More radically

50 Ibid., p. 169.

51 The eloquent burden of Damien's work is an argument to the opposite effect: while there was a contradiction between the 'secret logic of the confidant', allowing just twelve copies of his work to be printed, and the 'public logic of the counsellor', advertising the virtues of an open, universal library, it was the latter that prevailed over the former, assuming a use of reason that could be practised by all—the library acting as a matrix of readers that would one day give birth to voters, the promise of a democratic republic to come: *Bibliothèque et état*, pp. 29, 310 and throughout. For Damien's critic Sophie Gouverneur, the *libertins* of the age were not inconsistent: they were always committed to subversive publication of what was secret, but lacked any more collective political project, which would have been hard to reconcile with their negative anthropology of the masses. In Naudé's thought, there was an irreducible distinction between the 'public' and the 'people', which excluded any prospect of a republican education of the populace: *Prudence et subversion libertines. La critique de la raison d'état chez François de La Mothe Le Vayer, Gabriel Naudé et Samuel Sorbière*, Paris 2005, pp. 428–35.

than for Machiavelli, since not just politically but ontologically, mutability was the rule of all things:

> Since it began its course, the great circle of the universe has never ceased to carry away kingdoms, religions, sects, towns, men, beasts, trees, stones and everything that is found and enclosed within this great machine; the heavens themselves are not exempt from change and corruption.

Only 'weak minds imagine that Rome will always be the seat of the Holy Fathers, and Paris that of the kings of France'.[52] In the face of such cosmic caducity, the mark of an *esprit fort* was 'to see all things, hear all things, do all things, without being troubled, unbalanced, astonished'. Required for such a temper was an ability 'to live in the world as if one were outside it, and below heaven as if one were above it'.[53]

That could seem especially necessary in the conditions of the period when Naudé was writing, the bright impudence of *La Mandragola* long gone in what would become the crepuscular world of the *Trauerspiel*. By 1639, when he committed his work to print, the Thirty Years War had been tearing Europe apart and devastating Germany for twenty years, with still a further decade to go. 'If we consider well the state of Europe', he remarked in *Considérations*, 'it is not difficult to see that it will soon be the theatre of many tragedies.'[54] Two years later his cardinal-patron, who with French backing had high hopes of succeeding Urban VIII, expired and he returned to Paris to work with Richelieu, who in turn died a few months later, after which he secured the post of librarian to Mazarin. Naudé then spent the next seven

52 Ibid., p. 148.
53 Ibid., pp. 182–3.
54 Ibid., p. 150.

years criss-crossing France, Germany, Switzerland, Flanders, Holland, Italy and England in pursuit of manuscripts and books for a library which came to hold some 35–40,000 texts, probably the largest collection in Europe. A few months later, the Parlement of Paris revolted against the fiscal costs of keeping French armies in the field in Germany and Spain, detonating the Fronde. The common people threw up barricades, driving Mazarin and the royal family out of the city, and to raise cash for its cause, the Parlement decreed that the library be auctioned off. The Peace of Westphalia, bringing the war in Germany to an end, allowed the royal army to retake Paris, suspending the sale. But in the second round of the Fronde, when Mazarin again had to flee Paris, the Parlement enforced the sale and dispersal of the library in 1652. Amid this turmoil, about whose causes—the burdens of the war on the poor, the religious hatred left by persecution of the Huguenots—he was clear a decade earlier, Naudé attempted to intervene with a long imaginary dialogue between a bookseller and printer about the polemics swirling around Mazarin, hoping in vain to inflect events with appeals to reason. But as if he had foreseen it, everything he had once written of the savagery and ignorance of the populace came to life before his eyes, in bourgeois *parlementaires* and plebeian mobs alike. His life's work ruined, Naudé found a post with Queen Christina in Sweden. Like Descartes and Grotius before him, he did not last long in Stockholm, dying on a trip back to France in 1653. It was a typical seventeenth-century ending. A precursor of Bayle, who admired him, he was judged by his successor too advanced for his time.[55]

55 Bayle's epigraph for him went: 'I hold M. de la Mothe le Vayer and M. Naudé the two best read scholars of this century, and their minds most purified of popular sentiments, but because they overplayed the role of *esprits forts*, they often land us with doctrines whose consequences are dangerous': see Louis Marin's 'Pour une théorie baroque de l'action

IV

The world of Naudé was already distant from that of Machiavelli. We live in a world much further away from Naudé's. Militarized absolutism and religious fanaticism, princely generals, feudal estates and clerical ministers, civil wars and urban barricades, famines and witch trials: excepting plagues, what have they in common with a tranquil landscape of ballot boxes and opinion polls, shopping malls and social media, product regulation and quantitative easing, vegan picnics and emancipated pronouns? Yet between *Considérations* and *The Passage to Europe* there is a connexion. Coups d'état, in the now received sense of a military putsch have, of course, long since disappeared from the continent: the last came in Greece in 1967. But Naudé's definition was ampler, and did not require violence. What links the two works is the celebration of a coup as the courageous founding act of a positive statecraft. For both authors, it is a stroke prepared out of sight, behind closed doors, whose blade precludes consent. What it depends on is surprise, of which a classic form—St Bartholomew's Day—is the ambush. That, as it happens, is just what Craxi, conductor of the coup in Milan, vaunted his skills at, adopting the name of Ghino di Tacco, a thirteenth-century brigand (one of his killings recorded by Dante in *Il Purgatorio*), for the columns he wrote in the Italian Socialist Party newspaper. The coups of *Passage*, by contrast, are not only bloodless, but their success—just as Naudé had envisaged in such cases—depended on being so inconspicuous, appearing even so innocuous. What

politique. *Les Considérations politiques sur les coups d'état* de Gabriel Naudé, in *Politiques de la Représentation*, Paris 2005, p. 191. Marin cites a striking letter by Naudé of 1642, reporting that Poussin found the turbulence in Paris so great and disagreeable that Rome, to which he wished to return, was a paradise by comparison, and though Naudé had tried to dissuade Poussin, he shared his view of the two cities: p. 198.

could be more banal than a procedural motion about yet another meeting, or more trivial than a judicial decision over the price of a humble resin? Yet as at Wittenberg, so at Luxembourg, in the smallest beginnings were hidden the largest consequences—the division of a unitary faith that had lasted five hundred years, the abrogation of sovereignties that emerged in its wake.

Van Middelaar situates his writing in the tradition of Machiavelli, and in the literature of the EU, not without reason. But in the structure of his argument, he is closer to Naudé. For Machiavelli valued 'tumult' as the lifeblood of a flourishing republic, whose foundation was inconceivable without an active citizenship. Van Middelaar has no time for tumult, and no hesitation in welcoming the foundation of a union in which citizens were all but completely passive, neither playing any significant role in its construction nor even taking much notice of it. But why should that matter? The constitution of the United States, after all, was born of a procedural coup, accepted after the fact by its citizens, long internalized as their own and today near worshipped by them. Why shouldn't the European Union reproduce the same happy outcome?[56] The answer is plain enough. The thirteen colonies had fought a victorious revolutionary war and already declared themselves an independent nation. The colonists, united in a prospect of continental expansion, were of one language and origin. The constitution did not undercut such democracy as uniquely in that time each of the states possessed, but assembled and centralized it in a federation. The EU of today was neither the creation of a revolution, nor enjoys any homogeneity of culture or language, nor is united by the intoxicating prospect of any expansion. Moreover, and decisively, what degree of federation it has achieved has been bought by crippling rather than enhancing what democracy

56 *The Passage to Europe*, pp. 82–7.

its constituent nations possess. Comparison with 1783 is a paralogism.

That to date the EU has been unable to reproduce the bonds of identity and loyalty which tie Americans to the United States and Europeans to their nation states van Middelaar readily acknowledges, and supplies the memorable concluding meditation of his book, with its taxonomy of approaches for overcoming the lack of them. Of the trio of strategies he sets out, the tenor is not quite even. All are approved, but German and Roman lines of advance, 'creating companions in destiny' and 'securing clients', are treated more briefly and sceptically than Greek, on which the final emphasis falls, under the aegis of a solemn epigraph from Hannah Arendt (already a culture heroine of *Politicide*) on the historically unique character of the *polis*, where the other two have to make do with Julien Benda and Monty Python. Here, it could be thought, democracy would at last acquire its place, hitherto all but entirely absent, in the problematic of *The Passage to Europe*. What part does van Middelaar accord it? Since the Greek public, he explains, was at once spectator and participant, its example offers two opportunities for a political body in search of an analogue today. 'First, politics can give the public a say in decision-making. Second, politics can provide the public with drama, with on-stage action that captivates it. The genius of Athens bound these two aspects together, inventing both democratic freedom and a public arena.'[57]

There follows a painstaking attempt to show how in various ways—notwithstanding the 'calamity' of Danish utterance of a no to Maastricht, happily finessed on the morrow—'Europe has made a huge effort to give the population a say in decision-making'. That the adjective is risible hardly matters; it is the

57 Ibid., pp. 273–4.

indefinite article and feeble monosyllable of the penultimate phrase, to which van Middelaar reduces Athenian democracy, that delivers the message of his Greek conclusion. The assembly where all important political issues were directly debated and determined by citizens, which was most famously what Athens actually invented, is never so much as mentioned. Instead, what Athens gave the world was the chorus in Greek drama, which for van Middelaar combined the roles of spectator and participant in the play, being indeed—*apud* Nietzsche—more important than the action itself. That the chorus observes and comments on, but plays no role whatever in the action, is a historical detail that would impair the function of van Middelaar's construction of it, which is to collapse voter into spectator as the higher truth of the polis. The title of his chapter is franker: 'The Greek Strategy: Seducing the Chorus'. For a European public to come into being, needed is not a democracy determined by citizens, but a drama that entrances—'thrills'—them. Politics at its best, Ankersmit had argued, is an exercise in aesthetics.

Why was Ankersmit so taken with Naudé? After citing the lightning-streaked sky in which we see 'the thunderbolt before one hears it growling in the clouds', and 'all is done at night, in obscurity, in fog and darkness', Ankersmit went on:

> The coup is a sudden disruption of, or infraction upon, the natural social and political order: effects precede their causes; everything takes place in obscurity and darkness and belies our natural expectations. In this way the coups d'état seem to anticipate in the domain of history and politics the speculation of eighteenth-century philosophers on the sublime. We need only recall here how Kant related the sublime to what transcends the imagination's application of categories of the understanding. For in a similar manner

> the coup d'état transgresses all our moral expectations: the moral world we are living in is shattered to dust, although a great collective good may have been served by the prince's immoral behaviour. As the sublime transcends the apparently insurmountable opposition between pain and pleasure or delight, so do the *arcana* transcend the opposition between moral and immoral ... The well-being of society can sometimes only be achieved by crime.[58]

This was no passing aside. In an aesthetic politics, the sublime logically occupies the place of an *idée maîtresse*, and Ankersmit went on to devote his longest work to it, *The Sublime Historical Experience*. Breaking our normal epistemological framework, the sublime is the experience of an overwhelming reality connected with trauma, a compound of majesty and terror, fear and rapture, taking historical form in such great collective ruptures as 1494, 1789, 1861, 1917 or 1989, and to which Tocqueville's response to the French Revolution stands as the classic reaction. The same kind of experience, a sudden heightened apprehension of another, intenser reality could also, as Huizinga had shown, be aroused in the eyes of the historian by simple everyday objects of the past. Today, an uncanny elision of the two registers of the sublime, the monumental and the microscopic, was under way, in an invisible revolution. Out of sight, a huge number of small-scale changes in daily life were so altering our world that their 'sum may amount to little less than a permanent French Revolution'.[59] But there was a crucial difference. 'We live, as it were, in the negative' of the sublime of 1789: 'a revolution of the same scale, without ideals'.[60] The state was being demolished and the market

58 *Political Representation*, p. 24.

59 Marcin Moskalewicz, 'Sublime Experience and Politics: Interview with Frank Ankersmit', *Rethinking History* 11: 12, 2007, p. 260.

60 Marc van Dijk, 'De onzichtbare revolution van Frank Ankersmit', *Trouw*, 30 November 2007, reporting a panel discussion with Ankersmit.

worshipped, leaving us floating rudderless with flapping sails in a windless sea, in which it was only a matter of time before a storm broke and we could be lost. If a Hobbesian war of all against all was not to ensue, the state—the indispensable modern vector of collective self-awareness and self-determination—must be capable of imposing its order once again.

Van Middelaar, early exposed to his teacher's conception of the sublime as a paradoxical experience of the transcendent in this-worldly form, and the new ways in which it was taking shape, saluted it. 'We seem to be in control of the world more than ever, but we can see the consequences of it less than ever—ecology, nuclear bomb, genetic engineering', he would remark. 'The paradox is therefore an extreme polarization of certainty and uncertainty, of satisfaction about that certainty and of fear of that uncertainty—that is, the kind of paradox in which the sublime typically manifests itself.' But van Middelaar had another view of the market. If an example of Ankersmit's case were to be sought, there was

> no finer microcosm of sublime unintended consequences than the bourse. All its traders have the same goal, to get richer, but at times the paradoxical result of this joint endeavour is that they all lose a great deal of money in one fell swoop. That was not their intention. But it is exciting. Last Monday, the impending stock market crash in Amsterdam was definitely a sublime spectacle: the animal roar of the traders and the delighted smile of red-head AEX director George Moller who thought it 'beautiful', remarking 'We're now waiting for Wall Street to open this afternoon'.

Longinus may have held that 'slaves of money' were insensible to the sublime. But today

> Mammon itself is an important source of the sublime. Pessimists may think their view that the chances of moral elevation by the sublime are smaller than ever. They are wrong. The first-century rhetorician and the twenty-first century stockbroker learn the same lesson from the sublime: respect for indomitable reality.[61]

That was in 2000, fresh from *Politicide*. When van Middelaar returned to Ankersmit's work after his time in Brussels and The Hague, he was characteristically no less upbeat, but now the object of his admiration, and difference with Ankersmit, had altered. The fall of the Berlin Wall and 9/11 had changed international relations, permanently. They were ruptures of the kind Ankersmit had written about. But did that mean the state was on the way out? Far from it. Before these great events, Europe had become a mere marketplace between East and West. Now, however, states were taking more collective responsibility for the destiny of the continent than ever before. 'The flight from politics and history that Europe was for so long is over.'[62] The sublime was reverting to a more traditional décor.

V

Published in Dutch in 2009, *The Passage to Europe* had a triumphant local reception. Though still unknown to a wider European public, its success in the Netherlands was enough to secure van Middelaar the post of speechwriter and special adviser to the Flemish politician Herman Van Rompuy when this Belgian prime minister took office as the first full-time president of the European Council, a position newly created by the Treaty of Lisbon. Van Middelaar would now step onto the stage of the great

61 'Het beestachtig bulderen van de beursbedienden', *Trouw*, 20 April 2000.
62 'De onzichtbare revolution van Frank Ankersmit'.

events to which he had looked forward at the end of his book. Earlier that year, hailing Obama's inauguration in Washington, he set out their global context, updating his conception of the Modern Man's Burden:

> Obama makes America more powerful. The ability to cast the national interest in terms of a universal mission is deeply embedded in American consciousness. America is a force for good. That is its imperial trump card. Anyone who can credibly identify power with virtue is strong. The president himself knows this very well, and spoke to it in his masterly inaugural speech. Why did he move hundreds of millions? Certainly, because of the colour of his face, the sound of his voice, the moment in time. But also because he said that America, 'the wealthiest and most powerful nation on Earth' is and will remain a beacon of light and freedom, a country that is 'a friend of every nation' and 'willing to lead again'. Obama's audience, inside and outside America, yearned for this message.[63]

That was all the more important since anti-Americanism had been gaining ground worldwide. 'The Statue of Liberty was no longer the symbol of America, but Guantánamo Bay. That's why Obama decided to remove that blemish immediately. Symbolism is power politics.' That the Netherlands, which had relied on America for its safety since 1945, should 'refuse to help polish up the American blazon by accepting a few Guantánamo prisoners' was 'completely incomprehensible'. It was in the Dutch interest 'to strengthen our military protector against rivals like China or Russia'. But there was more to US paramountcy than simple might. Just as barbarians had been attracted to Rome by its aqueducts, villas with underfloor heating, and fine wines, so

63 'Obama maakt Amerika machtiger', *NRC Handelsblad*, 26 January 2009.

> besides its military and economic superiority, America's power lies in the global appeal of its lifestyle, racial equality and education. In this sense, Obama won on November 4 not only because he was able to promise a New Deal-like break with a deep crisis. It was striking that not only the poorest but the wealthiest voted for him. For in the long-run the richest too served the cause by the display of their lifestyle.

Equipped with these background convictions, van Middelaar made his way to Van Rompuy's cabinet, and out of the four years spent with him, produced *Alarums and Excursions: Improvising Politics on the European Stage.*[64] Reception has matched that of *Passage*—some thirty-plus dithyrambs posted on his website; pre-publication superlatives galore, this time topped by the incumbent president of the European Council himself, Donald Tusk ('quite simply the most insightful book on Europe's politics today') and Britain's former ambassador to the EU Sir Ivan Rogers ('brilliant'—sixth award of this epithet). But the two books are not on the same level. *The Passage to Europe* could legitimately claim to be a work of political realism. It laid bare central *arcana imperii* of European integration, as Naudé reproached Machiavelli for having done of princely practice—not all of them, of course, nor with any of his predecessors' sense of moral ambiguity, but as no other of the plethora of eulogies, official or academic, of the Union had ever done. *Alarums and Excursions*, though a sequel awash with many of the same tropes, is a different kind of exercise.

'During seventy years', the book begins, 'the preconditions of the miracle play that is a free society disappeared from view', while talk in Europe was all of growth, education, healthcare

64 Dutch original: *Die nieuwe politiek van Europa*, Groningen 2017; English translation, London 2019.

and such-like, with little care for the overarching questions of 'state and authority, war and strategy, security and the border, citizenship and opposition'. Then suddenly, crises came one after another: 'banks collapsed, the euro wobbled, Russia attacked Ukraine and annexed Crimea, vast numbers of desperate people attempted to cross into Europe, and Donald Trump pulled the US security rug from underneath the European continent'. Faced with this political cataract, new qualities were required to save the Union: 'speed and determination, visible gestures and authoritative words: leadership'. After some missteps, these were forthcoming. 'The Brussels backroom rule-making factory is giving way to political drama on a continent-wide stage', just as he had hoped would occur in *Passage*. The title of its sequel, an Elizabethan stage direction indicating tumult and clamour, captured the nature of the spectacle which this kind of drama offered its audience. No longer Sophocles: Shakespeare. 'Conveying the feverish mood when action becomes imminent, *Alarums and Excursions* tells the inside story of Europe's political metamorphoses and deciphers its consequences for political actors and the public alike.' Happily, all would end well, as through its ordeals the Union reached political maturity. By 2017 'we saw Europe's new politics rise to its full height, not just improvising and taking shape despite itself but acquiring self-knowledge and vitality'.[65]

First had come the troubles of the single currency. There, Merkel's declaration that 'if the euro fails, Europe fails' was decisive, heralding the rise of Germany's power in the Union. Did the measures which followed respect the Treaty of Maastricht? No, and so much the better. '"Europe" trumped Maastricht.' For Merkel's 'seemingly naïve' words concealed a rarely noticed truth: 'the states had committed themselves at the Union's

65 *Alarums and Excursions*, pp. vii–ix.

foundation not only to adherence to Union law but to the continued existence of the Union as such. In emergency situations, therefore, breaking with the rules could actually equate to being true to the contract.' The same held good of the tough financial and political measures taken by Berlin, Frankfurt and Brussels to oust weak governments in Southern Europe, crack down on the gambler Varoufakis, and circumvent the blackmail of Britain's opposition to the Fiscal Compact. Responsibility and solidarity were 'the root melodies of the Union' in conducting Europe away from the 'incalculable risks' of a Greek exit from the euro, while Tsipras's acceptance of medicine harsher even than that just rejected by voters was true to their deeper desire, which was not for a return to the drachma, but the preservation of their dignity. 'Miraculous' was the green light for banking union won in 2012. Draghi's bond-purchasing programme to prop up the euro was 'likewise a miraculous mixture of solidarity and responsibility'. Even if it was a bit above their head, 'the "Save the Euro" show captivated the public', and 'brought out the best in the players'.[66]

In the Ukraine, admittedly, the Commission over-reached itself at the outset, failing to realize how important the country was to the Kremlin. But once the street had thrown out Yanukovych, Putin had annexed Crimea, and in the ensuing civil war a Malaysian airliner was shot down with a Russian missile, the Council swung into action under the sagacious leadership of Merkel. First backing US sanctions with its own firm blows to Russia's economy, it then negotiated a deal at Minsk restoring the Donbass to Ukraine in exchange for a tacit right of the region to prevent Kiev from joining NATO. This was less than a complete victory, since in the Ukrainian civil war neither side has been willing to implement Minsk, and 'the West did

66 Ibid., pp. 40, 46–50, 53, 60–6, 259–61.

not have the will to win and Russia was not willing to lose'. But it was a watershed in Europe's role in the world, marking its 'geo-political emancipation from America' as an authoritative strategist in its own right—one that had come to understand the 'tragic dilemmas and hard choices' of power politics.[67] Just as the Council had mastered the euro crisis by discarding orthodox rules in the interests of financial stability, so by bracketing the issue of Crimea at Minsk, in the crisis of the Ukraine the Council discarded rigorous enforcement of international law in the interests of peaceful stability. But sanctions were not slackened: they would remain until Russia disgorged its prey.

Refugees posed an even more tragic dilemma for Europe, since they fostered so many tensions between the northern and southern, western and eastern member states of the Union. The task confronting the EU was to set an ethics of responsibility 'alongside' an ethics of conviction. After the Commission blundered with bureaucratic over-reach in trying to set quotas for the reception of refugees, it was left to Merkel to resolve the crisis by reaching an agreement with Erdoğan that may have been 'ethically and legally questionable', but was vital to prevent populist reactions threatening Schengen within the Union. A deal with Sisi in Egypt would no doubt be needed too, as one had been with Gaddafi, to keep the time-bomb of demographic explosion in Africa away from Europe's shores. Warning of 'political catastrophes' if the Union's borders were not secured, no one saw the magnitude of the problem more clearly than Donald Tusk, or expressed more eloquently the pride of Europe in nurturing during these difficult years a 'spirit of love and freedom'.[68]

Lastly came the double blow of Brexit and Trump. As Pocock had shown, it was 'out of the experience of a democratic republic's

---

67 Ibid., pp. 3, 72, 85, 87.

68 Ibid., pp. 4, 93, 111, 109, 114.

own transience and mortality that there may arise a political will to manifest itself as a sovereign player in historical time', remaining morally and politically stable in the irrational stream of events.[69] So it was with the EU. At this Machiavellian moment, Europe—in Merkel's memorable saying—showed itself able 'to take its destiny in its own hands'. In Paris, Macron stepped forth to the sound of Beethoven's 'Ode to Joy', and the EU united behind a determination to punish Britain for its desertion. Its stance was perfectly rational: 'Bluntly put, it would not be in the Union's interests for things to go well in the post-Brexit UK. Leading European voices considered that the political costs of a "soft" Brexit outweighed the "economic" costs of a hard Brexit.' So Tusk gave Ireland a veto on the withdrawal process, with Brussels compactly behind Dublin. Yet it was above all the awakening of the decisive power of Germany to the stakes at issue that made Brexit the Union's finest hour, enabling it to perform more convincingly than in any of its previous crises.[70]

Alarums and Excursions ends with an assessment of the balance sheet of these years for the character of the EU. What they had wrought was a transition from 'the politics of rules' to 'the politics of events'[71]—unforeseeable events, requiring impro-

---

69 Van Middelaar's gloss from Pocock's 'brilliant' work *The Machiavellian Moment*, Princeton 1975, cited three times in *The Passage to Europe* and five times in *Alarums and Excursions* without mention of Pocock's scathing opinion of the European Union.

70 *Alarums and Excursions*, pp. 116–17, 123, 132, 137–8, 140.

71 Ibid., p. 11. Van Middelaar's discovery of the numen of 'events' dates from a text he wrote on Nietzsche in 2006, 'Over het historische geluk', published as an annexe to the reprint of a Dutch translation of Nietzsche's *Vom Nutzen und Nachteil der Historie für das Leben* in Groningen. In a tripped-out collage that contains ruminations on an essay of 1969 by Gadamer in honour of Heidegger, van Middelaar links Gadamer's concept of a 'passage' to his use of the term 'an epoch-making event', as one that is at once passive and active, as in the birth of a child, which yields 'happiness' when it is named: p. 191. The same volume contains a no less

vised responses. The institutional consequence was to deepen the change in the relationship between the Union's constituent parts that had begun with the formation of the European Council in the seventies and been a leading theme of *Passage*. In its day, the rule-factory of the Commission in Brussels had done sterling work as 'an unrivalled pacifier and creator of prosperity', and now with Brexit continued to show its value by revealing to the public at large 'just how difficult it is to escape its clutches'.[72] Yet though technically it retained a monopoly of legislative initiative, in practice its proposals often originated in the Council of Ministers. The Commission might then elaborate them, but its federalist instincts had become counterproductive. It was no longer 'the site of development and renewal'.

That had passed to the Council. For if member states were to defend themselves against external attack, and offer their peoples a powerful role in the world, an 'emancipation of the executive' of the Union was vital. Meeting six to ten times a year as something like a Provisional European Government, the Council handles *Chefsachen*—the stuff of high politics, not low regulation—in closed sessions. At these, van Middelaar can report, all twenty-eight heads of government call each other by their first names, and can find themselves agreeing to decisions they had never imagined beforehand, then emerging together for a beaming 'family photograph' before the cameras of the one thousand reporters assembled to hear their tidings, whose presence makes 'failure impossible', as every summit (just one upsetting exception ever recorded) ends with a message of common hope and resolve. Flanked by its trusty 'Eurogroup' of

---

high-flown, but considerably more sober afterword by Ankersmit. For an English-language version of Gadamer's own text, see 'Concerning Empty and Ful-Filled Time', in *The Southern Journal of Philosophy*, Winter 1970, pp. 341–53.

72 *Alarums and Excursions*, p. 17.

finance ministers and above all by the European Central Bank, 'a monetary version of the passage to Europe's new politics' capable of equally decisive action in defence of the single currency, this is a Council not to be garlanded with the academic ribbon of mere legitimacy. For what it now wears is something older, firmer and more capacious—the uniform of authority.[73]

True, the Union still wants for one final complement. Opposition is 'oxygen for political life', lack of it a danger to any system. The technical, legal and procedural workings of the Commission and the Court were low-profile, but their 'dullness was a price worth paying to subdue national resistances, idiosyncrasies and pretentions'. For a time, depoliticized progress towards a closer union was valuable, but by obstructing protest it eventually had the unfortunate side effect of driving it into mobilization outside the arena of Brussels. The Council does not proceed so bureaucratically. But even the politics of events as opposed to rules can be depoliticizing, its decisions presented as so many necessities imposed by a series of emergencies, making opposition impossible. The risk of declaring measures *alternativlos*—a favourite formula of Merkel's—is the same. 'A strategy of *faits accomplis* feeds scepticism. The public hears this as "like it or lump it".'

What is to be done? It would be better if opposition could be fostered democratically within the system, 'to stage-manage and pacify social and political conflicts symbolically'. But that could hardly take the form of partisan division in the Union, since the diversity of politics in its member states precludes uniformity of governments in the Council, or blocs in the Parliament, since left or right parties never prevail simultaneously across the EU. In the Council and Parliament alike there is, on the contrary, always a de facto grand coalition of conservatives, Christian Democrats, social-democrats and liberals. Only political fringes

73 Ibid., pp. 175, 185, 189–91, 191, 211.

on the far right and far left lie outside it, but these hold power nowhere in Europe, and their 'polemical' opposition is futile, as Syriza and Podemos have discovered. So where is the right sort of opposition to be found? These problems are 'not easily resolved', van Middelaar concludes lamely, his last pages tailing away into the tritest of bromides from Brussels. The Union, of course, needs 'dissensus'—inspired by 'the conviction that what unites us as Europeans on this continent is bigger and stronger than anything that divides us'. In effect, consensus by any other name smells as sweet.[74]

VI

The product of services to Van Rompuy at the apex of the EU, *Alarums* belongs to a sub-class of literature of which *The New Machiavelli: How to Win Power in the Modern World* by Jonathan Powell and *The World as It Is* by Ben Rhodes are other recent samples: what might be called spin-doctorates of the equerry. Van Rompuy was never a ruler in the sense Blair or Obama were, and van Middelaar never enjoyed the power of Powell and Rhodes. He was, on the other hand, incomparably more intelligent and literate, so *Alarums* is a superior exercise in the genre, without need to beat the personal chest typical of it. But the deterioration since *Passage* is plain. The first book was the work of a historian who was an enthusiast for the EU; the second is the product of an apologist in its service. The difference lies in the quotient of evasion and hyperbole in each. *Alarums* retains flashes—in its description of the EU response to Brexit; its depiction of the operations of the Council and complexities of the institutional machinery of the new Europe; its emphasis on the strategy of the fait accompli in the 'Union method'—of

74 Ibid., pp. 239, 225, 231, 256–7, 265, 267.

the realist candour that was the leading virtue of *Passage*. Talk of coups is, naturally, no longer acceptable. But the gist of the story is still the same. With the demotic touch required of any decent publicist, this time van Middelaar places at the head of his book an epigraph not from Tolstoy, but from Miles Davis. It reads: 'I'll play it first and tell you what it is later.' The politics of the EU encapsulated in a pop one-liner.

But the price for these moments of frankness has risen. For along with acknowledgment of the 'coercive consensus' of the Council meetings, the charades of Union summitry, the demotion of the Commission, now come longer and more laboured efforts to magic into existence a 'public' at one and the same time spectators in a gallery (or in a more popular variant, fans at a football match) and actors in the scene they are watching (players in the game they are cheering or booing). The contradiction in terms, hazily sketched in *Passage*, where the image of choice is a Greek chorus, becomes an extended comedy in *Alarums*, whose concluding chapter—the largest in the book—is entitled 'The opposition takes the stage', only to reveal that there is no such opposition. Deontologically, it would be nice if there were, provided it was not polemical, but so far it hasn't materialized in any acceptable form. Nothing could be worse than expressions of the popular will that contravene the Union method. Think of the referendums on the draft European constitution—mere destruction, not opposition.

As for the main burden of *Alarums*—Europe rising to its full height in dealing with the crises besetting it—the roll-call of triumphs rarely rises above the language and level of public relations. Saving Europe, by saving the euro, by withstanding Grexit? Restoring dignity to the Greeks, by cancelling their votes? That the Union was never in danger from a departure or—Schäuble's proposal—a suspension of Greece from the single currency, only the stake of German and French banks in its debt; that the humiliation of commissioners from Brussels dictating laws, policies, regulations in Athens—dignity *à la hollandaise*—aside, the Troika's regime inflicted misery on the poor, the elderly and the young in Greece; that Greek public debt today stands higher than when Papandreou was forced by Berlin and Paris to call off one referendum, or Tsipras capitulated after another. None of this rates a mention.

Ukraine: geopolitical emancipation of Europe from America, resolute sanctions against Russia for annexing Crimea, enlightened interim compromise at Minsk? The realities: EU sanctions tailed US sanctions, uniting stupidity and hypocrisy. Stupidity—does any Western politician, no matter how ignorant, really believe that Russia will ever relinquish Crimea, an accidental province of Ukraine, whim of a paper shuffle by Khrushchev for a couple of decades, when it was a hallowed part of Russia for over two centuries, populated overwhelmingly by Russians? What possible gain could come from making relations with the country an indefinite hostage to the fiction that its recovery could be reversed? Hypocrisy: Europe has never lifted a finger over the annexation of East Jerusalem and the Golan Heights by Israel; South Sahara by Morocco; or the occupation of half of Cyprus by Turkey—though in all these cases seizure was against the will of most or all of the population, enforced by violent repression and ethnic cleansing, unlike Crimea where it was undoubtedly welcomed by a majority, if one exaggerated by Moscow. Borders are inviolable only when it suits the West to say so. As for Minsk, its upshot has been zero.

Refugees: what is there to be proud of in the European record? Attacking Libya (France, Britain, Spain, Italy, Belgium, Denmark), bombing and fighting in Afghanistan (contingents from virtually every member state of the Union) and Syria

(France, Britain), with the well-known result of increasing refugee flows in each case: a copybook case of the ethics of responsibility? Bribing Erdoğan with €6 billion to block fugitives from getting to Europe by penning them within Turkey, under a regime boasting 100,000 or so political prisoners: an exercise in the ethics of conviction? Not a line on the payoff to Erdoğan in *Alarums*, though it mercifully spares us Euro-cant on human rights, confining itself to talk of love and freedom, as internment camps fester in Lesbos and boats capsize off Lampedusa.

Brexit: a triumph of European statecraft? If the Union's great breakthrough was to advance beyond a politics of rules to one of events, overturning one rule after another in pursuit of financial stability and border security, wouldn't it have made more sense to concede Cameron the brakes on migration he was asking for to win his referendum, rather than risk Britain's desertion by invoking immovable principles that are continually being moved? If, when necessity calls, the Treaty of Maastricht's precise and detailed clauses on budgetary discipline—and prohibition of Central Bank purchase of government debt—can be dismissed in the shake of a lamb's tail, why not the far vaguer provisions of the Treaty of Rome on the free movement of labour? From the *Realpolitiker* standpoint advertised by van Middelaar, the logic of pragmatically dodging the blow to the EU from across the Channel should have been obvious. No such thought crosses the mind of *Alarums*.

In effect, the expressions of the Union's new political maturity —saving Europe by dignifying Greece, breaking strategically free from America, reconciling responsibility and morality in the Mediterranean, treating sagely with Britain—belong with the splendour of white man's colonialism, the abundance that bombs would bring to Afghanistan, the closure of Guantánamo by Obama, the global beacon of America's racial equality:

figments in the mazes of magical realism. But it would be a mistake to dismiss their author on that account. Fantastications can be politically functional, if they answer to the needs of rule. Van Middelaar occupies a unique position in the landscape of the Union today, as the one significant theorist of Europe to marry long-range thought with proximity to power. The balance in his work between genuine insight and glib ideology may form a shifting terrain, but not one that is to the detriment of his ambition. Having served with Bolkestein and Van Rompuy, he has since attached himself as special adviser to the new vice-president of the European Council, Frans Timmermans, another Dutch bruiser who would probably now be its president, had he not—after years spent buttering up Erdoğan as the Commission's point-man in the Union's cash-for-stopping-fugitives deal with Turkey: he claimed most of them were just economic chancers—hectored Poles and Hungarians too stridently for failing to uphold the rule of the law. A loud-mouthed transfuge from D66, a Dutch equivalent of Britain's SDP of old, who is today operative on the right wing of the ultra-moderate Dutch Labour Party, Timmermans was the most vociferous champion of the European Constitutional Treaty—of which he was one of the drafters—rejected by Dutch voters in 2005, and a key figure in sliding its core back into the Lisbon Treaty of 2010. Alongside him is a natural berth for an intellectual with an eye to a yet more organic future, as special adviser to Europe itself.

VII

With whom might such a figure be compared? Not to any contemporary, but there is a historical parallel. *Mutatis mutandis*, the person and career of Friedrich Gentz, 'Secretary of Europe', as Golo Mann dubbed him in an admiring biography of 1946, suggests a resemblance. Bourgeois son of the director of the Prussian mint, after studying under Kant in Königsberg, where he corrected the proofs of *Critique of Judgment*, Gentz won fame by producing the first European translation of Burke's *Reflections on the Revolution in France*, with an impassioned preface amplifying its summons to battle against the 'despotic synod' in Paris, whose theories were bent on 'rooting out all that gave happiness to millions'; published single-handed a *Historische Journal* with an international readership, in which he wrote the first systematic comparison of the American and French Revolutions, translated into English by John Quincy Adams; and set out in his *Political Condition of Europe before and after the French Revolution* the first strategic theorization of the need for the anciens régimes of Europe to transcend traditional balance of power politics for a confederate accord to stamp out subversion wherever it raised its head, without consideration of borders or sovereignties[75]—today's *droit d'ingérence*, before it was draped in human rights. Hired as 'the best political writer in Germany' by the court in Vienna to sway public opinion in favour of the

75 For currently available editions, see *The Origins and Principles of the American Revolution Compared with the Origin and Principles of the French Revolution* (tr. John Quincy Adams, 1800), Carmel (In.) 2010; *On the State of Europe before and after the French Revolution* (tr. John Charles Herries, 1802), reproduction, London 2018. In the latter, Gentz declared: 'There are cases in which sound policy suggests, and the law of nations permits, an active intervention in the internal proceedings of a foreign country. Such a case arises when there happens in any, especially if it be one of the principal states of Europe, a disorder so great, general and permanent (it must have all these qualities), as to endanger all the neighbouring powers.' The French Revolution was an event of this kind, 'not merely permitting, but requiring, the active interference of other nations', given 'the all-destructive principles upon which it was founded, the criminal excesses and contempt of every right that attended its progress', and the manner in which it had 'subverted and demolished every pillar of the balance of power, and converted the federal constitution of Europe into a scene of anarchy and confusion': pp. 198–9, 209.

Habsburg monarchy, he was lionized in London—by then he was on Pitt's secret payroll too—where the French envoy observed that 'if there is one man who can be called the champion of the counter-revolution, it is he'. An implacable foe of any settlement with Napoleon, who had trampled on the balance of power in Europe,[76] he became an early associate of Metternich, serving as the secretary to the Congress of Vienna, and under the Restoration drafted the famous Circular of Troppau authorizing the assembled monarchies to invade any country afflicted by revolutionary disturbances and crush them in the common interests of order and tranquillity in Europe.

For fifteen years Gentz was Metternich's closest continuous collaborator as policy adviser and propaganda chief, roles in which he displayed, according to Metternich, 'real genius'. Contrasts in background and character set the two men apart, in a common commitment to legitimism. Nine years older than his patron, Gentz was an outsider in the social and political system of Austrian absolutism, as a Prussian and a commoner of no independent means. Metternich was a wealthy aristocrat from the Rhineland, scion of Vienna's plenipotentiary in the Austrian Netherlands when the French Revolution broke out, a consummately cool, controlled and self-confident diplomat and politician, where Gentz was explosive and emotional, a gambler and spendthrift—class differences aside, a lesser temperament. In the current hagiography by Wolfram Siemann, Metternich features as a prince in name and nature alike:

76 Anticipating the contemporary critique of this term by the great conservative historian Paul Schroeder, who prefers that of 'political equilibrium', Gentz observed of the balance of power: 'it perhaps would have been of more propriety called a system of *counterpoise*', since it was not so much a question of a perfect balance as 'a constant, alternate vacillation in the scales of the balance, which from the application of *counterweights*, is prevented from ever passing certain limits': *Fragments upon the Balance of Power in Europe* (1806), reproduction, London 2017, p. 63.

visionary statesman of peace; masterly strategist of war; pioneering modern capitalist; impassioned humanitarian; devoted husband to his wife; yet as a connoisseur of women, tender lover of many another; before his time in understanding the intellectual equality of the sexes; not to speak of the true path to responsible liberty and prosperity. In a portrait in which no other figure in a potentially crowded canvas is allowed the smallest detraction from the monopoly of limelight accorded a hero who termed himself 'the saviour of the world' (the author assures his readers it can only have been in jest), Siemann dismisses Gentz in a paragraph as an 'ambitious journalist'.[77] The reality is that, far better educated than Metternich, and a much better writer, Gentz was also an original thinker of the European counter-revolution, in whose essays and books can be found the leading ideas of the Restoration long before they found scattered expression in the letters and papers left by Metternich, whose only sustained composition was self-serving memoirs put together posthumously by his son.

So too Gentz had an independence of mind capable of detaching him from the cause he served. In 1810 he could envisage a rational reorganization of post-Napoleonic Europe into no more than eleven states, including a politically united Germany and Italy, and the independence of Poland and Greece—just what the Congress of Vienna denied, and even as he helped conduct it five years later, could deliver a lucid judgment on it:

---

77 *Metternich: Strategist and Visionary*, Cambridge (Mass.) 2019, p. 341; compare with the way he figures in Mark Jarrett, *The Congress of Vienna and Its Legacy: War and Great Power Diplomacy after Napoleon*, London–New York 2013, where his work at successive congresses of the Restoration (not least its conclave at Laibach, where he invented a six-day 'journal' of its proceedings) is judged 'prodigious': p. 273. Gentz wrote memoranda or official circulars of the Congresses of Vienna, Aix, Troppau, Laibach and Verona: for these documents, see Vols II and III of Metternich's *Memoirs*, spatchcocked into them by his son.

> The magniloquent phrases about 'restitution of the social order', 'the recovery of European politics', 'enduring peace based on a just apportionment of power' and so on were trumped up only to quiet the masses and to confer on the Congress some semblance of import and dignity. But the real sense of the gathering was that the victors should share with one another the booty snatched from the vanquished.[78]

Gentz was never a steadfast follower of the grandee he came to serve, writing of Metternich and Austrian policies to a Scottish friend in 1813: 'They are not what I am, what I would like to be, so while I can defend Metternich and his system in certain respects from the false opinions others have of them, I will never adopt or espouse either out of my own conviction.'[79] Towards the end of his life, he could see the ultimate futility of the enterprise on which he and Metternich had embarked, writing in 1827:

> I have always been conscious that despite the majesty and power of my superiors, despite all the single victories we achieved, the spirit of the age would prove mightier in the end than we; that thoroughly as I have despised the press for its extravagancies, it will not lose its

78 Opening paragraph of his memorandum on the Congress, composed four months before its Final Act, for the full text of which see Metternich, *Memoirs*, Vol II, London 1980, pp. 553–86; I have preferred Mann's more vivid translation.

79 Letter to Sir James Mackintosh, in Raphaël Cahen, *Friedrich Gentz 1764–1832: Penseur post-Lumières et acteur du nouvel ordre européen*, Berlin 2017, p. 60. While Cahen justly views Paul Sweet's *Friedrich von Gentz: Defender of the Old Order*, Madison 1941, as still the most complete and scholarly biography of Gentz, his own study is now the best treatment of Gentz's ideas. Concerned to clear Gentz of the image of a reactionary, in the conviction that he was essentially an heir of the Enlightenment (if not an entirely consistent one) whose ideas were anti- rather than counter-revolutionary, Cahen—while pointing out for the first time the extent Gentz's rapprochement with Bonald and de Maistre in 1819–21—shows how far his political views had drifted away from Metternich by 1830.

> ascendancy over all our wisdom; and that guile will no more than force be able to stay the wheel of time.[80]

Such reflections were beyond Metternich, whose encomiast takes care not to let them ruffle his pages. The memoirs of the prince, ending in 1815 and devoting 200 of their 265 pages to his opinions and defeat of Napoleon, offer a self-satisfied story much of whose tenor, like his official papers, is nondescript and evasive, unlike his private correspondence, which is often terse and vivid. The exception is a striking portrait of Napoleon, acute, elegant and balanced, well above the level of what surrounds it. Forming a separatum within the text, its composition is dated 1820, whereas the *Memoirs* were completed in December 1844. There is no doubt that its substance corresponds to Metternich's view of Napoleon, whom he justly says he knew better than any other statesman of the period, having served as Austrian ambassador at the emperor's court for three years, on the friendliest of terms with him. Significantly, however, in 1825 Metternich addressed a letter to 'my dear Gentz', in which, after characteristically explaining that 'I alone possess the clue to the greatest events of modern times', he confessed 'how little I think of my talent as a writer' and 'how much better you would express what I wish to think and say than I ever can.' Asking him to 'read and polish it without changing the features of my Napoleon, who would otherwise cease to be mine', he urged Gentz 'not to weary of the work', assuring him that 'if we learn in the other world that my picture of Napoleon is the most successful, I will proclaim you as its author.'[81]

---

80 Golo Mann, *Secretary of Europe: The Life of Friedrich Gentz, Enemy of Napoleon*, New Haven 1946, pp. 213, 292. Mann's biography was completed in 1941, but published five years later, no doubt due to a mixture of the time required to translate the original and conditions of printing during the war; the original German text appeared a year later, in 1947.

81 *Memoirs*, Vol IV, London 1881, pp. 196–7.

What is clear from Metternich's pronouncements on Napoleon is that, unlike any other of the architects of the emperor's downfall, he had felt a real attraction towards him—there was a 'charm' in his conversation—and an appreciation of him as the one man who had 'mastered the Revolution', as neither Louis XVI nor Louis XVIII was able to do, and became deservedly popular in France for doing so. Napoleon could have been a pillar of a satisfactory European order after Austerlitz and Wagram, but his thirst for conquest was unslakeable, and its hubris undid him. But while his immense weight pressed down on good and bad alike, both were released after he was gone, and while 'the elements of good were distorted or paralyzed', the elements of evil sprang to life and 'the revolutionary spirit was soon seen to take a new flight':[82] words written in a memorandum to the tsar proposing that a Central Commission of Austria, Russia and Prussia be set up in Vienna to crush the dangers of continental subversion, of which Metternich had earlier warned him in a secret memorandum bordering on hysteria: they were faced with 'total ruin' of the glorious efforts of the Restoration and 'indescribable calamities to society' if the 'moral gangrene' of the middle classes, with their talk of 'constitutions' and 'reform', to be heard not only in Spain, Germany and Italy but in England as well, was not checked and the secret societies plotting the overthrow of the established order not vigilantly repressed.[83]

It is customary among historians to contrast the calm and good sense of Metternich, on which he prided himself in the struggle against Napoleon, with his increasing ideological rigidity after it. But there was no real contradiction between the two.

---

82 *Memoirs*, Vol III, London 1881, p. 667.

83 'The evil exists and it is enormous', ibid., pp. 464–5. His son dubs this epistle 'Metternich's Political Confession of Faith'.

Napoleon, though socially an upstart, was politically an equal, a guarantor of order with whom cordial relations were possible till he lost his way in Russia. In Metternich's imagination, the radicals, liberals and utopians of the 1820s belonged with the sinister secret societies infesting the Europe of the Restoration: a rabble menacing the very order that Napoleon—author, after all, of a 'counter-revolution'[84]—had in his fashion upheld. Just here, however, is where contemporary conservatives can find inspiration. For Siemann, Metternich's career after 1815 offers a premonition of our own times, and inspiration for how to handle them. The epoch of the Restoration? Banish the term, which is a misleading description of the objectives of the prince and his fellow statesman in those years. 'It would be much more appropriate to describe their aims, and the constraints under which they acted, as giving rise to "security policies".'[85]

These were required to defend 'the system of international law established in 1815' from 'attempted revolutions and rebellions, or assassinations and seizures of power', such as the Greek revolt against the Ottomans (best for it to 'burn itself out beyond the pale of civilization' was Metternich's humanitarian response). For the brand-mark of the period was 'the hitherto unwritten history of European-wide terrorism, which developed between 1817 and 1825. It was only because of this terrorism that nationalism was able to become an unassailable social power'. In Greece and elsewhere, 'modern nationalism presented itself as a form of religious salvation and exploited a context of social economic backwardness', thereby 'generating a universally usable myth' of utopian dimensions. It is easy, Siemann remarks, to accuse Metternich of repression, but if we look around us today, the counter-measures he took against the

84 *Memoirs*, Vol. IV, p. 14.
85 *Metternich: Strategist and Visionary*, pp. 518 ff.

jihadis of the period, comparable to 'the activities of modern intelligence services and other state institutions responsible for safeguarding constitutions', have continuing relevance in our own time. For do not 'the holy warriors of 1789, 1813 and 1819 have something in common with those of today'?[86]

The security policies set in place by Metternich were far-sighted not only in dealing firmly with a nationalism spawned by terrorism, but in furnishing the antidote to it. That lay in the 'historically evolved legal orders' of the Holy Roman Empire and the Habsburg monarchy, and the fashion in which these were folded into the German Confederation set up at Vienna. In this, Siemann goes on, Metternich was astonishingly modern, as we can see if we consider the contemporary scene in this respect too. 'The European Union follows the same model, guaranteeing national identity under the umbrella of composite statehood', in a way that 'advances the common interests of all'. Perceiving the deadly bacillus carried by the nation state whose unity 'led only to war', and rightly suppressing it in Italy, Metternich pioneered the vaccine against it.[87] The Concert of Europe created at Vienna has found its historical successor in Brussels.

The political connexion between the two is a descent freely affirmed in *The Passage to Europe*, where the founding states of the Community were possessed from the outset of 'a profound consciousness' of the 'legacy of the Concert of Europe', and the meetings of their heads of government, informal at first, then institutionalized as the European Council in 1974, formed 'a contemporary "Vienna 1814–15"'.[88] The historical circumstances of the Union of the twenty-first century, of course,

86 Ibid., pp. 554, 631–2, 412, xv, 753.

87 Ibid., pp. xv, 441–2, 531. Siemann observes that Metternich's opinion that Italy could not become a unified state might well be thought confirmed today.

88 *The Passage to Europe*, pp. 23–4.

differ vastly from those of Metternich's system. Composed not of aristocratic monarchies but of electoral democracies, it is in no danger of internecine fighting or revolution. Front lines in the war on terror are in other continents. The commonest arena for nationalism is the football field. Nevertheless, it is equally clear that tension, mostly submerged but sporadically visible, is widespread between the elites and the peoples of Europe, as it was in the days of the Restoration, requiring extra-territorial interventions to keep public order once again. No longer military expeditions of the kind sent to crush Spanish or Italian liberals, these now take economic form: dictates of Berlin, Paris or Frankfurt evicting unsuitable governments in Rome and Athens; commissaries of Brussels invigilating taxes, labour laws, pension systems of other lands for their conformity to neo-liberal principles, today's legitimism.

In defending and illustrating this system, van Middelaar is the closest thing the Union has produced to a modern Gentz. Like the secretary to Europe, he won his spurs with a philippic against ideological toxins coming from France: the ideas of 1789, the ideas of 1917. *Politicide*, denouncing latter-day philosophers of terrorism, was his translation of Burke for moderns. Both propagandists, yet also original thinkers, each would combine gifts of literary eloquence with calculations of *raison d'état*. Both would enjoy a European reception for their political writing beyond that of any contemporary. Gentz exercised real power—Metternich's first modern historian thought his overall system could equally well be called Gentz's—though always as a subordinate, never in his own person. Van Middelaar to date has not. On the other hand, compared with Gentz's prolific writing, remarkable though it was in its age, van Middelaar's work is of another order of intellectual complexity and sophistication, as befits the distance between the relative simplicities of the

Congress system and the labyrinths of the EU in the pedigree of descent linking them.

If Ankersmit gave the original impulse to van Middelaar's outlook in much the same way as Burke to Gentz's, can it be said that in exalting the Restoration as the cradle of democracy, Ankersmit offers another connexion between the worlds of the two? Not exactly, since his Restoration was that of Guizot, not of Metternich—the censitary rather than absolutist variant of oligarchic rule. In that nuance lies a difference between the teacher and his pupil. Ankersmit transmitted to van Middelaar, along with a conventional anti-communism and commitment to capitalism, his distinctive conception of politics as fundamentally an aesthetic enterprise, his lofty sense of the state, and his cult of the sublime. But Ankersmit has also in his way been politically anti-elitist, attacking what has become of democracy in the West as 'an elective aristocracy'.[89] That note is entirely missing in van Middelaar's writing. There, the enemy is, on the contrary, just what the elites of Europe themselves decry, and fear, most: 'populism'. Democratic systems have effective oppositions, that one day may govern. The European Union is organized in such a way that it does not. But since it is good form to regret its 'democratic deficit', it would be better if it at least appeared to do so. Hence van Middelaar's successive attempts to supply an ersatz opposition—a chorus, a gallery, an audience—that could offer a façade of democracy to the construction he extols. No thinker agitated the young van Middelaar more than Jean Baudrillard. But the public invoked in protean guises across so many of his pages is always in substance the same, as depicted by Baudrillard, the neutered onlooker of a spectacle. European democracy? Less diplomatic than his aide, Van Rompuy has voiced the

89 See 'What if Our Representative Democracies Are Elective Aristocracies?', *Redescriptions*, January 2011, pp. 21–44.

truths of Brussels more bluntly. In Greece, 'the performance of the troika may have taken place a little too much in the media spotlight': better in a blackout.[90] What of the continent at large? 'I believe the Union is overdemocratized': in so many words.

90 'Reflections after Five Years in Office', in Luuk van Middelaar and Philippe Van Parijs (eds), *After the Storm: How to Save Democracy in Europe*, Tielt 2015, pp. 14–15.

3

THE RIVETS OF UNITY

Quantitatively speaking, the shift in the centre of gravity of work on the EU from America to Europe itself has been a product of a now vast academic industry: some five hundred Jean Monnet chairs currently planted across the Union. Most of this is impassable to the general reader. But amid a sea of conformity, it has also seen the emergence of a cluster of thinkers whose writing represents a qualitative advance in critical understanding of the Union. In independence of spirit closer in type to Gramsci's 'traditional' intellectuals, as distinct from the 'organic' variant represented by van Middelaar, these are not to be found nestling in official positions; form no collective school of thought; and are of diverse national and generational backgrounds. A short list would include Giandomenico Majone (Italy), theorist of regulation; the jurists Dieter Grimm (Germany) and Thomas Horsley (Britain); the sociologists Claus Offe and Wolfgang Streeck (Germany); the political scientists Chris Bickerton (Britain), Morten Rasmussen (Denmark) and Antoine Vauchez (France); the historians Kiran Klaus Patel (Germany) and Vera Fritz (Luxembourg). In the work of these and other scholars, the dynamics of European integration emerge in a cooler, more searching light than in van Middelaar's panegyrics, revealing what these omit and scrutinizing what they don't with a finer lens.

I

The Union, as we know it today, is a complex composed of five principal institutions: the European Commission, the European Court of Justice, the European Parliament, the European Council and the European Central Bank. A consideration of these can begin with the term conventionally encompassing the story of their development, 'European integration'. This came from America, as Patel has shown,[1] adopted to avoid another term too pointed for tactical purposes in the politics of the fifties. The word it replaced was federation, rejected by governments and what interested opinion at large then existed, if ardently espoused by a small, but committed minority of activists. For these and their academic sympathizers, integration supplied a more neutral term for progress towards an ideal best kept, for the time being, *in petto*. Nowhere was it more helpful than in characterizing the work of the Court of Justice which was, as van Middelaar emphasizes, the first mover in the 'passage to Europe' after the Treaty of Rome.

Today the Court remains, of all Union institutions, the most withdrawn from the public. Discreetly situated in Luxembourg, not exactly a European crossroads, and composed of judges appointed—one per country—by member states, its proceedings are hidden from public scrutiny; its decisions permit no admission of dissent; its archives grant minimal access to researchers. In modus operandi, the ECJ is the antithesis of the Supreme Court in America, whose emoluments it comfortably tops—its president receives a salary worth some $400,000, plus

1 Kiran Klaus Patel, *Project Europe: A History*, Cambridge 2020, pp. 35–6.

many an allowance, the chief justice in Washington a measly $267,000. Historically, its origins date back to the first stage of integration, the European Coal and Steel Community born of the Schuman Plan, endowed with a Court of Justice that was rolled forward into the European Economic Community set up by the Treaty of Rome five years later, and then the European Union created at Maastricht.

Thanks to the pioneering work of a young historian from Luxembourg, Vera Fritz, we now have a detailed scholarly study of the composition of the Court in the first twenty years of its existence. Her findings are illuminating. There were seven founding judges, and two advocates general.[2] Who were they? The Italian president of the ECJ, Massimo Pilotti, had been assistant secretary-general of the League of Nations in the thirties. There he had acted as the long arm of the fascist regime in Rome, personally advising Mussolini on what countermeasures to take in manoeuvres to shield Italy from condemnation by the League for its actions in Ethiopia. On resigning his post in 1937, Pilotti took part in the celebrations at Genoa of the conquest of Ethiopia; and during the Second World War headed the high court of occupied Ljubljana after Italy's annexation of Slovenia, where resistance was met with mass deportations, concentration camps, and police and military repression. The German judge on the court, Otto Riese, had been so devoted a Nazi that without any duress—he spent the war as an academic in Switzerland—he retained his membership of the NSDAP down to 1945. His compatriot Karl Roemer, advocate general to the Court, had spent the war in occupied Paris managing French companies and banks for the Third Reich; after the war, when he married

2 Vera Fritz, *Juges et avocats généraux de la Cour de Justice de l'Union européenne (1952–1972): Une approche biographique de l'histoire d'une révolution juridique*, Frankfurt 2018, pp. 34–55.

Adenauer's niece, acting as defence lawyer for the Waffen SS charged with responsibility for the massacre of Oradour. The French advocate general Maurice Lagrange had served as a senior functionary in the Vichy government, fully committed to the ideology of a 'National Revolution' to sweep away the legacy of the Third Republic. Acting as linkman between the judicial apparatus of the Conseil d'Etat and the political apparatus of the Council of Ministers, Lagrange was the specialist in charge of coordinating the first wave of anti-Semitic persecution of the Jews.[3] When Laval took over the reins of Vichy in 1942, transferring him back to the Conseil d'Etat from which he came, Pétain thanked Lagrange for his 'rare perseverance' in the legislative and administrative work of the regime, to which he replied that 'for me it has been a great privilege to be so closely associated with the enterprise of national renovation you have undertaken for the salvation of our country. I am convinced that every Frenchman can and should take part in this work.'[4] After the war, he was chosen by the Americans to help them democratize the civil service in Germany, and by Monnet to help draft the treaty establishing the Coal and Steel Community.

That figures like these were the ornaments of Europe's first Court of Justice reflected, of course, the general closing of political ranks after the Cold War set in, when what mattered was not the misdeeds of the fascist past but the menace of communist present. It was a time when the last commander of

---

3 See Laurent Joly, *Vichy dans la 'Solution Finale': Histoire du commissariat general aux Questions juives (1941–1944)*, Paris 2006, pp. 88–92, 133 ff.

4 Marc Olivier Baruch, *Servir l'État français: L'administration en France de 1940 à 1944*, Paris 1997, pp. 325–6. In May–July 1944, Lagrange published three pieces in the *Revue des deux mondes* lamenting the subsequent lack of devotion that had weakened reconstruction of public administration in the spirit of 1940.

the Charlemagne Division of the SS, fighting to the last bullet to defend Hitler in his bunker in 1945, could reemerge as best choice for the Robert Schuman Prize for services to European unity.[5] Why should European justice too not let bygones be bygones? More generally, appointments to the Court had little or nothing to do with juridical qualifications. Nearly all were political. The Belgian judge was a leading figure in the Catholic Party of his country; the Dutch judge was the brother of a pre-war foreign minister; the French judge, Jacques Rueff—former deputy-governor of the Banque de France—was one of the founders of the CNIP, Antoine Pinay's post-war version of his pre-war Radical grouping; a Catholic trade-unionist from the Netherlands and a Socialist magistrate from Luxembourg rounded out the set.

Nor did this change when the next levy of judges arrived. Among these were a founder of the CDU in Berlin, later deputy for the party in the Bundestag; the son of a leader of the Anti-Revolutionary Party (Calvinist) in the Netherlands; a former aide to Dino Grandi, minister of justice for the Duce, now brother of the finance minister in Italy; a co-founder of the Christian Social Party in Belgium; a one-time Nazi and stalwart of the SA (1933 vintage), latterly become a Social Democrat in Germany; a long-time functionary in the Italian colonization of Rhodes; a former *chef de cabinet* to the civil and military governor of Algeria.[6] *Justice à l'européenne* was never blindfold: its eyes were wide open, and round its head was a bandana gaudy with the colours of the assorted establishment parties of the time.

---

5 See the remarkable portrait of his grandfather, Gustav Krukenberg, by Peter Schöttler in *Du Rhin à la Manche: Frontières et relations franc-allemandes au XXe siècle*, Tours 2017, pp. 177–203.

6 *Juges et avocats généraux*, pp. 60–77.

Decisive among the second wave of appointees was one in particular: in the words of an admirer, Europe's equivalent of John Marshall, the patriarch of the Supreme Court in the US, responsible for establishing its authority across the land. Robert Lecourt was a leading politician in the French version of the Christian Democratic parties in Italy and Germany, the MRP (Mouvement Républicain Populaire), which formed part of every government of the Fourth Republic, of which it supplied the second and second-last prime ministers. The most significant difference between the MRP and its opposite numbers in Rome and Bonn was that France possessed a large colonial empire of which the party was a zealous defender, resolute in prosecuting the country's wars in Indochina and Algeria. Joining de Gaulle's government with the arrival of the Fifth Republic, the MRP split over his announcement of a referendum on self-determination in Algeria. The party's long-standing leader Georges Bidault joined the right-wing paramilitary OAS, which launched armed resistance against de Gaulle in the name of *Algérie française* and narrowly failed to assassinate him, while his colleagues in the party hewed to de Gaulle. Lecourt, who like Bidault and others in the party was active in the Resistance, had a doctorate in law, serving as minister of justice in 1948, 1949 and 1957. Under de Gaulle, he held portfolios for France's colonies in Africa and elsewhere. In May 1962, he was appointed to the European Court of Justice.

Lecourt came to Luxembourg with a specialized set of associations and convictions from the MRP. Alongside his role as a deputy and minister for the party in the National Assembly, he had been active since the late forties in Nouvelles Équipes Internationales (NEI), the undeclared international of Christian Democracy in Europe, participating in its annual congresses devoted to such themes as 'firmness in the face of communism in crisis', and in due course becoming head of its French section. He continued without compunction to lead it at the NEI congress in Vienna in 1962, after he had taken up his post as judge in the Court of Justice. The NEI was in favour of European unity, and Lecourt was himself a member of Monnet's Action for a United States of Europe, formed in 1955. He was an ardent federalist.[7]

With this background, Lecourt's arrival in Luxembourg could not have been more happily timed. For on the docket of the Court lay the case that would produce its first landmark decision, *Van Gend en Loos*, a suit brought by a small transport firm against the Dutch government for imposing a customs charge on its import of an adhesive from Germany. To all appearances, a dispute of minor significance. In the shadows, however, powerful forces had been gathering around it. One was the European Commission in Brussels. There, heading its Legal Service was the Frenchman Marcel Gaudet. When working in the same capacity for the ECSC before the Treaty of Rome, he was already determined to ensure that the future ECJ would not be an international court along conventional lines, but a federal supreme court on the American model. Corresponding with Donald Swatland, a Wall Street lawyer who had been a wartime associate of Monnet, he explained in 1957 that 'federal ideas are still very new in continental Europe', and sought guidance from Swatland in promoting them.[8] He also developed a close relationship with the American legal scholar Eric Stein, the first person anywhere to hail the promising judicial future of the Court in Luxembourg. In 1959 Stein invited Gaudet for

---

7 Ibid., pp. 241–8.

8 See Julie Bailleux, 'Michel Gaudet, a Law Entrepreneur: The Role of the Legal Service of the European Executives in the Invention of EC Law and the Birth of the *Common Market Law Review*', *Common Market Law Review*, April 2013, pp. 359–68.

a six-week trip to the US to learn about federalism first-hand. In return Gaudet planted Stein, while he was on a sabbatical in 1962, in the offices of the Legal Service with a desk of his own, and invited him to sit in on the briefings with lawyers preparing the Commission's case on Van Gend en Loos for the ECJ. Stein, proponent of a set of fundamental axioms for a constitutional order in Europe, could be counted on as a transatlantic zealot of federalism for the Old World.[9]

Meanwhile, associations of jurists concerned to promote European law had been springing up in each of the countries of the Six, of which the German *Wissenschaftliche Gesellschaft für Europarecht* (WGE) was the largest and most important, followed by the *Association Française des Juristes Européens*. In close touch with these organizations, the Commission supplied financial support for their meetings, and in 1961 Gaudet created an umbrella organization bringing them together, the *Fédération Internationale de Droit Européen* (FIDE), 'with the explicit aim of facilitating exchanges across political, bureaucratic and scholarly boundaries.' In the words of its first president, FIDE acted as 'a private army of the European communities.'[10] The spirit informing the federation would be recalled by a member of its German branch: 'In Europe around 1950 the idea of European unification was capable of evoking almost religious enthusiasm among young lawyers. We believed in the United States of Europe.'[11] In the Netherlands, the Dutch section of FIDE was particularly active: one of its members acted as counsel for Van

9 Anne Boerger and Morten Rasmussen, 'Transforming European Law: The Establishment of the Constitutional Discourse from 1950 to 1993', *European Constitutional Law Review* 10, 2014 pp. 216–18 ff.

10 Stephanie Lee Mudge and Antoine Vauchez, 'Building Europe on a Weak Field: Law, Economics and Scholarly Avatars in Transnational Politics', *American Journal of Sociology*, September 2012, p. 467.

11 See Karen Alter, *The European Court's Political Power*, Oxford 2009, p. 67.

Gend en Loos. It can be surmised with some confidence that the case in question was set up by this lobby.[12] However that might be, supported by the Commission it found the right rapporteur in Luxembourg, where Lecourt, hotfoot from Paris, penned the historic verdict overturning a national law.

A year later came the second decisive act. In Italy two lawyers, outraged by nationalization of the electricity industry, set up a challenge to the constitutionality of its issuance of a $3 utility bill. When the Italian Constitutional Court ruled that nationalization was not a constitutional issue, and could not be challenged by reference to the Treaty of Rome, as passed subsequent to it, they appealed to the European Court. Two weeks after its advocate general argued that the Italian Court could not be overridden, though it should be encouraged to seek ways of integrating European into national law, the WGE held a meeting in Hesse at which three of the ECJ's judges were present. There, a participant recorded, they sat with 'red ears' as a leading authority of the WGE, Hans Peter Ipsen, instructed them on the supremacy of European over the national law of any member state.[13] Ipsen's opinion would prevail: five days later Lecourt issued the ECJ's ruling on *Costa v. Enel* to the same effect. The cornerstone of European justice was laid.

Who was Ipsen? A jurist from Hamburg who joined the SA in 1933, and the NSDAP in 1937, becoming a full professor at the age of thirty-two on the strength of a doctorate, subsequently published as a book, *Politik und Justiz*, dealing with 'sovereign acts' by the state that dispensed with considerations of justice. Exalting the German version of these based on the *Führergewalt*

12 For particulars, Morten Rasmussen, 'Establishing a Constitutional Practice of European Law: The History of the Legal Service of the European Executive', *Contemporary European History*, August 2012, pp. 385–6; Alter, 'As Lawyers and Judges, FIDE Helped Create Cases the ECJ Could Rule On', p. 36.

13 Alter, *The European Court's Political Power*, pp. 77–8.

of Nazi power—finding expression since 1933 in arrests, purges, expropriations, *Gleichschaltung* of trade-unions—as superior to earlier merely 'governmental' legislation in France, and the fascist variant in Italy based on legislative authority in a division of powers system, the book understandably attracted the interest of the Nazi party's central chancellery.[14] Active in Brussels and Antwerp during the war, Ipsen served as a commissar for universities in occupied Belgium, where in April 1943 he extolled the 'external administration' of the Third Reich that now covered Norway, Belgium, the Netherlands, France, the Ukraine, the Baltics, the *Generalgouvernment* of Poland, occupied areas of Serbia and Greece, not to speak of Alsace, Lorraine, Luxembourg, Southern Styria and the protectorates of Bohemia and Moravia—an area comprising some 2,865,000 square kilometres and 154 million inhabitants, in addition to the nearly 700,000 square kilometres and 90 million inhabitants of the enlarged 'inner Reich' itself, amounting in all to 46 per cent of the total population of the continent. These lands held the promise of a future *Grossraumordnung* of Europe, to which Germany could look forward, organized around it.[15] Before the war was out, Ipsen became dean of the Law Faculty at the University of Hamburg and adviser to the Ministry of Justice

---

14 *Politik und Justiz*, Hamburg 1937. Visibly indebted to the writing of Carl Schmitt, the work was greeted with an admiring review by Ernst Rudolf Huber, a leading Nazi jurist, whose only reservation would be that Ipsen had not fully appreciated the difference between Schmitt's subjective decisionism, a product of chaotic Weimar conditions, and the objective criteria laid down by the Third Reich to defend 'the people's way of life against existential hardship and danger'. See ' "Politik und Justiz": Zu Hans Peter Ipsens Schrift über das Problem der "justizlosen Hoheitsakte"', *Zeitschrift für die gesamte Staatswissenschaft*, 1938, Bd 38, H 1, pp. 199–200.

15 Hans Peter Ipsen, 'Reichsaussenverwaltung', *Brusseler Zeitung*, 3 April 1943, reproduced in Hans-Werner Neulen, *Europa und das 3. Reich: Einigungsbestrebungen im deutschen Machtbereich 1939–1945*, Munich 1987, pp. 111–15.

in Berlin. In 1945 he was briefly deprived of his chair, but soon recovered it. A better than average Nazi career, it was capped with post-war honours as he became the doyen of European law in the Federal Republic, authoring a monumental summary of the subject in 1972.

Three years later Lecourt became president of the ECJ. In this position, he wooed national judges with regular invitations to learn from Luxembourg—a systematic 'campaign of seduction', assorted with champagne brunches, to disarm resistance to the supremacy it claimed. By the end of his tenure, some 2,500 magistrates from across the member states had enjoyed his hospitality. In the other direction, judges of the Court were encouraged to pay ceremonial visits to the governments of the Community, where they were typically received, an assistant could report, 'like emperors'. Since so many of them had come from political backgrounds, or were scions of well-placed family dynasties, they could take these as opportunities for insider exchange of news and views of an informal kind, oiling the wheels of ECJ presence and influence. Lecourt, with a long experience of journalism and politics, also encouraged his colleagues to give lectures and write articles—for the cognoscenti—to spread the glad word of the Court, setting an energetic example himself.[16]

In all this he was seconded from 1967 onwards by the arrival of Pierre Pescatore, another kin appointment, brother-in-law of the prime minister of Luxembourg and a more outspoken and prolific champion of federalism even than Lecourt—his legal opinions serving in the words of one witness as the 'shock troops' of supranational advance.[17] Together they propelled

16 *Juges et avocats généraux*, pp. 149–50, 159–67; *The European Court's Political Power*, p. 36.

17 *Juges et avocats généraux*, p. 150.

European justice forward in what would later be seen as its heroic age: one bold judgment after another sealing the Court's authority over successive aspects of the life of the Community. Lecourt's record as its president, Pescatore declared after his chief had retired, was nothing less than 'a jurisprudential miracle'.[18] His own contribution was to uphold still more firmly a 'teleological', rather than merely literal, reading of the Treaty of Rome. For whatever its clauses might or might not say, it was inspired by ideals inherent in 'the common liberal and democratic traditions of the peoples of Western Europe' that should acquire legal force.[19] After Lecourt had gone, it was Pescatore who delivered the last key judgment of the Court as a driver of European unity, the market-levelling verdict of *Cassis de Dijon* of 1978, ruling that any product on legal sale in one country of the Community was vendible in any other. Lecourt's strategy had always been to move gradually, avoiding any blatant provocation of national governments, deflecting their attention from momentous juridical pronouncements by attaching them to matters of seemingly minimal commercial importance. In this case, the commodity in question was a blackcurrant liqueur.

After *Cassis de Dijon*, strategic initiative passed to the European Council which gradually took shape after its creation by Giscard in the mid-seventies, and to the Commission after it came under the command of Delors in the mid-eighties. The Court handled an increasing number of cases and its judicial activism scarcely abated. But it now reinforced rather than led the Hayekian turn in the Community that crystallized with the Single European Act of 1985. In the new century, it has enjoyed an extra shot of neo-liberal adrenalin with the arrival in

---

18 William Phelan, *Great Judgments of the European Court of Justice*, Cambridge 2019, p. 22.

19 *Juges et avocats généraux*, pp. 157–8.

Luxembourg of converts to free market principles from Eastern Europe, resulting in two judgments in 2007—*Viking* and *Laval*, pitting Baltic freebooters against Nordic trade-unions—undermining labour rights. These were a departure from the tactical precepts of Lecourt, arousing adverse public attention of the kind the Court had always sought to elude, and conspicuous further steps did not ensue. After Maastricht an important task would still fall to the Court, but of a different character. Its pioneering work—celebrated by van Middelaar as the coup that essentially founded today's Union—had been accomplished.

II

Where did this achievement lie? The two jurists who have spelt it out with greatest clarity are Dieter Grimm, for twelve years a judge on the German Constitutional Court, and Thomas Horsley, two generations younger, a senior lecturer in the Liverpool Law School. The decisions of the Court in the sixties, Grimm has observed, were 'revolutionary because the principles they announced were not agreed upon in the treaties' that created the ECSC and EEC, and 'almost certainly would not have been agreed upon had the issues been raised'. It was a Court with an agenda that did not correspond to the intentions of its founders, seeing itself 'neither as a guardian of the rights of the signatory states, nor as a neutral arbiter between the states and the Community, but rather a driving force of integration'.[20] Its assertion of the supremacy of Community over domestic (let alone constitutional) laws, Horsley remarks, had no basis in the Treaty of Rome, which granted it rights of judicial review only 'with

20 Dieter Grimm, *Europa ja—aber welches? Zur Verfassung der europäischen Demokratie*, Munich 2016, pp. 12–13 (In English: *The Constitution of European Democracy*, Oxford 2017, pp. 4–5. Henceforward *TCED*.)

respect to acts of Union Institutions', not of member states. 'Yet, in effect, this is exactly what the Court now does on a routine basis', proceeding as if 'the Treaty framework, as the touchstone on the internal constitutionality of all EU institutional activity, has never actually meant what it so clearly states'.[21]

But is there anything particularly unusual about this, it might be asked? Isn't creative interpretation of laws by judges almost as familiar as of figures by accountants? On an alternative and less cynical view, isn't what matters the outcome? For an Ankersmit or van Middelaar, we would be looking at an instance of the judicial sublime. Without having to go so far, it is reasonable to enquire what's wrong with the upshot. The answer lies at the level both of principles and of consequences. As to the first, Horsley opens his study with the following grave statement: 'Among EU institutions, the Court remains uniquely distinguished as an actor in the integration process. It is the only Union institution whose activities are not routinely scrutinized (by itself or by others) for compliance with the EU treaties.' Yet the 'Treaty framework provides no basis whatsoever to justify differentiating between the Court and the Union's administrative and political institutions with regard to compliance with its demands. The Court is formally designated an institution of the Union under Article 13 TEU. As such, along with the Union's political institutions, it is irrefutably subject to compliance with EU Treaties.'[22] But once, from the moment of its 'coup', the Court had authorized itself as the guardian of a constitution which had

21 Thomas Horsley, *The Court of Justice of the European Union as an Institutional Actor*, Cambridge 2018, pp. 125, 129.

22 However obvious or central the issue should be, Horsley notes that 'none of the leading textbooks on EU law or works on the Court of Justice addresses the application of the EU Treaty framework *to the Court* as a source of normative restraint on the exercise of its attributed functions'. *The Court of Justice of the European Union*, pp. 5, 7.

no basis in the Treaties, but supposedly corresponded to their 'ultimate purpose', what other institution could bring it to book? Its circular self-validation ruled out any such challenge.

The Court thus became not just a unique institution within the Community, but unique within the range of supreme or constitutional courts at large, endowed with powers which no analogue in a democracy has ever possessed. For in all other cases, the rulings of such courts are subject to alteration or abrogation by elected legislatures. Those of the ECJ are not. They are irreversible. Short of amendment of the treaties themselves, requiring the unanimous agreement of all member states, 'which, as everyone knows, is all but out of the question', there is no recourse against them. They are set not in stone, but in granite, and are far from neutral in effect. Written in 'opaque, technical language', the Court's decisions will often cloak highly political issues in an apolitical fashion, 'below the threshold of public attention', rendering their effects difficult *ex ante* to perceive; but should they subsequently be protested, become accomplished facts which citizens are told it is too late to do anything about—'there is now no alternative'.[23] Since these rulings have constitutional force, much of what would be ordinary legislation at national level became built into successive sequels to the original Treaty of Rome—Maastricht, Amsterdam, Nice, Lisbon—in documents of such 'epic length' that the Ireland's EU commissioner declared of the last that 'no sane person' could read it, after his prime minister admitted, after signing it, he had not done so: amounting, in effect, to enormous cryptograms beyond the patience or grasp of any democratic public.

The effect of 'constitutionalizing'—the quotation marks are needed because the treaties remain international pacts, not federal charters—issues like the permissibility of state aid to

23 *Europa ja—aber welches?*, pp. 16, 18, 28 (*TCED*, pp. 8, 10, 19).

industries, or subsidies to public services, is to immunize judicial ukases on them against any ordinary exercise of the popular will. As Grimm writes: 'The stronger the substantive content of the constitution, the narrower the leeway for politics.' Typically, 'whatever is governed in the constitution is removed from the realm of political decision-making. It is no longer an object, but a premise of politics.' In the EU, 'it cannot even be influenced by the outcome of an election.'[24] That the judges who deliver the decisions of the ECJ are themselves unelected is, of course, common though not invariable practice in constitutional courts. What is not, is the European Court's 'insatiable jurisdictional appetite.'[25] Its current president, the Belgian Koen Lenaerts, has spelt out the extent of that hunger. In his words: 'There is simply no nucleus of sovereignty that the Member States can invoke, as such, against the Community.' The Court aims at 'the same practical outcome as the one that would be obtained through a direct invalidation of Member State law.'[26]

To such self-aggrandizing presumption corresponds neither judicial nor political competence. Even setting aside its systematic disregard for the limits on its scope in the treaties, writes Horsley, 'the Court fares poorly in comparison to its counterparts on the classic measures of comparative institutional analysis: democratic legitimacy and technical expertise. Its judges are not elected, its deliberations are secret, and, as a court of general jurisdiction, it enjoys no special expertise in the wide range of policy fields over which it intercedes to adjudicate.'[27]

24 Ibid., p. 18 (p. 9).

25 Ibid., p. 23 (p. 14).

26 'Constitutionalism and the Many Faces of Federalism', *American Journal of Comparative Law*, Spring 1990, pp. 221, 256.

27 *The Court of Justice of the European Union*, pp. 192, 200. In compensation, what it has enjoyed is the complicity of the community of European legal scholarship, about which the two authors concur. Grimm: 'European law was studied primarily by experts who overwhelmingly identified with their

But if it has no special expertise, it had from the start a particular orientation, 'a settled and consistent policy of promoting European federalism', and once the turn of the eighties came, a decided social inclination, which it has pursued, in Grimm's view, with 'missionary zeal'. Interpreting 'prohibitions of discrimination against foreign companies so widely' that 'almost any national regulation could be understood as a market access obstacle', and pushing 'privatization regardless of the motives for entrusting certain tasks to public services', the Court effectively deprived member states of 'the power to determine the borderline between the private and public sector, market and state'.[28]

Such judgments come, not from any eurosceptic standpoint, but from authorities committed to, in their view, the achievements of European integration. For Grimm, what is needed to restore legitimacy to the process is essentially the de-constitutionalization of political decisions to allow their discussion by voters and revision by legislatures. Horsley, after explaining what in his opinion have been the benefits of judicial intervention along with its costs, assures readers that he does not seek to undermine the Court of Justice, let alone add to

---

subject and who viewed the discipline as part of the European project', so 'there prevailed an unspoken ban on criticism, so as not to endanger the European project', *Europa ja—aber welches?*, p. 18 (*TCED*, p. 12). Horsley: 'The Court robustly defends a view of the EU as a "new legal order" that is defined in opposition to international law and, further, considers the domestic effect of EU norms as an exclusive matter for the Union, not Member State law. The source of this judicial vision is external to the Treaty framework. It represents the Court's projection onto the Treaty framework of a model of political federalism. To a great extent, that vision was also "co-produced" with an influential body of legal scholars advocating a shared political vision for EU integration', in 'a uniquely proximate relationship between officials at the Court (and those working within the Union institutions more generally) and the academic community'. *The Court of Justice of the European Union*, p. 255.

28 'The Power of Restraint in the European Union', in van Middelaar and Van Parijs (eds), *After the Storm*, p. 117.

'denigration of the Union', but to enhance the legitimacy of its lawmaking. Yet if their accounts of the ECJ are those of friends of the Court, it is not clear what its enemies would be left to say. The truth is that, on any reasonable reckoning, it would be difficult to conceive of a judicial institution in the West that, from its tenebrous outset onwards, was purer of any trace of democratic accountability.

III

The European Commission, whose evolution has been more winding, was in its early years the crucial partner of the Court. Its history can roughly be divided into three phases, corresponding to the three figures who alone would hold its presidency for a full decade across two terms: Walter Hallstein (1958–67), Jacques Delors (1985–95) and José Manuel Barroso (2004–14). Hallstein, a German lawyer and diplomat—a Christian Democrat best known for the Cold War doctrine lasting until 1972 to which he gave his name, making West German recognition of any state dependent on its refusal to recognize East Germany—was an outspoken federalist, who conceived the Commission as a proto-government of the Community, declaring national sovereignty a 'doctrine of yesterday', and awarding himself the status of 'Prime Minister of Europe'. De Gaulle put a brusque end to his pretensions in 1965, and he left Brussels a mocked and deflated figure. However, in his heyday, between 1958 and 1964, Hallstein presided over a Commission that was a dynamo of energy in finding ways and means to circumvent the Treaty of Rome in the higher interests of European unity.

Brussels, as the French scholar Antoine Vauchez has shown, quickly became a magnet for corporate lawyers and investors from America on the lookout for market opportunities, and bringing with them the expectations and practices of a powerful ongoing federation, who soon formed close relations with the substantial number of high-flying Belgian commercial jurists. This common milieu offered smooth intermediation between arriving multinationals and the Commission, and a propitious setting for exchange of ideas with its key Competition and Legal Services. The European Economic Community created by the Treaty of Rome was not conceived as a free-fire zone for the market, giving birth to a heavily subsidized and regulated Common Agricultural Policy that was anathema to liberal economists, prompting Hayek's fellow thinker Wilhelm Röpke—taking aim at its Belgian founder—to denounce it as nothing more than a miserable 'Spaakistan'. From the outset, however, the Competition Service of the Commission was a fortress populated by German ordoliberals, whose devotion to market principles and determination they should not be impeded by improper meddling on the part of any state made them natural proponents of federalism, as Hayek had been already before the war. In this cause, the Legal Service led the way, supplying the Court of Justice with the overwhelming majority of cases on which, as intended, its verdicts could build an ever more extensive edifice of European law trumping the rights of national legislatures. Between 1954 and 1978 the ten most frequent plaintiffs before the Court brought a total of 1,371 cases before it: of these 1,082 came from the Commission or its adjuncts—just under 80 per cent. The loop of collusion was tightly wound. By 1964, Hallstein could announce triumphantly that Europe had achieved 'the beginnings of a real and full "political union"'.[29]

---

29 Antoine Vauchez, *Brokering Europe: Euro-Lawyers and the Making of a Transnational Polity*, Cambridge 2015, pp. 81, 28. Adjuncts were the executives of the ECSC and Euratom.

A year later he was a busted flush, and it took another twenty years for the Commission to recover its dynamism. When it did so, it came under other colours. Delors, whose youthful background was in the Catholic trade-union confederation in France, in due course joined the Socialist Party, where he advocated a 'social Europe'. But when there was a conflict between the adjective and the noun, the noun came first. As finance minister under Mitterrand, it was Delors who made sure that the socialist programme on which Mitterrand had been elected and had at first been implemented, was ditched in the famous U-turn of 1983 for austerity to keep the franc in the European Monetary System. At the head of the Commission, Delors was profuse with declarations of the need for social solidarity and did in the end secure Cohesion Funds to help less advantaged regions in the Community. His main achievements, however, were to pass the Single European Act—crafted under him by an emissary of Thatcher—unifying and deregulating markets across the Community, and to drive through the monetary union that became the centrepiece of the Treaty of Maastricht. In his mind, these were the necessary preambles to European-wide social solidarity. Not only were they economically efficient in themselves, promoting a growth that would eventually lift all boats; without them, governments could not be persuaded of the need to redistribute wealth across classes and regions, essential if Europe was to win the full adhesion of its citizens. A far more charismatic and commanding figure than Hallstein, a politician who dealt on equal terms with all the national leaders of the day, Delors led them to the single currency, but failed to achieve the social objectives he had thought he could buy with it. All governments save Britain and Denmark signed up to the first. Few wanted much of the second. Delors did manage to get Cohesion Funds—help for disadvantaged regions, not classes—out of

Maastricht, but these were the crumbs of solidarity, not the loaf: compared with the subsequent impact of the single currency, little more than the alms of an instrumental charity.

Barroso, installed four years before the global financial crisis of 2008 and exiting just as Syriza came to office in 2014, was the second sitting prime minister of a member state to become president of the Commission. A politician of the Portuguese right, whose main previous claim to fame was hosting the Azores Summit between Bush, Blair, Aznar and himself that launched the Iraq war, his appointment to Brussels the following year demonstrated how hollow was the nominal opposition of France and Germany to Operation Iraqi Freedom. An usher of austerity in his own country, his tenure marked the apogee of the neo-liberal drive that followed the introduction of the single currency, with the promulgation of Bolkestein's General Services Directive in 2004 and the arrival of the Treaty of Lisbon in 2010. But though personally as ambitious for his role as Hallstein or Delors, the ideas he represented were conventional wisdom by the new century, while the power of the European Council had grown significantly at the expense of the Commission since Maastricht, a body that in Barroso's second term enjoyed its own president in Van Rompuy, a rival for the limelight with whom his relations were never good. His tenure was less consequential than that of his predecessors.

Today, twenty-eight commissioners, one per member state, each allocated a portfolio—naturally, of vastly differing importance: Competition has long since become the top prize —formally enjoy equal status under the president, currently CDU politician Ursula von der Leyen. In reality, as the veteran director-general of its Legal Service, the all-purpose Brussels fixer Jean-Claude Piris (twenty-two years in the saddle) has pointed out, since this would mean that the fourteen commissioners from the Union's smallest countries, representing a mere 12.65 per cent of the population of the Union, could easily outvote the six commissioners from its biggest countries, representing 70 per cent of its population, decisions are always taken by 'consensus'—that is, behind a façade of unanimity, under the impulsion or veto of the six major states. Likewise the president of the Commission, responsible for liaison with the heads of government of member states, normally confers only with those of the same select group, or perhaps just with Berlin and Paris at the top of it: to do otherwise would be 'too time-consuming'.[30] So composed, the Commission is formally vested with the sole power to propose legislation for the Union, but here the reality differs: more than two-thirds of its proposals are in fact now hatched jointly with representatives of the member states in the dense undergrowth at Brussels, in which COREPER—bringing together their permanent envoys to the EU—holds pride of place, and then rubber-stamped by the relevant Council of Ministers when passed up to it.

Below the commissioners, appointed for five-year terms, sits the permanent bureaucracy of the EU, some 33,000 strong—the 'Eurocrats', as coined by the *Economist* in 1961 and popularized with no pejorative intent by a book of Altiero Spinelli in 1966. In its higher echelons, where heads and assistants of the Commission's thirty-two directorates-general are to be found, recruitment was heavily weighted up to the mid-eighties towards functionaries with a legal background; while below them, in the body of the administration, a general European orientation of humanistic stamp was encouraged, a Master's in European studies an advantage, preferably from the College of Europe in Bruges. Thereafter, and with the subsequent

30 Jean-Claude Piris, *The Future of Europe: Towards a Two-Speed Europe?*, Cambridge 2012, pp. 26–7, 30–1, 33.

enlargement of the Union to the East, the pattern changed. Under Romano Prodi (president 1999–2004), Neil Kinnock was entrusted with the task of modernizing the system of pay and recruitment, bringing the tidings of New Labour to Brussels, with predictable outcomes. By 2014, two-thirds of the directors-general were trained in economics, receiving commensurately higher salaries to compete with the private sector, and lower down, in the name of democratizing future intakes, knowledge of foreign languages or of any general culture faded as requirements, giving way to MBAs.[31]

For observers of the course of the EU since Maastricht, such changes might be logical enough—neo-liberals were being neo-liberalized—but they were not appreciated by many of those affected by them, their Anglo-Saxon origin rubbing post-Brexit salt in the wounds. 'After having broken Europe from the inside for years, they're breaking it from the outside by destroying its political legitimacy', said one. Another, not as angry: 'It's insane when you think about it. They are leaving after having imposed their administrative model on us.' Caustically commented yet another: 'The new model is the Procter & Gamble one.'[32] Barroso's elevation, from presidency of the Commission to chairman of the International Division of Goldman Sachs, was a natural sequel to these reforms. But the alteration of outlooks and mores in the Commission has also to be understood in terms of its surroundings. There are some 30,000 registered lobbyists in Brussels. In 1994 only 5 per cent of these represented trade-union, environmental, feminist or other 'public interest' groups: over 90 per cent were business organizations,

31 Didier Georgakakis, *European Civil Service in (Times of) Crisis: A Political Sociology of the Changing Power of Eurocrats*, Cham (Switzerland) 2015, pp. 26, 204, 276, 288.

32 Ibid., pp. 206, 288.

seeking prebends and favours.[33] That is over double the number infesting Washington, reckoned at a mere 12,000. That Europe's executive could resist infection from the vapours of this swamp is implausible.

Since Delors, the Commission has had to play second fiddle to the European Council, which is unlikely to appoint a figure of his political stature to lead it again. Contemporary popular suspicion of the Commission as the bureaucratic demi-urge of the Union is in that sense misplaced. But it remains a considerable power within the complex machinery of the EU, by reason of three attributes peculiar to it. The first is simply its size as a corps of permanent functionaries compared with that of any of the Union's other institutions, and the closed citadel of its workings—thirty-four different 'procedures' that no lay person is equipped to understand. The second lies in the volume of the rulebook that it wields as an instrument of power within the Union—the *acquis communitaire*, impenetrable to its citizens, but inescapable for its states, forming the primary means of the *Gleichschaltung* of Eastern Europe to EU norms, over which commissioners presided as proconsuls from Brussels. Originally put together as a codification of EEC regulations to which the UK, Denmark and Ireland would have to adapt on entry into the Community in 1973, when it already came to 2,800 pages, the *acquis* now runs to 90,000 pages, the longest and most formidable written monument of bureaucratic expansion in human history. (The notorious US tax code is a mere 6,500.) Foucault's over-blown identification of knowledge with power here finds literal embodiment.

33 Jan Zielonka, *Counter-Revolution: Europe in Retreat*, Oxford 2018, p. 66 (see also note 24, p. 143); Stefano Bartolini, *Restructuring Europe: Centre Formation, System Building and Political Structuring between the Nation-State and the European Union*, Oxford 2005, p. 288 (see note 50).

'This technical and cognitive equipment', writes Vauchez, going on to quote Joseph Weiler,

> is not only the instrument that officially defines and authenticates that 'Europe' to which candidates are applying in phases of enlargement; it equally inserts itself into the most routine operations of the EU, turning into Europe's 'constitutional operating system ... axiomatic, beyond discussion, above debate, like the rules of democratic discourse, or even the very rules of rationality themselves, which seem to condition debate but not be part of it.'

Nor, of course, is it institutionally neutral.

> As it formalizes a stable figure of Europe (its foundations, its missions) and of its value objects (its body of law), the *acquis* implicitly locates the ability and responsibility for the 'rational guidance' of European affairs in particular institutions (here: the Commission and the Court) and professional groups (Euro-lawyers and EU civil servants), while dispossessing others (here: Member States, constitutional courts, national diplomats, bureaucrats, etc).[34]

At the same time, along with the *acquis* as a disciplinary instrument, the Commission possesses a mollifying implement of power in the apportionment and disbursement of its Cohesion Funds, the *annona* of van Middelaar's latter-day Roman strategy for securing clients. These form a significant source of patronage, usable to induce compliance or reward loyalty, whose promise could be critical in winning local elites to the will of the Union, if also conditions bent where it was politic to overlook corruption

---

34 Antoine Vauchez, 'Methodological Europeanism at the Cradle: Eur-lex, *the Acquis* and the Making of Europe's Cognitive Equipment', *Journal of European Integration* 37: 2, 2015, p. 194.

in the interests of ideological subsumption, as in Romania and other candidates for membership. Little noticed at the time, geographical enlargement of the Union to the East produced the greatest operational enlargement of the Commission since Hallstein's time, as it took charge of the task. That some of its fruits have since become thorns in its side, as the more advanced states of Eastern Europe, once their elites were safely inside the Union, became less submissive to it, has been another of the unintended consequences, or counter-finalities, of which there have been so many in the history of integration.

IV

What of the European Parliament? Composed now of some 700 deputies, apportioned between the Union's twenty-eight countries to reduce somewhat the weight of the largest (Germany in particular), and shuttling monthly between Brussels and Strasbourg, it has historically been an ally of the Commission and Court in aspirations to a federalist future for Europe. The Commission would have liked to become, as Hallstein expected it to be, the governing executive of Europe, and the Assembly—it only came to be officially styled a Parliament in the eighties—sought to become the legislature of Europe to which this executive would be responsible: hopes that did not materialize. Nevertheless, over time the Parliament has acquired a substantial bureaucratic infrastructure of its own—presently, some 7,000 functionaries service it—and a limited number of powers, of which the three most significant are the right to 'co-decision' with the Council on legislation proposed by the Commission; to reject—but not amend—the budget proposed by the Commission; and reject—but not elect—commissioners chosen by the president of the Commission. What it does not possess are the rights to elect a government, to initiate legislation, to levy taxes, to shape welfare or determine a foreign policy. In short, it is the semblance of a parliament, as ordinarily understood, that falls far short of the reality of one.

Voters are aware of this and have shown scant interest in it. Turnout at European elections is notoriously poor, falling steadily across four decades to a point where its recovery to just over 50 per cent in 2018 could be hailed as the sign at last of a robust European democracy, though this was still 10 percentage points below the figure in 1979, when the first such election was held. Nor are most of the citizens who do take the trouble to go to these polls voting on European issues. Rather, in casting their ballots for or against local parties, they are expressing their views on the performance of their national governments of the day. The result is an assembly composed of some 200 heteroclite parties, which then group themselves into some six or seven blocs, whose unity does not run deep—ties between deputies are often closer within national delegations than with their pan-European affiliates. No division between government and opposition can emerge, because there is no government to be formed or opposed. The pattern instead is for grand coalitions along German lines, bringing together centre-right and centre-left blocs to control the proceedings, and electing the chief officers and key committee chairs of the Assembly from their ranks, with variable input from Liberal and Green auxiliaries. The political difference between the two main blocs, in general faded enough at national level, becomes all but completely invisible in the successive *GroKo* combinations at Brussels and Strasbourg.

As might be expected, in this huge, heterogeneous, largely ceremonial body, deputies have little appetite for going through the motions of actually being there. Average attendance is around 45 per cent. Virtually all its work is seconded to committees, where behind closed doors the mysteries of 'trilogue' are enacted: that is, representatives of the Parliament confer with representatives of the Council of Ministers and of the Commission as to what legislative proposals emanating from the Commission, and typically pre-cleared by member states and their permanent representatives in Brussels, can be accepted for transmission to a vote in the chamber—discussion mostly revolving around matters of procedure rather than substance. As Christopher Bickerton notes: 'Between 2009 and 2013, 81 per cent of proposals were passed at first reading via the trilogue method. Only 3 per cent ever reached third reading, which is where texts are debated in plenary sessions of the Parliament.'[35] Such is the alchemy of co-decision.

In 2014, when turnout was just 42.3 per cent, the Parliament launched a campaign with wide media support to convert the elections to it into a pan-European exercise in the democratic will: each of the political blocs would nominate a candidate for presidency of the Commission—legally in the gift of the Council—and the bloc securing the largest number of seats would, equipped with the backing of the whole Parliament, then elevate its *Spitzenkandidat* to the command of the Commission, as any other legislature might vote a government into office. The centre-right gained most votes; its candidate was the 'malodorous fixer' Jean-Claude Juncker. After some tergiversation, Merkel prevailed on the Council to accept him and Juncker became president of the Commission on the strength of 10 per cent of the European electorate. Had she not done so, Habermas told his readers, it would have been 'a bullet to the heart of the European project.'[36] Five years later Macron put his foot down,

35 *The European Union: A Citizen's Guide*, London 2016, p. 27.

36 See Susan Watkins, 'The Political State of the Union', *New Left Review* 90, November–December 2014, pp. 20–2.

and the next president was picked according to the rules by the Council, as always in the past, ignoring the hapless *Spitzenkandidat* of the hour. Indignant at this rebuff to its pretensions, there was talk of a rebellion in the Parliament, which though it has no right to select, can reject a Commission president. But wouldn't that provoke a crisis of the European project? The terrifying prospect of an open disagreement between its institutions quelled enough spirits for Ursula von der Leyen to sidle into office.

The function of the European Parliament, which neither aggregates nor channels the wishes of voters, from whom once the polls close it becomes completely detached, is, as the Italian scholar Stefano Bartolini has put it, 'elite consolidation'.[37] That is, a process in which the assorted parties collude with each other to present the appearance of a democratic assembly, behind which oligarchic coteries are comfortably entrenched. These would be happy to gain more powers than they enjoy, but they have no interest in ceding any to those they nominally represent. The width of the gap between the institution and the populations beneath it can be judged from the rare occasions on which the latter have been able to make their voice heard directly. In the Netherlands, turnout for the European elections of 2004 was just 39 per cent. A year later, it was 63 per cent in the referendum on the Draft Constitutional Treaty—which, supported by 80 per cent of the Dutch delegation at Strasbourg/Brussels, was rejected by 62 per cent of Dutch voters. The Parliament is not what it seems, and is the component of the Union of least consequence. Does that mean it is little more than a glorified fig-leaf? Not quite. Appearances matter, and in its fashion the Parliament plays a constructive role for the Union, supplying a measure of the legitimation that any self-respecting liberal order

37 *Restructuring Europe*, Oxford 2005, p. 331 ff.

requires. However limited citizen investment in them may be, synchronized pan-European polls are better than none, and their beneficiaries can continue to hope that a vibrant federal polity will one day arise from them.

V

Of an altogether different order of political avoirdupois is the European Central Bank, created to manage the single currency that came into force in 1999. Today it is one of—some would say, the—most powerful of EU institutions. Based in Frankfurt, its Governing Council is composed of the heads of the central banks of the eurozone countries and the six members of its Executive Board, meeting every two weeks. Its proceedings, unlike those of the Fed or the Bank of England, but in keeping with those of the European Court of Justice, are secret. Occasionally, unlike the ECJ, a member of it may resign, but its decisions are formally unanimous. No dissent from them is ever published. The Treaty of Maastricht conferred absolute independence on the ECB, which operates without any of the counterweights—Congress, the White House, the Treasury—that surround the Fed, embedding the latter in a political setting where it is publicly accountable. Nor, unlike any other central bank, is the independence of the ECB merely statutory, its rules or aims alterable by parliamentary decision: it is subject only to treaty revision. Nor—unlike the Commission, Parliament, Court or even Council—are its proceedings in any way cumbersome. It can act with a speed and impact no other EU institution can match.

The Treaty charged the ECB with a single objective. Where the Fed is charged by Congress with ensuring maximal employment as well as stable prices, the single responsibility of the ECB was to ensure monetary stability in what would become the eurozone. From the outset, as economists were aware and not a few pointed out, the economies due to adopt the euro, differing widely in size, composition and level of development, in no way met the criteria of an 'optimal currency area' as set out by Mundell and others. Quite the contrary. But this did not deter the Delors Committee which drove the project through, since its aims were political rather than economic—in part to tie down a reunified Germany within the Community, but more broadly to create a currency that would lock those states which adopted it so closely together that they would be obliged to follow a monetary with a political union. As an explicit goal, that was a bridge too far at Maastricht, where federalist hopes were dashed by inter-governmental bargaining of a traditional sort. Still, the Treaty created a European Monetary Union, the assembled politicians who signed the document characteristically giving little thought to what its consequences might be when they were no longer in office. The portals of a political union were not entered; but nor were they foreclosed.

The disjunction between means and ends soon made itself felt. Wim Duisenberg, the crude Dutch banker who became the first president of the ECB, prided himself on being a rough-hewn champion of financial orthodoxy along the best Anglo-Saxon lines. Yet he was overjoyed when Greece, after suitably cooking its books, promptly adopted the euro. His reasons were not economic, but political. For though the single currency was not, for those administering it, simply a short-cut to federalism, it was—as Giandomenico Majone, a thinker truer to classical principles, would put it—a 'prestige project' designed to raise the profile of the EU in the world.[38] A decade later, the eurozone would be paying for this vanity. Jean-Claude Trichet,

38 *Rethinking the Union of Europe Post-Crisis: Has Integration Gone Too Far?*, Cambridge 2014, pp. 29, 58.

the Frenchman next at the helm in Frankfurt, was a smoother figure, but no less blind. His response to the global financial crisis was pro-cyclical: raising interest rates to force governments to cut public spending, imposing austerity as a cure for the crash. His successor Mario Draghi was widely celebrated for reversing course, spraying money into the eurozone economies with purchase of government bonds and a generous dose of other forms of liquidity. In fact, there was more overlap between the two than generally believed. Draghi, responsible for a sweeping privatization programme in Italy, was the more outspokenly neo-liberal, openly pronouncing Europe's social contract obsolete in the pages of the *Wall Street Journal*. But in August 2011, the two jointly penned a secret letter to Berlusconi, the Italian prime minister of the time, demanding that he resort to a Cold War emergency mechanism to cut pensions and other public expenditures—an unprecedented violation of its mandate by the Bank. Three months later Berlusconi was gone. For his part, Trichet had by the end of his tenure come round to schemes to circumvent the ban in the Treaty of Maastricht on purchase of public debt by the Bank. Praising her chief, the former head of research at the ECB, Lucrezia Reichlin, told the *Financial Times* in February 2012: 'The whole concept of getting around European rules and doing QE without calling it QE was extremely clever.'[39]

Six months later, Draghi famously announced to an audience in the City: 'Within our mandate, the ECB will do whatever it takes to preserve the euro.' After boasting of the superiority of the eurozone's economic performance to that of the US and Japan (the latter held less 'socially cohesive' than the Union, where half the youth of Italy, Spain and Greece were unemployed), he ended by making clear what was ultimately at stake

39 *Financial Times*, 8 February 2012.

in the crisis. No one should 'underestimate the amount of political capital that is being vested in the euro'.[40] It was to safeguard this that the *extrema ratio regis* of the hour was required: 'targeted longer-term refinancing operations', 'outright monetary transactions', and the rest, or clever ways of getting around European rules, 'within the mandate' of the Bank—that is, in blatant breach of Articles 123 and 125 of the Treaty of Lisbon forbidding these. In due course, their legality would be challenged before the European Court of Justice. But just as it had no compunction in interpreting the Treaty of Rome to arrogate powers to itself of which no trace can be found in the document signed by the Six, so the ECJ had none in deciding that Lisbon meant the opposite of what it said. Since it was now a question, not of reading into a treaty what it did not contain, but of purging one of what it did contain, the contortions required were, in Horsley's words, 'herculean'.[41] The comedy of judges solemnly explaining that financial assistance under the European Stability Mechanism constituted an act of economic, not monetary, policy, and was therefore perfectly in order, while outright monetary transactions were an instrument of monetary, not economic, policy, and therefore were also perfectly in order, calls for the pen of a Swift. What did the 'no bailout clause' of Article 125 actually mean? That bailouts were fine, so long as they served 'the higher objective' of preserving the euro. Or in van Middelaar's gloss, to break the rules was to be true to the contract.

In Germany, successive attempts in 1974, 1986, 1993 and 2009 to contest the validity of laws or treaties of the Community before its own Constitutional Court have all yielded the same result. The judges in Karlsruhe have declared that Germany's *Grundgesetz* may not be overridden by the European Court,

---

40 Speech at the Global Investment Conference in London, 26 July 2012.
41 *The Court of Justice of the European Union as an Institutional Actor*, p. 96.

but since no such infringement has 'so far' or 'yet' occurred, the plaintiffs have no case. This year, it was called upon once more, this time to pronounce on the legality of the blessing the ECJ had given the ECB's bond-purchasing programme. Once again it declined to say this was illegal, while observing that the proportionality of its effects had not been adequately appraised, and instructing the German government and the Bundesbank to conduct such an appraisal and ensure appropriate proportionality. There was uproar in the Euromedia. The *Financial Times* was apoplectic. 'The German Court throws a grenade under Brussels' legal order', cried Martin Sandbu. The Court had 'launched a legal missile at the heart of the EU. Its judgment is extraordinary. It is an attack on basic economics, the central bank's integrity, its independence and the legal order of the EU', thundered Martin Wolf. 'Future historians may mark this as the decisive turning-point in Europe's history towards disintegration.'[42] They need not have turned a hair. The *Bundesverfassungsgericht* is a mostly toothless body, as its studiously suspended judgments indicate. Best known for meekly overturning Germany's Basic Law to allow Schröder and Merkel in 2005 to stage an unconstitutional election before polls were due, it takes care to avoid serious offence to the *Obrigkeiten* of the day. Berlin and Frankfurt are unlikely to have much difficulty sending Karlsruhe back to sleep.

No piety is intoned so frequently by the EU, or identified so complacently with itself, as the rule of law. *Fatta la legge, trovato l'inganno* holds popular wisdom in Italy. The adage implies that those who make and those who trick the law are not the same. What distinguishes the Union is that the two are one. In the hands of the European Court and the chorus of its admirers, the rule of law has more or less come to mean the misrule of

42 *Financial Times*, 6 and 13 May 2020.

lawyers who will stop at nothing to bend texts to their pleasure, at the expense of ordinary understandings of what a principled justice should direct. So what, it may be asked, if higher needs are served—the survival of a monetary union on which rational labour markets, taxes and transfers, the prosperity of all depend? But as more than one writer has replied, are bankers and judges the most competent authorities to determine what pensions or wages should be? Certainly, in these matters they do well enough for themselves. Is that the most appropriate qualification? Fritz Scharpf's dictum stands: in the EU, it is precisely those institutions which have the greatest impact on the daily life of most people that are furthest removed from democratic accountability: the European Court of Justice, the European Central Bank, the European Commission.

VI

Less removed is the last of the Union's institutions, the European Council, since it comprises heads of government enjoying majorities in genuine parliaments, the product of meaningful elections. As such, it has become the peak authority of the Union. Van Middelaar's *Passage* is largely the story of its rise to this position, and its claim that the Council is now the principal driver of European integration is warranted. What it does not do is look beneath the hood. What kind of a vehicle has been advancing? That is the subject of the most fundamental of all works on the EU of the past decade, Christopher Bickerton's *European Integration*, whose anodyne title, shared by dozens of other books, conceals its distinction, which comes in a subtitle, *From Nation-States to Member States*, that delivers its argument. Everyone has an idea what a nation state is, and knows that twenty-eight countries are member states of the European Union. What is the conceptual difference between the two? Bickerton's definition is succinct. 'The concept of member state expresses a fundamental change in the structure of the state, with horizontal ties between national executives taking precedence over vertical ties between governments and their own societies.' This development first struck him, he explains, at the time of the Irish referendum on the Treaty of Lisbon.

> When the No was announced, members of the Irish government expressed a mixture of surprise and embarrassment: surprise as they were unfamiliar with the sentiments prevailing within their own population, and embarrassment because this compromised many of the promises they had made to their peers at previous meetings in Brussels.[43]

(The description is something of an understatement. Spotted outside a pub in Dublin that evening, Brian Lenihan, minister of finance at the time, was white around the gills).

How did the transition from nation state to member state come about? After the Second World War—Bickerton follows Alan Milward and John Ruggie—a class compromise between capital and labour was reached in Western Europe, taking the organizational form of a corporatist state committed to full employment, a range of welfare services, and a set of transfer payments. Based on steady economic growth, the ideological consensus of this period presumed a strong measure of government involvement in economic life, and delivered rising popular living standards. Yet at the same time 'a more egalitarian and redistributive social contract' than in the pre-war years 'coincided with a narrowing of the political spectrum':

---

43 Christopher Bickerton, *European Integration: From Nation-States to Member States*, Oxford 2012, pp. vi–vii.

deradicalization of the left presaging a broader depoliticization to come, and lack of political experimentation leading to dominance of centrist parties.[44] The general economic crisis of the seventies saw the unravelling of this class compromise, as growth sputtered, industrial unrest grew and Keynesian ideas gave way to Hayekian or Public Choice doctrines dismissive of any conception of a social contract. For a time, governments continued to try familiar recipes, but by the early eighties neo-liberalism had arrived, pioneered by Thatcher, followed by Mitterrand's U-turn, and the crushing of Danish, Belgian and British strikes. Liberated from the pressures of organized labour, governments converged towards deregulation and privatization to liberate markets for innovation and competition according to the prescriptions of the new period. The Single European Act of 1985 marked their transposition to the plane of the Community.

The relaunching of the dynamic of integration under Delors was thus the outcome of a pattern of domestic political change in which policy priorities had become fiscal retrenchment, wage repression and a return to financial orthodoxies of classical stamp. Achieving sustained voter assent to this course was never easy, but as processes of integration deepened, involving ever closer ministerial coordination across borders, governments could present unpopular measures as necessities flowing from the constitution of the Community. From the time of Montesquieu and Madison onwards, constitutionalism had involved the idea of a self-limitation of the political will to safeguard the liberties of the subject: a set of internal constraints—division of powers, checks and balances—to insure the nation against tyranny, whether rule by monarchs or mobs. In due course such became the standard liberal format of the nation state. With the advent of the European Community, once the Court of Justice

44 Ibid., pp. 82–3.

had succeeded in effectively, if not formally, constitutionalizing it, member states accepted a set of external constraints whose form was radically different. Bickerton writes:

> The active subject, namely the people, is not doing the binding. Rather national governments commit to limit their own powers in order to contain the political power of domestic populations. Instead of the people expressing themselves qua constituent power in this constitutional architecture, national governments seek to limit popular power by binding themselves through an external set of rules, procedures and norms. An internal working out of popular sovereignty that serves to *unite* state and society is replaced with an externalization of constraints to national power intended as a way of *separating* popular will from policy-making process.[45]

By the time the Cold War had ended in 1990, European executives had consolidated the transition to member statehood. With Maastricht and the proclamation of monetary union, the constraints this involved naturally increased, as would the convenience of these to governments seeking to impose neo-liberal ordinances of one kind or another on their citizens. In 1992–93, Giuliano Amato famously put through a 'fiscal correction'—that is, austerity package—amounting to no less than 6 per cent of the GDP of Italy in the name of the *vincolo esterno* of Union necessity. When the single currency, far from bringing the renewed growth and prosperity promised of it, plunged Italy into prolonged stagnation and regression, and the eurozone as a whole into crisis, the upshot was not to loosen the corsets of member statehood, but to tighten them still further, with a spectacular constriction of popular sovereignty in the Fiscal Compact of 2012. In this, the external restraints of the Union were for the first time written,

45 Ibid., pp. 66–7.

at German behest, into the very internal constitutions of successive member states, and their annual budgets, at the traditional heart of domestic politics, became subject to invigilation and instruction by envoys from Brussels.

Though friction is rarely absent from such visitations, the discipline they represent has for the most part come to be accepted as part of the natural order of things. 'For member states, the eurozone is not just a currency union but also a collective framework for coordinated macroeconomic policymaking to which all belong and which in multiple ways is constitutive of their identities and interests as member states.'[46] Not least in shielding them from the intrusion of potential protest, as the outcome of expert committees—ratified in ministerial conclaves, announced by heads of government, and presented to citizens at home as faits accomplis—becomes the norm. In this process, what sets the EU apart, as a political structure unlike any other, is the presumption of consensus and the protocols that follow from it, which form the working code of its being. In Brussels emissaries from the different nations confer together on questions in their specialized fields, developing a common *esprit de corps* and professional identification with the technical side of their discussions, in a system designed to exclude the unpredictability of public debate or political disagreement. The same pattern then holds higher up, as decisions are passed to the Council of Ministers in any given area, and—where required—finally up to the European Council itself, anointing the upshot with its family photographs and unanimous communiqués. The imperative of consensus is all. 'This is what explains why EU policy-making is so secretive and lacks what is elementary in political life at national level', where conflict is open and normal.[47]

46 Ibid., p. 148.
47 Ibid., p. 33.

Structurally, Bickerton judges member statehood to be a 'fragile and contradictory' social form, at once powerful in immunizing national governments from domestic social pressures, and weak in lacking any roots remotely comparable to the vertical bonds between governments and populations of the classical nation state.[48] The form of national politics to which it gives rise, often held to pit a dominant technocracy against an oppositional populism, tends rather towards a malign combination of the two, leaders such as Sarkozy mixing a populist stance on immigration with a technocratic approach to the economy, or Blair posturing as a pragmatic manager close to the feelings of ordinary people; Macron offering the latest version of the blend. The shallowness of the attachment of elites to the citizens they represent inevitably strengthens their sense of solidarity with each other in the club of Union leaders where they gather together every two months or so. But the fellowship it offers is not—so Bickerton asserts—a stable refuge. Viewed historically, member statehood is a 'hard but hollow state form.'[49]

Institutionally, however, it has been filling up. Since 2017, the European Council possesses for its bimonthly sessions a new symbol-saturated seat in Brussels—lantern in shape for the warm glow its deliberations radiate, polychrome in fittings for the diversity of peoples illuminated by them—where the twenty-eight heads of state and government, plus the presidents of the Commission and of the Council itself congregate. They in turn are flanked by the 'Eurogroup' of the finance ministers of the eurozone, meeting monthly, whose president may also attend the Council when so invited, as too the high

48 Ibid., p. 14.

49 Ibid., p. 69: the formula comes from Vincent Della Salla, 'Hollowing Out and Hardening the State: European Integration and the Italian Economy', *West European Politics* 20: 1, pp. 14–33.

representative of the (considerably less important) foreign affairs and security pillar of the Union. Though the supreme political authority of the Union, the European Council does not itself legislate: laws are lower-order matters for the tractations of the trilogues beneath it. Its business is with the big decisions of the Union: essentially, crisis management, treaty revision and foreign policy. That is, urgent economic and 'security' (viz refugee) problems; constitutional questions (the word is banned by the Treaty of Lisbon, but the thing remains); relations with other powers (and the periphery of the EU, where enlargement lingers in the Balkans). These are where the 'alarums' arise that call for the valiant 'excursions' of van Middelaar's tales of the Union. Notable examples: handling Greek delinquency; utilizing Turkish venality; riposting to rejection of the draft constitution with a recension of the same at Lisbon; punishing Russia for annexation; and Britain for desertion.

In principle, the weak link in the Council's jurisdiction of *Chefsachen* is economic, since it has no authority over the ECB, whose independence is absolute and power over the economies of the Union unrivalled. In practice, the Eurogroup provides informal liaison, a representative of the Bank attending its meetings, which are even more confidential than those of the Council itself, not least since the presence of the Bank at them, in derogation of its independence, requires a veil of discretion. By training and outlook, finance ministers tend to be like-minded—as Varoufakis discovered in his brief stint with the Eurogroup. Higher up, disagreements are more frequent in the Council. Before its meetings, participants can stake out contentious positions, while during and after them, leaks—typically garbled sound bites for media consumption—will report clashes of opinion, victors and losers in argument, to the taste of the leakers. But the proceedings themselves remain concealed from the public, and issue in decisions which are virtually always announced *nem. con.*, in keeping with common practice across the institutions of the EU.

In the case of the Council, more is at stake in such displays of unanimity than the generic *omertà* of the European political class. For the truth behind them is uncomfortably at odds with the formalities of its composition, in which all member states are technically equal, and can block decisions in conflict with what they believe to be vital national interests. The reality, of course, is that with vast disparities between countries ranging in population from 80 million to half a million, two states—Germany and France—de facto command the proceedings by reason of their size and power. Of the pair, heirs of the Treaty which de Gaulle sealed with Adenauer, Germany is now the stronger and larger economically. But though this advantage makes it *primus inter pares*, its margin of superiority, and relative weight within the eurozone as a whole, is too limited to give it the hegemony its bolder theorists claim.[50] France remains militarily stronger, and diplomatically more seasoned, in a relationship on which each depends in equal measure. Since they do not always agree, and when they do, may not always insist, this does not mean that every decision of the Council is a translation of their will. Simply, without need of any hint of a veto, no proposition that is not to their liking has any chance of passage, while any proposition behind which they unite with joint force may be inflected, but will not be resisted by the other two dozen or so states of the Council. The Treaty of Maastricht was the fruit of a pact between

---

50 For its general position in the EU, see Susan Watkins, 'The Political State of the Union', p. 15 ff. In the same sense, Majone points out that, for all its manufacturing prowess, Germany—comparatively weak in financial and digital performance—is 'hardly a leader in the services sector' that accounts for the bulk of GDP in all the advanced economies: *Rethinking the Union of Europe Post-Crisis*, pp. 262–3.

Mitterrand and Kohl; the Treaty of Lisbon, between Merkel and Sarkozy; the current Covid package, between Macron and Merkel. In each case the initiative came, unstoppably, from Berlin and Paris. In each case, details of the arrangement were adjusted to accommodate lesser states, without its direction being altered.

The only case when a major proposition on which Germany and France insisted met intransigent opposition, the Fiscal Compact of 2012 vetoed by Britain, lit up the realities of the structure of power in Europe. Without delay Berlin and Paris simply bypassed the Council with an international instrument outside the legal framework of the EU, the 'Treaty of Stability, Coordination and Governance', to which all the other member states dutifully signed up. The effect was exactly the same. Cameron was left to complain that Merkel and Hollande had not even bothered to respect appearances, stitching together this extra-Union arrangement on Union premises in Brussels. The lesson was clear: should the two European hegemons, in the unlikely event of encountering—post-Brexit—similar obduracy in a matter to which they attach importance, they can respond with a bilateral (or multilateral) international treaty making an end run round the obstacle in the same way. It is scarcely a coincidence that Jean-Claude Piris of France, the legal linchpin of the Commission for twenty years, should have ended his 2012 book *The Future of Europe* by pointing out how convenient and fruitful resort to such 'additional' treaties might be. With Britain out of the way, however, as things stand there is little call for the device. One incongruous fact alone is enough to bring home the outlook, and power, of the Franco-German duo. There have been three presidents of the European Council since the office was created in 2010. Of these, two have been Belgian—a country with just over 2 per cent of the population of the Union. Why? Because inconspicuous politicians of a weak state, handily placed between France and Germany, can be relied on not to cross the will of either, but to help out the good intentions of both.

VII

It has often been remarked that the institutional ensemble of the EU is *sui generis* as a polity, a creation more easily defined negatively than positively. It is not, obviously enough, a parliamentary democracy of any sort, lacking division between a government and an opposition, competition between parties for office, or accountability to voters. There is neither a separation between executive and legislative powers, along American lines; nor a connexion between them along British or Continental lines, in which an executive is invested by an elected legislature to which it remains responsible. Rather it is the inverse that holds: an unelected executive holds a monopoly of legislative initiative, while a judiciary, self-invested with an independence subject to no constitutional audit or control, issues decisions which are effectively unalterable, whether or not they conform to the treaties on which they are nominally based. The rule of the Union's proceedings, be they presided over by judges, bankers, bureaucrats, deputies or prime ministers, is wherever possible secrecy, and their outcome, unanimity.

In the words of Majone, its most clear-sighted liberal critic, the world which the Union inhabits is one in which 'the language of democratic politics is largely unintelligible'. Unique in modern constitutional history, he observes, 'the model is not Athens but Sparta, where the popular assembly voted yes or no to the proposals advanced by the Council of Elders but had no right to propose measures on its own account'. The political culture of Union elites resembles that of the European Restoration and its sequels, before the reforms of the franchise in the nineteenth century, 'when policy was considered a virtual monopoly of cabinets, diplomats and top bureaucrats'. The mental and institutional *habitus* of Old Regime Europe is still alive in the 'supposedly post-modern system of governance of the EU'.[51] In sum, the order of the Union is that of an oligarchy.

The historically minded can reply yes, but the Restoration brought peace to Europe that lasted for forty years, or on a looser reckoning even a century. Hasn't European integration, however undemocratic in structure, achieved the same for three-quarters of a century, after the terrible internecine wars of 1914 and 1939? In the official credo of the EU, probably no other claim is repeated so insistently, nor movements questioning the Union so frequently attacked as carriers of the bacillus of future wars. The truth, of course, is that after 1945 there was never any risk of another outbreak of hostilities between Germany and France, nor any other of the countries of Western Europe, because of the Cold War, which made the whole region an American security protectorate. NATO, not the EEC, was what laid the military conflicts of the past to rest. As Albert Hirschman once caustically put it: 'the European Community arrived a bit late in history for its widely proclaimed mission, to avert further wars between the major Western European nations'.[52] A beneficiary of the Pax Americana rather than a progenitor of it, the Union faced its first test as an actual keeper of peace in Europe after the Cold War. It failed miserably, not preventing but stoking war in the Balkans, as Germany backed Slovene secession from Yugoslavia, the starting gun for successive murderous conflicts that the EU, dragged in the wake of Kohl, proved incapable of

51 *Europe as the Would-Be World Power*, Cambridge 2012, pp. 30, 33; *Rethinking the Union of Europe Post-Crisis*, p. 189.

52 'Three Uses of Political Economy in Analyzing European Integration', in *Essays in Trespassing*, Cambridge 1981, pp. 266–84.

moderating or bringing to halt. It was once again not Brussels but Washington that finally settled the fate of the region. Even the enlargement of the Union to the former countries of the Warsaw Pact, its major historical achievement, followed in the footsteps of the US, their inclusion in NATO preceding their entry into the EU.

Human rights are another *point d'honneur* in the public relations repertoire of the Union. The Council of Europe, whose members include twenty states not part of the EU, including Russia, Turkey, Georgia and Azerbaijan, established a Convention on Human Rights and a Court to protect them back in 1953, whose provisions were essentially reproduced in the EU's Charter of Fundamental Rights in 2000, much as the EU would purloin the Council's flag as its own. As elsewhere, proclamation and observation of such rights are not the same. Ordinary police brutality is certainly less than in the United States, where prison conditions are also worse, and inmates far more numerous. But this scarcely distinguishes the EU, the same holding for Canada or countries of Western Europe that don't belong to the Union. More pointedly still, when America required European cooperation in renditions, members of the EU complied with assistance in kidnappings and supply of torture chambers on Union soil, documented and denounced by a Swiss prosecutor to the Council of Europe, without a finger being lifted by the EU to bring those responsible to book.[53] Where infractions of its Charter come from governments it dislikes, as currently in Hungary and Poland, the Union will threaten sanctions. Where they come from governments with which it wishes to keep on good terms, it will turn a blind eye, or seek to render them acceptable, even if the infractions are far more extreme—as in the long-standing military occupation and ethnic cleansing of

53 See *The New Old World*, London–New York 2009, pp. 74, 76.

Union territory in northern Cyprus; let alone in Eretz Israel, early in the history of the Community invited to consider membership of it, and more recently described by the Union's first high representative for foreign affairs as an honorary member. As for refugees, the record of European inhumanity in the Aegean and Libya speaks for itself. Migration has largely become a security question.

Solidarity, another important term in the EU lexicon, refers to two features of its self-image. The first emphasizes its Structural and Cohesion Funds, the 30 per cent of the Commission's budget dispensed to poorer countries and regions of the Union for transport, environmental and other projects. Though not always well spent, these are genuinely redistributive and have historically had a significant impact on the biggest beneficiaries of them—Spain, Greece, Portugal and Ireland. Larger is the Common Agricultural Policy, which disburses over 40 per cent of the budget and is regressive, the great bulk of the money going to the richest farmers, above all in France, though titled millionaires in Britain have collared the largest bonanzas of all. Combined, the equity effect of the two kinds of expenditure is probably neutral, possibly negative. The second sense of solidarity refers to European 'social policy', broadly defined as measures to reduce the vulnerability of wage-earners and their families, and less well-off citizens in general, to the vagaries of the market. Wolfgang Streeck has traced the evolution of these from the sixties to the present. Originally, they comprised attempts to alter capital–labour relations by promoting industrial co-determination that would give workers rights of representation on company boards, resisted by business. The Vredeling Directive giving form to these hopes was ditched after the passage of the Single European Act, and attention shifted to questions of health and safety and equal opportunity.

At the insistence of Delors, proclaiming the need for a Social Europe, the monetary union created at Maastricht was accompanied, in the thicket of adjacent and subsidiary clauses in the Treaty, by a Social Protocol promising enhancement of labour rights, from which Britain opted out. So little came of this piece of symbolism, Streeck remarks, that its later adoption by New Labour 'did nothing to prevent the rise of inequality, the decay of collective bargaining and the deterioration of employment conditions in the UK over the years that followed'. EU-wide, these became years in which businesses successfully attacked public service provision in the name of competition law, while the Court of Justice dealt successive cold blows to trade-union rights. The current European Pillar of Social Rights, announced in 2017, does not redress the trend: as a uniform set of injunctions amid huge differences between member states, it is largely a dead letter. In public and academic arenas, Streeck comments, talk of a Social Europe has faded as the EU becomes identified primarily as a vehicle of 'universal peace, human rights and civilized speech, rather than as an alternative to unbridled capitalism'. His conclusion: 'What seems clear is that the project, reaching back to the 1970s, of a supranational European Welfare State giving political definition to a "European social model" has come to an end.'[54]

VIII

What about European economic growth, in that case? While the GDP of Western Europe grew at some 2 per cent a year between 1900 and 1950, it bounded forward at 5 per cent a year from 1950 to 1973, a speed without precedent in its history. But how far

54 'Progressive Regressions: Metamorphoses of European Social Policy', *New Left Review* 118, July–August 2019, pp. 126, 135–7, 139.

was that due to integration? In those years, West Germany and Italy grew by 5.0 per cent annually, France 4.0 per cent, Belgium 3.5 per cent and the Netherlands 3.4 per cent. But outside the ECSC and EEC, Austria averaged an annual growth rate of 4.9 per cent, Spain 5.8 per cent, Portugal 5.9 per cent and Greece 6.2 per cent. Pent-up pre-war demand, state intervention and international cooperation all played a role in this. Given that the boom started a decade before the EEC, integration alone cannot explain these fast rates of growth. Its impact on the boom has never been subject to research of real accuracy. But if it existed, in these years it was small and may even have been negative.[55] In Patel's view of this period, there was 'virtually no public pressure to present a clear account of the economic achievements of the integration process.' The Community was not at this stage particularly neo-liberal, as sometimes later alleged. While competition policy may have been shaped by German ordoliberals in the sixties, their impact was still highly selective, without incidence on most of its budget, dominated by concessions to French farmers they abhorred. Structurally, European integration was 'born technocratic', as it has remained. For its citizens, the Community was what Patel terms an 'adiaphoron': that is, according to Stoic philosophy, 'a matter having no moral merit or demerit.'[56] Such was popular indifference to it that by the end of the sixties only 36 per cent of its inhabitants could correctly name all six members of the EEC.

How have the lands of today's eurozone fared since 1973? In 2000 the Lisbon Agenda of the European Council promised productivity gains of 4 per cent a year, about double the US rate.[57]

55 See Patel, *Project Europe*, pp. 84–93.

56 Ibid., pp. 101, 138, 305; a term technically covering everything between vice and virtue, used metaphorically here.

57 *Rethinking the Union of Europe Post-Crisis*, p. 5.

In reality, they increased at somewhere between 0.5 and 1 per cent a year. As for overall growth, here are the OECD figures:

Table 3.1. GDP growth in eurozone

Years	*Average GDP growth (%)*
1973–1979	2.7
1984–1994	2.5
1994–1998	2.3
1999–2003	2.1
2004–2008	1.8
2011–2019	1.2

In other words, a steady decline since 1973, even before the collapse of 2020, when in the first six months of the year, GDP fell 15.7 per cent.[58] As for the contribution of integration to the record, Barry Eichengreen and Andreas Boltho—two economists committed to the benefits of European unity—reckoned in a paper of 2008 that over the long run, from the time of the ECSC to that of monetary union (EMU), 'European incomes would have been roughly 5 per cent lower today in the absence of the EU'.[59] Hardly a momentous achievement. Nor has intra-EU trade increased greatly since the Union, the overvaluation of the euro favouring imports from the US, PRC and other countries, while diverting trade from within the EU.[60] More generally, the socio-economic and geopolitical heterogeneity of the fifteen

58 Marcus Ryner, 'An Obituary for the Third Way: The Financial Crisis and Social Democracy in Europe', *The Political Quarterly*, October–December 2019, p. 561; Eurostat, *Real GDP Growth Rate—Volume*—14/08/2020; *Eurostat, Newsrelease Euroindicators*, 31 July 2020.

59 Barry Eichengreen and Andrea Boltho, 'The Economic Impact of European Integration', Discussion Paper No. 6280, Centre for Economic Policy Research, May 2008.

60 *Europe as the Would-Be World Power*, p. 109.

members of the Union in 1996, further stretched by the arrival of another twelve over the next decade or so, made it decreasingly possible to arrive at common Pareto-efficient decisions. In practical terms, enlargement to the East rendered 'Social Europe' as conceived by Delors impossible, since the average income of the new members of the Union was only some 40 per cent of the average of the fifteen West European members. EU resources were insufficient to close the gap.[61]

The contrast between West and East has not been the only fracture in the Union. For Bolkestein on the right, the single currency was afflicted with a birth defect from the start. Its fatal weakness, he told an audience in 2012, lay in 'trying to serve two groups of countries that differed greatly in their economic culture, lands of the North that respected rules and discipline and lands of the Mediterranean that sought political solutions to economic problems. The first group—Germany, the Netherlands, Finland and others—wanted solidity; the second wanted solidarity, which means other people's money. [Laughter in the auditorium. Bolkestein does not laugh.] That could not and did not go well. Herman Van Rompuy was right to call the Euro a sleeping pill: the Mediterranean countries could enjoy artificially low interest rates, which they did abundantly, dreaming of a *dolce far niente*.'[62]

For Claus Offe on the left, it is clear that 'the Euro has rendered European democratic capitalism more capitalistic and less democratic', disembedding financial markets from states and exposing states to their vicissitudes, in a system that Offe judges no more favourably, if for opposite reasons, than Bolkestein.

61 Ibid., p. 113.
62 'De Verenigde Staten van Europa?', Speech to Congress on Control of Assets, 26 July 2012.

> The Euro under the ECB's regime over-generalizes monetary policy across widely diverging economies and their given position in the business cycle. Instead of the 'one size fits all' we are left with a situation where 'one size fits none' due to the institutional incapacity of monetary policy to respond to the specifics of countries and their situations.[63]

No sooner has he casually said this, however, than he soberly retracts it. For there is one country of which this judgment does not hold, his own. Given the huge advantages that Germany derives from the euro, 'any conceivable German government will do everything in its power to keep the common currency intact by avoiding the default of any member of the Euro club. For this currency allows the German government to live in an ideal world where pleasure is not followed by regret, meaning that an export surplus is not followed, and its continuation thus limited, by the appreciation of the currency of the country.'[64] Matters are otherwise, of course, on the receiving end of such appreciation. Invocation of an even playing field is a sham, and consensual German leadership of the EU a non-starter. The Southern and Eastern belt of states are paying the price of a misconceived currency union that cannot now be reversed. For even if 'the introduction of the Euro into a fundamentally flawed currency zone was a huge mistake, the same applies to simply undoing that mistake', since the dissolution of the eurozone would be 'equivalent to a tsunami of economic as well as political regression.'[65] Hence the 'trap' in which Europe is in—it can neither move forwards, nor move backwards.

Fritz Scharpf, to whom Offe looks for counsel, is less categorical. He concluded that, as of 2015, the ongoing EU decision

63 *Europe Entrapped*, Cambridge 2015, pp. 43, 25–6.

64 Ibid., pp. 45–6.

65 Ibid., pp. 49–50.

to rescue the single currency rather than dismantle it was creating an economically repressive and politically authoritarian euro regime that was enormously counterproductive. By forcing member states in trouble to adopt fiscal austerity and internal devaluation, reducing labour costs with beggar-my-neighbour effects of permanent downward pressure on wage incomes, social transfers and public transfers, official policy was 'utterly devoid of democratic legitimacy'.[66] In future, Scharpf argued, much of the Community's *acquis* would have to be de-constitutionalized, returning it to the ordinary conditions of legislative re-examination and revision. For the moment, no responsible politician regarded this as feasible. But if a second big shock, comparable to the impact of the global financial crisis, hit the system, European democracy would have to be rebuilt from the bottom up, restoring the necessary barriers to market interference with it at both supranational and national levels.

The last and bleakest word comes from Dani Rodrik. Might the closest historical analogy to the euro, as we know it today, be the gold standard as it existed prior to the First World War, before there was any developed welfare state or counter-cyclical policies? Yet both of these now exist and complicate the tasks before the Union. Can democracy, sovereignty and globalization be happily combined? Regrettably, an EU-wide democracy does not exist, and the reforms adopted since the crisis of 2008—banking union, stricter fiscal oversight—have made the Union more technocratic, less accountable and more distant from European electorates. What American examples show is that European elites must make a choice, opting either for political union at the cost of national sovereignty, or for

66 'After the Crash: A Multilevel European Democracy', *After the Storm*, p. 144.

national sovereignty at the cost of political union. Intermediate solutions—a little democracy at national level, a little more at EU level—won't work. The reality, Rodrik concludes, is that it may be too late to take the first path, in the hope that a European demos will ultimately emerge to correspond with a European federation. If that were so, it is hard to see how a single currency can be reconciled with multiple democratic polities. It may be better to jettison the hope that one day economic union will prove compatible with democracy as eventually reconstituted, and ask instead what degree of economic integration is compatible with democracy as currently instituted.[67]

So, if we look for silver linings in the overall performance of the EU since Maastricht, it is not easy to find them. International peace, human rights, social solidarity, economic growth: the cupboard is pretty bare. Yet defenders can point out, not completely empty. Two features of the EU that make a genuine difference to the lives of many of its citizens are plain. The first is the convenience of travel without a passport in the Schengen zone, which still excludes Bulgaria, Romania, Croatia, Cyprus and Ireland of the EU, but also includes Iceland, Norway, Liechtenstein and Switzerland from outside the EU. More generally, there is the variety of products on supermarket shelves that followed the single market, the Union interpellating its citizens as consumers rather than political subjects. Loss of low-key facilities of this kind would not pass without discomfort among those affected. Habit is a powerful force in human affairs. In this century, too, political expectations in advanced societies have declined nearly everywhere. If the Union's advertisements for itself, on which it spends a fortune

67 'The Future of European Democracy', *After the Storm*, pp. 55–65.

in euros every year, meet no more than a listless assent—a passive acquiescence, rather than active endorsement—from the populations over which it presides, that is sufficient for its purposes. Fear of the unknown is the more important integument.

4

THE BREAKAWAY

What of Britain, which has now left the Union? Convinced of the superiority of its own economy and the strength of its ties with the US, the UK showed scant interest in the Schuman Plan in 1950, and little more in the preparations for the Treaty of Rome at Messina in 1955. The future of the world, so it believed, lay with joint Anglo-American hegemony. It was not until after the shock of American desertion at Suez, the fall of Eden and the re-election in 1959 of a Conservative government under Macmillan that this stance changed. By 1960, the poor performance of the British economy compared with that of the Six who had created the EEC was plain, and strongly encouraged by the new Kennedy administration in Washington, which saw Britain as a useful bridgehead into the Community, Macmillan applied for membership in 1962. Explaining that in these conditions Britain would be little better than a Trojan horse for American domination of Europe, de Gaulle vetoed his application in January 1963.

The following year, Labour came to power in London. Before his death, Gaitskell had rallied the party to vigorous opposition to British entry into the EEC, arguing that it would mean the end of a thousand years of history as an independent nation. Wilson could not make a speedy break with this position, but by 1967 British economic decline had become so pronounced that he was able to renew an application for entry into the EEC with all-party support, in a motion carried by 487 to 26 votes in the Commons—a high watermark of enthusiasm for Europe, never attained again thereafter. No dice: six months later de Gaulle reissued his *fin de non recevoir*. It would take two changes to alter the situation. In the summer of 1969, de Gaulle was succeeded by his prime minister Georges Pompidou, who had played no role in the Resistance, making a post-war career in Rothschilds before rising through the ranks of the Gaullist administration in the sixties. A year later, Edward Heath succeeded Wilson as prime minister, heading a Conservative government in a time of decolonization. Unlike any other British prime minister of the post-war epoch, Heath was overwhelmingly oriented to Europe—where he had fought during the Second World War—rather than to America. It did not take him long to hit it off with Pompidou, a politician who in any case did not share Gaullist reservations about the United States, to which he paid an official visit in 1970.

Pressing Britain's application for entry to the Common Market as soon as he was in Downing Street, it took Heath eighteen months to negotiate terms of membership that were satisfactory to him and to Pompidou, a period probably extended by the need for Ireland and Denmark to do the same (Norway having meanwhile opted out). The arithmetic in the Commons was not unfavourable. The Tories had a nominal majority of 330 to 288 Labour, twelve Liberal Democrats and fifteen others. But while at least forty Conservative MPs were against joining the EEC, some sixty-nine Labour MPs led by Roy Jenkins were in favour of doing so. There was thus never any real risk of the government being defeated on the issue. When the decisive third reading of the Bill of Accession came in July 1972, it passed by 301 to 284 votes. Britain had finally made it into Europe. But there was a substantial catch. While still in opposition, Heath had promised that he would not take the country into the EEC without 'the full-hearted consent' of the parliament and people of Britain. That was never tested. Heath flatly rejected any question of a referendum to ascertain the popular will, though events would show there was little risk of him losing one. More fatally, the case the government made for its terms of entry to the Community systematically avoided the fact that these instituted the supremacy of European over British law—meant, in short, a derogation of national sovereignty. Neither Rippon, Douglas-Home, Howe nor Heath himself—not a single minister—candidly admitted what the documents they were urging into law meant, constitutionally. For Heath, Europe would be a substitute for empire, and that was sufficient; likewise his colleagues. As Hugo Young put it: 'The deep, existential *meaning*, for Britain, of getting into "Europe" was not considered.' No serious thought was given to the implications of accession. In his judgment, 'Ministers did not lie, but they avoided telling the full truth', leaving subsequent Conservatives to feel that 'British entry was originally approved on false, even fraudulent pretences'.[1] To get the country into the Common Market, the government opted for obfuscation rather than openness.

From the opposition benches, Wilson had been obliged to denounce the Treaty, while ensuring that Jenkins and others suffered no penalty for having ensured its passage. Restored to government in 1974, Labour went through the motions of renegotiating the terms which Heath had secured from Pompidou, then staging a referendum on the revision of them. Wilson allowed his ministers to take whatever side they preferred in the

---

1 Hugo Young, *This Blessed Plot: Britain and Europe from Churchill to Blair*, London 1998, pp. 238, 248–9.

ensuing campaign, in which Benn from Labour and Powell from the opposition—he had by then left the Tories and joined the Ulster Unionists—campaigned for a No vote. In June 1975, on a turnout of 64 per cent of the electorate, more than two-thirds of those who voted—67 per cent—approved the deal that Wilson had obtained. British membership of the Common Market looked rock solid. When Thatcher took over four years later, and promptly abolished exchange controls, releasing the City for further European deals, it strengthened. By the mid-eighties, the British economy was out-performing its counterparts on the continent, even as the long general downturn of the period cut growth rates across the world capitalist economy. In confident mood Thatcher could recover two-thirds of the UK's (disproportionately high) net contribution to the EC budget, before helping to propel the next major stage of market integration with the Single European Act of 1985 under Delors, from which she expected British financial services in particular to benefit.

It was not long before any such linear prospect was in trouble. At the Treasury, Lawson had pressed for British entry into the Community's Exchange Rate Mechanism already in 1985, and when Thatcher vetoed this, shadowed it nonetheless. By 1989 the economy—pumped up by Lawson to secure Thatcher's third electoral victory in 1987—was visibly overheating, with a record balance of payments deficit, rising inflation and higher interest rates. For her part, Thatcher, sensing the direction in which Delors was heading with his committee on monetary union, dug in her heels over demands from her colleagues that she follow the trend in Brussels and Frankfurt, which was visibly gearing up for a single currency. By the end of 1989 Lawson was gone, and within another year Thatcher followed him, toppled by Howe for her growing hostility to the Community. She was still strong enough to ensure that her favoured successor, John

Major, took over, but it soon became clear that he had no more intention than Lawson or Howe of hewing to her vision of where Europe was heading. With scarcely over a year in office behind him, Major had signed the Treaty of Maastricht, after negotiating an opt-out from the single currency. On his return to London, the government's press release crowed that the upshot of the inter-state conference was 'game, set and match' to Britain.

In the wake of this ostensible triumph, Major called an election in April 1992 and won it comfortably. Less than two months later, the Danes voted on the same package their government had brought back from Maastricht, and rejected it. The Danish revolt sparked a British one, dissident Tories and Liberal Democrats demanding a referendum on the Treaty, the *Telegraph*, *Sun* and *Spectator* backing them, and polls showing public support for one. From the wings, Thatcher had become an increasingly vocal critic of Brussels.[2] Just at this point, British membership of the ERM—which the country had entered at too high an exchange rate—collapsed, destroying the credibility of the government. Limping through successive divisions over Maastricht without ever recovering politically, Major finally got ratification through in May 1993, a couple of days after the Danes had given up resistance in a second referendum. At the Treasury, Clarke presided over a return to growth, but it was of no electoral avail. The Conservatives were comprehensively thrashed in the elections of May 1997, leaving Blair with the largest Commons majority of any government since 1945.

Dramatic though the overthrow of Major proved to be, it did not substantially alter the position of Britain in Europe. Once he was gone, however, the Euroscepticism he had just managed to keep in check on his front and back benches broke loose, electing

2 For the circumstances, see Chris Gifford, *The Making of Eurosceptic Britain*, Farnham 2014, pp. 116–19.

three Conservative leaders in succession—Hague, Duncan Smith and Howard—all sworn opponents of Maastricht, none with any hope of winning an election. In government, Blair's initial doubts about adoption of the single currency, prompted by the hostility to the euro of the Murdoch press that had helped elect him, soon faded. But Brown's firm refusal to abandon sterling, from his position of strength at the Exchequer, maintained the status quo bequeathed by Major. London could sign up to the Social Chapter that Major had side-stepped, but despite increasingly frantic pressure from Blair, the UK would respect the rest of the package negotiated at Maastricht, retaining its opt-out from the single currency. Brown was emboldened in this course by the continuing success, as it appeared, of Britain's splendid isolation from the eurozone. Here was Blair, addressing the Labour Conference at Brighton as prime minister in 1997:

> We are one of the great innovative peoples. From the Magna Carta to the first Parliament to the industrial revolution to an empire that covered the world; most of the great inventions of modern times have Britain stamped on them: the telephone; the television; the computer; penicillin; the hovercraft; radar. Change is in the blood and bones of the British—we are by our nature and tradition innovators, adventurers, pioneers. As our great poet of renewal and recovery, John Milton, put it, we are 'A nation not slow or dull, but of quick, ingenious and piercing spirit, acute to invent, subtle and sinewy to discourse, not beneath the reach of any point that human capacity can soar to.' Even today, we lead the world in design, pharmaceuticals, financial services, telecommunications. We have the world's first language. Britain today is an exciting, inspiring place to be.[3]

3 Speech to the Labour Party Conference at Brighton, 30 September 1997.

Captivated by the 'rare brilliance' of Blair's speech to the National Assembly in Paris the following year, and the 'effortless aplomb' of his handling of questions about Europe, Hugo Young saluted his leadership of the country out of the 'darkness' of the past, even if he was 'not yet ready to name the day or the hour when the old world would end'.[4] In the view of the real architect of the outcome at Maastricht, Ruud Lubbers, the pro-European British elite had been unable to represent the realities of integration to their compatriots. 'It was as if the makers did not dare to tell the truth.' Blair was braver, Young believed: it was plainly his intention to call a referendum on British entry into monetary union before the euro came into effect in January 2002. He was 'unlikely to miss his opportunity to reposition the national mind' on Europe. No alternative to it had existed for fifty years. 'But now there was a Prime Minister prepared to align the island with the natural hinterland beyond.'[5]

No such luck. Young, star-struck by Blair in 1997, was cruelly disappointed by the time he died in the autumn of 2003, when the consequences of the war on Iraq, against which he had warned, and of the rift between Blair and Brown on Europe, were already plain.[6] Blair lacked the courage to tackle the issue until he had won re-election in 2001, when he began pressing for entry to EMU. Brown, however, master of the briefs the

---

4 *This Blessed Plot*, pp. 491–5.

5 Ibid., pp. 510, 514–15.

6 See his last seven columns, in one of which he called on Blair to resign, in the expanded posthumous edition of *Supping with the Devils: Political Writing from Thatcher to Blair*, London 2004, pp. 295–322. Yet he could still describe his lost hero as 'a great tragic figure' in the penultimate paragraph of the book: 'Tony Blair had such potential. He was a strong leader, a visionary in his way, a figure surpassing all around him at home and on the continent. His rhetorical power was unsurpassed, as was the readiness of people to listen to him. He had their trust. He brought credibility back to the political art.' The rest of the book destroys these sentimental illusions.

Treasury had produced for him, dug his heels in, and when the two clashed head-on in the spring of 2003 had no difficulty prevailing. Britain was star performer in the G-8, with no reason to truckle to the wishes of others. In the autumn, Brown told the party:

> While America and Japan have been in recession—while half of Europe is still in recession, Britain with a Labour government pursuing Labour policies has achieved economic growth in every year, indeed in every quarter of every year, for the whole six and a half years of this Labour government ... Britain can be more than a bridge between Europe and America: our British values—what we say and do marrying enterprise and fairness, and about public services and the need to relieve poverty, can and should in time make Britain a model, a beacon for Europe, America and the rest of the world.[7]

Brown's relationship with Blair, as he would later report, never recovered from the rebuff he dealt him.[8] So long as he was chancellor, his own political reputation remained intact. No sooner had Brown become prime minister in 2007, however, than the wheels fell off the triumphal chariot he thought he was riding. By that summer sub-prime mortgages in the US were already in trouble, and were soon taking down with them the British banks that had plunged recklessly into the American housing market. By the autumn of 2008, the Royal Bank of Scotland—at the beginning of the year the flushest in the world, with nominal assets at £2.3 trillion, larger than British GDP—was effectively bankrupt, saved only by a last-minute government takeover. Amid the disintegration of its braggadocio, New Labour was

---

7 *The Making of Eurosceptic Britain*, pp. 135–6.
8 *My Life, Our Times*, London 2017, p. 184.

left with the worst fiscal deficit of the G-8, and horizons of acute austerity. Few were surprised that it was trounced at the polls in 2010.

II

Three years before the financial crisis, Cameron had been elected to lead the Conservatives after promising to make them a more appealing alternative to Labour, after the serial fiascos of his predecessors. Unlike them, he was not a Eurosceptic and made sure he got into office without damaging commitments of the kind that had helped sink them. But the party he led had shifted steadily further away from the positions of Heath and Howe. To the original small group of bone-dry sceptics of 1972–75 was now added those who broke with the party's leadership over Maastricht, and yet more recently those who saw nothing positive in the arrangements of Lisbon that succeeded it. All were on their guard against further concessions to Brussels, and in early 2011 forced the European Union Act through parliament, making a referendum obligatory in the event that any further treaty revision was proposed. They were fortified in their position by the strength that the UK Independence Party (UKIP) had revealed in the European elections of 2009, when it had come second with 16 per cent of the vote behind the Tories with 27.4 per cent, but ahead of Labour with 15.2 per cent.

Helping Cameron, on the other hand, were the Liberal Democrats who had taken nearly a quarter of the vote in 2010, and provided the Coalition of the two parties with enough seats for a comfortable majority of seventy-seven against all comers in the Commons. Under Nick Clegg, who promptly scuttled his party's pledge to scrap tuition fees for higher education, the Liberal Democrats were at one with the Tories in forcing harsh austerity on the country, but as a party remained unconditionally pro-European. The first test of the Coalition's mettle came when Merkel decided, shortly before the British elections, that it was essential the EU revise its treaties with a Fiscal Compact binding every government to rigid budgetary discipline, to check the danger of the Union unravelling amid tensions over the fallout of the Wall Street crisis. By November 2011, the regimes in Dublin, Lisbon, Athens, Rome and Madrid had all been toppled under the pressure of the crisis, not infrequently the demands of Berlin and Frankfurt too. In December, the European Council met in Brussels to vote on the German package to save the euro. Cameron vetoed its adoption by the EU, whereupon Merkel pushed it through as an inter-governmental treaty outside the framework of the Union, a compact sealed in early 2012, making clear how ineffectual British opposition proved in practice to be.

Undaunted, Cameron held his second election in May 2015. By now Clegg's role as a parliamentary footstool for the Tories had discredited the Lib Dems, and its vote collapsed by nearly two-thirds, giving Cameron a small but workable majority of his own in the Commons. Buoyed by victory in the Scottish referendum the previous September—when warning of the economic dangers of a break with England had yielded comfortable support for the status quo—Cameron announced a referendum on membership of the EU for the following spring, expecting that with leeway from the Union on migration, which had become a running source of complaint in domestic politics, he could carry the day without much difficulty. His insouciance was wrong. The footling concessions he secured in Europe won him no friends at home, and the timing and terms of the referendum were set, not by him or his cabinet, but by the astute and clear-sighted strategists of the European Research Group in the Commons, implacable adversaries of what the EU had become.

Once the campaign was declared open, two of his leading cabinet ministers—Michael Gove the slyest and Boris Johnson the most popular of his colleagues, neither of them close to the ERG, both actuated by career rather than conviction—declared themselves for Leave rather than Remain.

In parliamentary terms, that still gave Remain a winning hand, since Labour, the Lib Dems, the SNP, Plaid Cymru and the Greens were all theoretically with Cameron, who retained the support of 52 per cent of the Tory delegation in the Commons, or 172 MPs, together comprising a majority totalling some 73 per cent of the House.[9] Such proportions, however, were detached from the politics of the time. When Edward Miliband resigned as Labour leader after his electoral defeat in 2015, the first poll in the party's history to be decided on a simple one-person-one-vote basis, rather than by the block union and parliamentary quotas of the past, produced a landslide victory for Jeremy Corbyn, an outsider from the left. Corbyn soon made it clear he did not intend to repeat Miliband's performance in lining up with Cameron in the Scottish referendum, but would argue for British retention of EU membership on his own, independent terms, with no support for the Tory government. Nor did the parliamentary statistics reflect the balance of opinion in the country, as would shortly become clear.

After a referendum campaign of ten weeks, some 61 per cent of Tory, 37 per cent of Labour and 96 per cent of UKIP voters opted for Leave, yielding an overall majority of 52 per cent for Brexit, rising to 64 per cent in the poorest three categories of the population, C2 and DE. The only socio-economic group where a

9 See Timothy Heppel, Andrew Crines and David Jeffery, 'The United Kingdom Referendum on European Union Membership: The Voting of Conservative Parliamentarians,' *Journal of Common Market Studies* 4, 2017, pp. 770–1, 774–5. Some 43.6 per cent of Tory MPs voted Leave.

majority voted to Remain was the most affluent stratum of the population, composed of members of income categories A and B. All others preferred to Leave. If voters were divided, however, not by income but by age and education, the result looked very different. Of those aged between eighteen and twenty-four who voted, 73 per cent chose Remain; of those aged between twenty-five and thirty-four, 62 per cent; of those between the age of thirty-five and forty-four, 52 per cent—as against all those aged over forty-four voting Leave. Similarly, 57 per cent of all those with university degrees opted to Remain, 64 per cent of those with higher degrees, and 81 per cent of those still in full-time education. Geographically, in England it was in university towns alone that Remain won handsomely.

Politically, the two camps were divided by contrasting perceptions of what was at stake in the referendum. The Remainers consisted essentially of two groups, those who were moved principally by cultural and those principally by economic issues. Among the first, composed of the young and (many of) the highly educated, the driving force of their vote was overwhelmingly hostility to chauvinism—a rejection of the blind xenophobia and racism that threatened, they believed, to make Britain a suffocating prison of reaction. Among the second, to leave the EU was a threat to the living standards of all, which were bound to drop cruelly on exit. On the other side, Leavers were also divided into two groups. For the first, overwhelmingly located in the plebeian categories C2 and DE, the key issue was control over their own, and the country's, destiny, which could only be secured by departure from the EU. For the second, it was recovery of the independence that had been the basis of Britain's prowess in the past. To these more general considerations, control of immigration and borders came in second place. Close to three-quarters of Remainers thought Britain a better land than thirty years earlier; nearly three-fifths of Leavers thought it had worsened.

Behind the clash of arguments and identities in June 2016 lay two critical legacies of New Labour. The first derived from Blair's decision in 2004 to reward his East European allies for their staunch role in the Iraq war. Poland, which had taken part in the US–UK-led invasion and hosted a CIA torture-chamber, received pride of place in the reception of immigrants to the UK. Some 700,000 Poles eventually came, many more than Blair had bargained for. No other European country knew an influx of comparable size and speed so early on. By 2017, another 400,000 Romanians and Bulgarians had joined them. The Cameron government, though acutely aware of the potential danger this cumulative influx represented to Tory stability, could do nothing to halt or mitigate it. When the referendum came, UKIP under Farage and Banks pulled no punches in the nativist operation it ran independently of Cummings's 'Take Back Control', along a parallel track but at some distance from it. In the opposite camp, Remainers made hay with UKIP's histrionics.

The second legacy of New Labour, unlike the first, attracted virtually no public attention, but was probably more decisive. Had Blair pushed through accession to EMU after 2001, or even after 2005, the outcome of the referendum would have been very different. It was his failure to override Brown, and lock Britain into the single currency when the economic going was still good for the country, that handed victory to Leave. For one lesson of monetary union is crystal clear. Once a country is inside it, fear of the consequences of departure, if the issue is ever tested at the polls, trumps all else. The nearest any people came to such a decision was the Greek referendum of 2015 rejecting the Troika's terms for a bailout. That vote, however, was a simple negative: *Ochi—No!* It lacked any positive proposal, and as soon as Tsipras capitulated, resistance to the worse terms he accepted dissolved virtually overnight. The reason was the same as that which made Salvini and Le Pen ultimately back off any talk of exit from EMU. Once the single currency was in force, all popular savings were in euros. To leave monetary union when it had become an accomplished fact was to destroy their value. No party with a popular base dared risk such a prospect.

It was the complete absence of this danger which secured the victory of Leave in Britain. The masses who voted for Brexit believed they were striking a blow at Brussels and the neo-liberalism under which they had suffered for a quarter of a century. In reality, that neo-liberalism—harsher than anything on the continent—was British in origin, and could be overthrown without paying any of the instant penalties that would have been incurred if the UK had been a loyal member of EMU. As for those who voted against Brexit, their warnings of disaster were for all immediate purposes irrelevant too. In the longer run, Offe's verdict may hold good: though imposition of the single currency was a huge mistake for Europe, unwinding it could risk even greater harm to ordinary citizens than introducing it. But in 2016, such a risk was an abstraction. In their different ways, the two sides in the battle of the referendum shared the same illusion: that in the world at large, defeat for their position would mean a loss of standing of the country which was bound to be fatal to its prosperity. Neither of them paid the slightest attention to the obvious fact that (if we exclude toy-states like Liechtenstein, Monaco or Luxembourg) the two richest countries in Europe, with the most advanced welfare systems, do not belong to the EU: Switzerland and Norway. Both rejected integration with the Union in popular referendums and have flourished since doing so. The cry from both camps says enough about their common motivation: what, be reduced to the rank of the Swiss or the Norwegians! Suppressed or blurted, nostalgia for the Great Power status of Britain in bygone days united the combatants of the referendum—ignorant armies, as in Arnold's imaginary, compulsively grappling with each other in the dark.

III

The morning after the vote, Cameron announced his resignation as prime minister, and in mid-July 2016 was succeeded by Theresa May, his home secretary, also a former Remainer, if a more cautious one. Anger at the result of the referendum in the Parliamentary Labour Party (PLP) was such that—even before May was installed as premier—it voted by 172 to 40 to evict Corbyn, as leader of the party held responsible for the defeat of Remain. A second poll of members returned him with an even larger majority in September. Buoyed by her success in local elections the following spring, and enjoying a large lead in opinion surveys, May called a snap election in the summer of 2017, counting on a much enlarged majority. It did not materialize. Though she increased the Tory vote by nearly three million, raising its share of the total from just over 36 to 42 per cent—its highest level since Thatcher—and did significantly better than her predecessor in Scotland, the total number of seats she won fell; while under Corbyn, Labour increased its vote by nearly double the Tory margin, hitting 40 per cent of the total for the first time since 2001. With just 317 seats, May put together a minority dependent on the ten-strong Democratic Unionist MPs from Ulster.

May soldiered on in the hope of a Chequers deal with the Union, trading concessions to it over Northern Ireland, where opinion was overwhelmingly against a hard border with the

South, for otherwise a smooth path to withdrawal from the Union. Small chance. In the summer of 2018, Foreign Secretary Johnson resigned from the cabinet over the proposed arrangement, followed in the autumn by Brexit Minister Dominic Raab. Successive attempts to get Chequers-lite arrangements through the Commons floundered in the face of opposition from the European Research Group, which could muster up to eighty votes against them. Tory ranks looked in complete disarray. Worse, however, had overtaken Labour. As May struggled to persuade her own party to support her, the Labour right, which had always commanded a big majority in the PLP, regrouped behind the broad front for a 'People's Vote' that took shape in the spring of 2018, campaigning for a second referendum to reverse the result of the first along standard EU lines, as successfully pulled off in Denmark and Ireland. Recovering its spirits, the *Guardian* was soon baying in support. The campaign was internally divided, formal ownership of the assets of Open Britain, the original impetus behind People's Vote, resting with millionaire public relations tycoon Roland Rudd, while most of the organizational work came from Blair's former aide Alastair Campbell and other veterans of New Labour, who unlike Rudd were chary of committing the campaign to explicit cancellation of the result of the referendum, preferring the pretence of simply asking voters what they now thought. Tensions between the two wings boiled over in the autumn of 2018, when Rudd staged a swift coup dismissing the Blairite operatives from their common offices in Millbank.

Distinct from these shenanigans, but within their general *mouvance*, the youthful cadres of Momentum that once formed the shock troops of Corbynism shifted to an increasingly militant pro-Europeanism. In this change, however, a substantial gap opened between aspirations and abilities. That a passionate internationalism moved the new recruits to the idea of a second referendum was clear. But what kind of an internationalism was it? Under New Labour, foreign languages ceased in 2004 to be compulsory in schools after the age of fourteen, command of any foreign language among fourteen- to fifteen-year-olds falling to less than a quarter of the EU average. A decade later, the number of pupils taking German at GCSE level had plummeted by half, those taking French by two-fifths. At A-level, where dropout rates are very high, the number taking German had by 2019 fallen to a third of that in 1996, and Spanish—chosen by just 1.1 per cent of candidates, about two-thirds of them female—had overtaken French as the most popular language. At university level, less than one in twenty undergraduates now studies a foreign language, a decline of a fifth since 2015. Noting that the use of English online had dropped from 51 to 26.8 per cent of traffic in the decade from 2001 to 2011, the British Academy and associated institutions warned that 'monolingualism' is 'the illiteracy of the twenty-first century'.[10] Among the young, an internationalism that remains so largely sentimental yields solidarity with other anglophones, of Commonwealth or other backgrounds. But in any wider or more lasting sense, sympathies without skills lack depth and staying power. In the background, the *London Review of Books* entered the fray from February 2016 onwards, publishing some 210 pieces invoking Brexit in 114 issues of the paper, with a further fifty-five letters and 167 items in its blog.

In these conditions, under pressure from the PLP, the

10 See Richard Adams, 'GCSE Results: Fall in Numbers Taking Foreign Languages "a Cause for Concern"', *Guardian*, 20 August 2015; Branwen Jeffreys, 'Language Learning: German and French Drop by Half in UK Schools', *BBC News*, 27 February 2019; Samuel Kerr, 'The Cost of Britain's Language Problem', *New Statesman*, 31 January 2020.

Guardian, the BBC and its own youth, the Labour leadership drifted towards a generic obstructionism in the Commons, as May's base in the Conservative Party disintegrated. When she finally threw in her hand, and Johnson romped home in the contest to succeed her, quickly reaching agreement with Dublin and Brussels on the terms of a Brexit, Labour was caught off guard, and bounced overnight by the Lib Dems and SNP into accepting the Tory demand of an early election, for which it had long clamoured but now had every reason to fear. Taking full advantage of popular exasperation at the three years of political deadlock since the referendum, and simply campaigning on a relentless refrain of 'Get Brexit Done', Johnson swept to an easy victory, coming close to Thatcher's electoral score in 1979 and comfortably exceeding its majority in the Commons. Labour collapsed by nearly eight points, to a level only just ahead of its debacle in 1983. When Corbyn stood down, Starmer secured a majority in the poll of the party that followed virtually as large as Corbyn's had been, and wasted no time in purging the shadow cabinet and National Executive of holdovers of the previous regime, restoring the traditional status quo of a right-wing Labourism, indistinguishable from the good sense of a mainstream establishment.

Leaving Blair's initial fumbling over Europe well behind—in 1983 he campaigned against membership of the EU, before rallying to it in 1987—in a somersault of scarcely a year between passionate calls for a second referendum to overturn the first and resolute enforcement of submission to the pact clinching it, Starmer would show a clean pair of heels to New Labour itself. The 'EU and UK Trade and Cooperation Agreement' was bundled through the Commons on 30 December in four hours, amid a *bien-pensant* consensus that while far from desirable—since it multiplies red tape on goods and excludes the financial services at which Britain excels—it's at least better than no-deal. If the cost will still be a 4, rather than 6, per cent loss of GDP, what else could be expected, given the disparity —the EU over six times the size of the UK in output and population—in the bargaining power of the two sides?

Macroeconomic predictions extending over a period of years are rarely foolproof; deviations from them cannot be discounted in either direction. In this case, perhaps more significant than standard reactions to them is what these generally overlook. The Lisbon Treaty, copied from the draft constitution of the EU thwarted by French and Dutch voters, proclaims the commitment of the Union to a 'highly competitive market economy', if naturally 'social' one, not to speak of 'peace, security, the sustainable development of the Earth, solidarity and respect among peoples, eradication of poverty and the protection of human rights' and other such worthy objectives. Among these comes 'free and fair trade'. Why the first adjective requires the second, or how exactly it consorts with it, is left unexplained. But that the first is coaxed by the second, in much the same way that the addition of 'social' soothes 'market', is clear. The drafters' delicate sense of words does not end there. For whereas the Union 'shall establish' a highly competitive economy, it will merely 'contribute' to free trade. The reality so nicely captured in this distinction is that, like the US or the PRC, the EU is a mercantilist bloc, replete with subsidies (think only of CAP) and protections (think only of services) of many kinds, aimed at barricading outsiders from privileges afforded insiders. That its neo-liberal admirers in Britain should burn so much incense in honour of its internationalist calling is not the least irony of the hour, only underlined by the contrast between its practices and the purer free trade dispositions, proceeding to unilateral abolition of tariffs, of mid-Victorian Britain.

IV

The honeymoon enjoyed by the Johnson government was brief. Elected on 12 December 2019, it celebrated British exit from the EU on 31 January 2020. By then Covid-19 was already circulating in the country. But it was not until 23 March that the government ordered a lockdown. Criticism of its performance came from all sides, not least from newspapers such as the *Guardian* and the *Mirror*—but as organs of the Labour establishment, these could be discounted. More telling attacks came from writers once close to the Tories themselves. Three stood out as authors of far the most effective critiques of recent British developments, all with a past at the *Spectator*: Ferdinand Mount, former aide to Thatcher, whose *New Few* had appeared in 2012; Peter Oborne, whose *Triumph of the Political Class* was published four years earlier; and Geoffrey Wheatcroft, whose *Yo, Blair!* came out the same year, in 2008: the first looking at the structure of wealth that had emerged in the new century, the second at the character of the ruling elite, the third at the role played by the architect of New Labour in the decline of the traditional political order.

In this trio, Mount was in some ways a figure apart, having transferred his admiration from Thatcher to Blair by the time of the wars on Yugoslavia and Iraq, adventures that he supported. In *Mind the Gap* (2004), he could write with unalloyed admiration of 'progressive reformers' such as Mandelson, Milburn and Byers, and of late has given voice to a robust defence of the 'constitutional and administrative reforms of the Blair Years'. In a similar mood, he would greet the 'thrilling' early episodes of the Cameron–Clegg Coalition with enthusiasm. But when he came to write *The New Few* (2012), an assault on the degree to which Britain had fallen into the grip of self-seeking oligarchies of one kind or another, he made it clear that the EU was a still more extreme case of the same disease, devoting a chapter to its manifestations entitled 'Stuck in the Eurostar'. Nor did these in any way leave Britain unaffected. 'Belonging to the EU brings us under a system of law that is new to us, both in kind and degree. It is far more abundant, much less responsive to public opinion, more or less irreversible [adding: whereas English law is in no way unalterable], and within its spheres of competence, unlimited.' The Union, advancing with a vast and virtually untouchable *acquis*, and decreasing connexion to public feeling, was expanding its powers at the expense of national parliaments. The truth was 'the EU began as an oligarchy, it continues oligarchic, and the oligarchs see no reason to alter their practices or their ambitions. No previous empire I can think of, certainly not that of the Romans or the British, not even the French carried centralization quite so far'; and no project revealed its nature so starkly as the single currency. The euro was 'the oligarch project to end all oligarch projects', a design careless in its hubris and heedless of its casualties, from which countries such as Portugal, Greece and Italy would do well to exit. Though he had always supported British membership of the EU, in the hope that 'over the years the EU would gradually cast off its elitist oligarchic origins and engage with the people, I have to confess that no such casting-off or engaging has been observable to date.'[11]

That was in 2012. Since 2016, a very different note would be heard, in a series of impassioned philippics against Brexit.[12] In these, Britain is now in the grip of an unpleasant and unscrupulous regime, populated by venomous paranoids determined

11 *The New Few*, London 2012, pp. 187–200.

12 'Nigels Against the World', *London Review of Books*, 19 May 2016; 'Just Get Us Out', *London Review of Books*, 21 March 2019; 'Après Brexit', *London Review of Books*, 20 February 2020; 'Superman Falls to Earth', *London Review of Books*, 2 July 2020.

to obstruct decent relations with Europe, whose vainglorious *Duce* not only has scrapped Thatcher's commitment to the free market and deregulation, but tolerates no equals. To denounce the misgovernment of Johnson is not 'to defend the ramshackle and blatantly imperfect institutions of the EU'. But what has Europe ever had to do with our domestic problems? Virtually all the changes that have occurred in the UK since it entered Europe were locally derived, with the partial exception of immigration. Had Britain joined the eurozone, its sovereignty would have been impaired, but, since it did not, we never lost control of our destiny. Under Johnson, Luttwak's prediction that, in conditions of massive middle-class job losses, capitalism could generate a soft variant of fascism, now seemed far-sighted. There was indeed a new puzzlement at the workings of capitalism. But timely measures to help farmers, small businesses, human rights and ordinary families, and revival of our links with European institutions, were perfectly capable of resolving it. In this threnody, forgotten or repressed are the charges once laid against not only the character of the Union, but its impact on the country—here too Remainer passion obliterating the Europe of its attachment.

Oborne, unlike Mount, welcomed the referendum on Europe and voted for Brexit. But looking back in the spring of 2019, as May stepped down but before her successor was chosen, he was seized with regret. 'Part of me still feels proud of Brexit. Well done Britain for challenging remote oligarchs based in Brussels.' But thirty months of angry and bitter debate had cut him in two. It was clear that Nissan, Sony and Panasonic were shifting their investments to the Continent, and Japanese financial firms might well follow, while even Brexiteer Dyson was moving his vacuum-cleaners to Singapore. Nor was there any widespread support for Brexit in Northern Ireland or Scotland, risking the unity of Great Britain. He had changed his mind, and urged others to do so. But where, he admitted, is 'the ringing declaration of love for the European Union? We have seen the passionate beliefs of the Brexiteers. Where's your own positivity? Where's your matching passion for Remain?' To which he could only reply: 'I have none. Only a deep, gnawing worry that we are making a significant mistake: a worry that is growing by the hour. Call that negative, if you like, but precaution is negative—yet it is part of our kit for survival.' In December, Oborne announced that to stop Johnson he would have to vote Labour.[13]

Describing himself as 'a somewhat tepid or critical Remainer', one who had long viewed the notion of a United States of Europe as misguided and foredoomed, Wheatcroft attacked the referendum of 2016 a week beforehand as a demagogic distraction. Maastricht had combined two mistakes, premature enlargement of the EU to the East before it had achieved sufficient economic convergence with Western Europe, and imposition of a disastrously misjudged single currency on Southern Europe. The Union needed drastic reform if it was to survive. But Brexiteers offered none. When the referendum was lost and Cameron produced an apologia for his time in office, Wheatcroft compared it to 'Blair's gruesome memoir *A Journey*', as 'one more apology that doesn't apologize'. Cameron was refusing to admit that the referendum could never have had a good outcome, since 'by trying to appease the unappeasable, he was on a hiding to nothing: if the Europhobes had lost, they would simply have come back another time'. It was as if Cameron had told Spaniards in the summer of 1936: 'We are a sadly divided nation. Let us clear the air and bring the country together, by

13 'I Was a Strong Brexiteer. Now We Must Swallow Our Pride and Think Again', *openDemocracy*, 7 April 2019; 'Johnson Wants to Destroy the Britain I Love. I Cannot Vote Conservative', *Guardian*, 11 December 2019.

fighting a Civil War.' As for the foreign policy of those who won the referendum, the Tories, defiant of the EU and subservient to the White House, had become '*résistants* towards Brussels, but *pétainistes* towards Washington.' Johnson, aptly depicted by Mount as 'a seedy treacherous character', was both ruthlessly ambitious and totally unprincipled. For Wheatcroft, as a writer for the *Spectator* when Johnson was editor of it, 'our dealings were perfectly cordial, but then I've dealt with plenty of affable rascals in my time.'[14]

Vengeful, remorseful, critical: such was the gamut of the best one-time Tory reflections on Brexit. Striking in every case is the weakness of the case made against it. Although all three writers are well versed in matters European, in these interventions none pays any sustained attention to the institutions of the EU, or the direction they have been taking in the decades since Maastricht. Europe is scarcely even a sideshow. What matters is what has happened in Blighty. Mount's lone proviso—*if* Britain had entered the eurozone, the issue wouldn't be the same—scarcely affects the upshot. Central to these positions and their wistful retellings of the downfall of the UK is the same contradiction. Europe has been vital to the liberty and prosperity of Britain, without which it would have withered in isolation: Europe is marginal to the life of the country, which has never submitted to the Caudine Forks of Frankfurt. The reality, of course, is that the country and such patriots cannot have it both ways. If Britain has never joined the single currency or the Fiscal Compact, and in the most intense heat of the battle over the referendum, no one any longer dared—as they might have done a decade earlier—suggest that it should do so, it is pointless to imagine

14 'Europhobia: A Very British Problem', *Guardian*, 21 June 2016; 'How Europe Stumped Conservatives', *New Republic*, 12 November 2019; 'The Opportunist Triumphant', *New York Review of Books*, 11 March 2020.

the UK could ever play a significant role in the construction of a yet more integrated Union to come. Insularity is always in the eye of the other. Without benefit of any referendum, Britain had long ago locked itself out of the arena where such questions would be decided.

The antidote to anguished Remainer ruminations lay close at hand, but was all but universally ignored. The world's two leading authorities on Thomas Hobbes, the foremost modern theorist of sovereignty, are at different ends of the political spectrum: Noel Malcolm of All Souls, editor of *Leviathan* for Oxford, on the right; Richard Tuck of Harvard, author of the finest contextualizations of Hobbes's thought, on the left. Differing in outlook in so many ways, their convergence on Brexit is all the more arresting. For Malcolm, who intervened in 1991 before the Treaty of Maastricht was signed, sovereignty was being systematically confused with power by those hoping to consign it to an irrelevant past, from Heath onwards. In fact, sovereignty was a question of authority, not of power, and could be described as a set of rules for the legitimate exercise of government—in Britain, statutes passed by parliament. Such authority could not be delegated, though its exercise might for limited purposes be devolved (for example, collective defence by NATO). But it could be abolished, as British sovereignty would be if its attributes were transferred upwards to a federal Europe, reducing Westminster to a mere regional assembly.[15]

Returning to the charge four years later—Maastricht was now in force, and there was a question whether Britain should enter the Economic and Monetary Union which the EU was preparing to set up—Malcolm identified the project of Europe as the creation of just such a federal union. Could that yield

15 *Sense on Sovereignty*, Centre for Policy Studies, Autumn 1991.

any economic advantages to a state participating in it? The fate of CAP and its costs was clear: it could not. Nor would EMU be any better, acceptance of its exchange-rate rigidity spelling economic regression—either collapse of industries under competitive pressure, or mass migration of the labour force to lands with less depressed wages. It was an illusion to think the nation state was obsolete: the most successful economic models of the time were all classic nation states—the US, Japan, West Germany. What the European Union stood for was the decaffeinated ideal of a Eurocratic class, bent on extracting politics from the management of economic affairs in a fashion that was incompatible both with inevitable national divergences of situation and interest, and with popular politics of any kind. What the EU offered instead was a prospect of log-rolling by Councils of Ministers behind closed doors, elite corruption—witness the recent flight or suicide of premiers in Italy, Germany and France—and popular impotence. Such a combination was bound to boil over in outbursts of aggressive nationalism.[16]

Two decades later, Tuck broke his silence on Europe as Britain prepared to vote on Brexit. Facing the referendum of 2016, the left risked throwing away democracy, the one instrument for popular sovereignty available to it, rather than to global capitalism and managerial power. In considering the options before the country, it should never forget the lesson of the National Health Service, when Labour had been able to override all medical and sectional opposition to the nationalization without compensation of private 'charity' hospitals because it had the authority of parliament behind it, an action inconceivable in today's European Union, whose rules forbid any such expropriation. In stark contrast, the EU was an essentially technocratic construct,

16 'The Case against "Europe"', *Foreign Affairs*, March–April 1995, pp. 52–68.

designed much like central banks or constitutional courts to give immense power to select bodies whose prejudices were inevitably those of the class from which they were recruited. Varoufakis was proposing vast institutional changes to the EU, which were nowhere on the agenda, while Labour risked quietus because of its decline in Scotland, whose independence could only be halted if Brexit prevailed. Rapidly rising immigration was a symptom of a more general loss of power by the masses, and could only be controlled by its recovery. The left was in disarray, if not despair, believing that Britain was a country of such ingrained conservatism that the EU could be a safeguard against that native tendency, despite its lack of democracy and bias for capitalism. Belief that it was too late to change any of this was a rationalization of defeat in advance.[17]

A year later, in the wake of an unexpected victory in the referendum, Tuck adopted a more theoretical position. In the eighteenth century, theorists—most conspicuously, Rousseau—established a critical distinction between government and sovereignty. The former could be exercised by a small group of people, whereas the latter was inherently a prerogative of the people. The identification of the two still to be found in Bodin and Hobbes was indefensible. Today the European Union was not a super-state, but a set of states which had enacted a constitutional order between themselves that cannot be amended in the same way that it was introduced, by any conventional—that is to say, governmental—legislation. Only a process, subject to veto, issuing *per impossibile* in inter-governmental unanimity can alter this constitutional structure. As such, the idea of an unamendable constitution was new in Europe, even if the German *Grundgesetz* comes closest to it. The British left would do well to reflect that even Sanders's three basic

17 'The Left Case for Brexit', *Dissent*, 6 June 2016.

demands—reject or modify NAFTA and the TPP; raise taxes on Wall Street; free university tuition—would be out of reach if the country were still in the EU. Correctly, from its own point of view, the Labour right had always supported membership of the Community as a prophylactic against proposals of this kind. Were the Labour left to be tempted to join with it in blocking May's attempts to implement the referendum, the result would only be the restoration of a Blairite or Macronesque neo-liberal regime in Britain. Brexit was the greatest prize for Labour in two generations, among other things making Scottish independence less, not more, likely. The left should not let go of it.[18]

Finally, joining forces with Christopher Bickerton, Tuck warned against any reversal or suspension of Brexit as hardening the pathological divisions in British society and convincing millions that democracy in the UK was a sham. Having been told there was nothing they could do about immigration because of the EU, the masses had demonstrated they no longer wanted to play a secondary role, but to become sovereign once again and put government back where it belonged—not a quixotic or esoteric point to take. The old left was in irreversible decline in Europe, and neither Syriza nor Podemos could revive it, since the EU did not represent an attack on the old nation states of Europe in the name of a new one, but an assault by capitalism on politics as such. The European treaties radically diminished the power of national legislatures, while expanding the power of national executives. The British were not used to this kind of arrangement, as the only people whose legislature was the sole source of authority in the country. The left viewed the Constitution and Supreme Court in America as formidable barriers to political democracy, without realizing that the EU was far worse in this respect—a judgment of the ECJ being for all practical

18 'Brexit: A Prize in Reach for the Left', *Policy Exchange*, 7 July 2017.

purposes unalterable. The 52 per cent who voted for Brexit still lacked any common identity or coherent will, as the British political class intended they should. But they ought not to be intimidated by threats of violence in Northern Ireland or job losses in England if Brexit was ratified. The first had raged after Britain joined the Common Market, the second had jumped after 9/11. What was holding Brexit back was something else—the lack of a political vision capable of giving effect to popular longings to regain control of society.[19]

To proceed from Mount, Oborne and Wheatcroft to Malcolm and Tuck is to move from surface to substance—from emotional reaction to critical reflection on the gulf that had opened up between Britain and the EU by 2016. But addressing essentially the same audience, the two sets of responses share a negative premise that is unspoken. Which is? Essentially, avoidance of any direct comparison between the political structures of Westminster and the complex of institutions centred in Brussels, with its flanks in Luxembourg and Frankfurt, as two patently different systems of representation. Neither, it should go without saying, is remotely matter for idealization: the vices of each are without number. But that a stark contrast between them exists is plain. It can be put most simply like this. In design, Westminister is a pre-modern construction that has survived long past its due date, while Brussels is a post-modern fabrication that is determined to outlive every alternative to it.

Much of the anger aroused by Brexit in once-Tory circles that have broken with the party comes from an acute sense of the anachronism of leading advocates of departure, the ostentatious old-fogeyism of Rees-Mogg, Bone, Baker and others, defenders of the indefensible in the age of climate change, crowd

19 'A Brexit Proposal', *The Current Moment*, 20 November 2017; republished in Cambridge, 17 August 2018.

sourcing and correct speech. What is the order they uphold? A first-past-the-post electoral system dating back to the sixteenth century, before most constituencies were even contested, which regularly produces results that bear no resemblance to divisions of opinion in the country; an unelected upper chamber crammed with flunkies and friends of the two dominant parties; an honours system devised to reward bagmen and sycophants; a parliament with so little sense of fixed terms that it can be bundled into a poll at a day's notice; a judiciary capable of covering any administrative enormity. Little wonder its admirers quote Latin statutes from the time of Richard II or Henry VIII in praise of its workings.

Yet through all this, the fact remains that British governments can only survive if they enjoy a majority in the Commons—which can be eroded by dissension within a party, as in 1940, or defection of an ally, as in 1979, or sheer attrition at by-elections, as in 1996—and if they fall, new elections to replace them must ensue. In the EU, by contrast, executives are appointed by governments, not put into office by the votes of citizens; legislative elections yield neither a government nor an opposition; proceedings at every institutional level of the Union, including its judicial and financial arms, are shrouded in secrecy; decisions of the supreme court are immutable. In post-modern style, all this is presented as the last word in an up-to-date polity: in practice, it is the simulacrum of a sentient democracy. It may grate that, for all its woeful shortcomings—think only, beyond England, of the place of Scotland or Northern Ireland in the composite realm—Westminster is vastly superior to this lacquered synarchy. The difference can be regarded as a historical fluke. But it is the indisputable bedrock of the quarrel between London and Brussels.

V

The European Union, as it has come to take shape and looks to the future, speaks continuously of democracy and the rule of law, even as it negates them. No ill intention need be ascribed it. What it has become was inscribed in what it was intended to be, in the minds of those who took possession of the project: a unification of the continent from above, by stealth where possible, by diktat where necessary. Europe was ultimately too large and too various for the results to be otherwise. With a population of now some 446 million, the third largest of any polity on the planet, divided by some twenty-six official languages —another eight or so lie waiting in the Balkans (with a further 17.5 million people)—the EU is more linguistically and culturally divided than India (twenty-two official languages) or China (one official language), each vastly bigger in population. Of the twenty-seven countries comprising the Union, none has a continuous parliamentary history comparable to the record in England, which with the exception of the eleven years of Charles I's personal rule avoided the absolutism that snuffed out representative assemblies across most of the continent from the sixteenth century onwards. Quite a few of them, indeed, date their modern experience of constitutional politics no further back than a quarter of a century. In these conditions, the extension of internally representative political systems into a quasi-confederation of continental dimensions was virtually bound to produce a structure of power fundamentally oligarchic in nature, whose only *lingua franca* is that of the country that has abandoned it. 'The most hopeful sustained trend in Europe today', writes a commentator on the left of the political spectrum, 'is the rapid spread of English among the younger generation', which promises a wider 'linguistic justice' to come.[20] That there is nothing specific to Europe about such second-order anglicization, in a continent where half the population knows only its own native language, is no objection for the champions of a global transnational democracy in which nostalgic attachments to national linguistic diversity wither away.

For the foreseeable future, however, the layer of the population that is fluent in either two or three of the official languages of the EU, or—perhaps more relevantly—commands just the oncoming lingua franca of one, is necessarily restricted, probably comprising not more—perhaps less—than a tenth of the total population of the Union. Those from the EU actually living and working outside their country of birth in the Union form a number smaller still—less than 4 per cent of the total population of the Union in 2015, of whom the large majority were manual labourers of one kind or another; in 2008, less than 2 per cent of the population of Western Europe.[21] Such expatriates, however, include what can be described as the European political class *stricto sensu*, composed of executives and professionals from the centre-right-to-centre-left continuum of parties comfortable in the institutions of the EU and accustomed to running its affairs. It would be a mistake either to demonize or to idealize this stratum.

That its top ranks have long been corrupted by immunity in their exercise of power is plain. It is enough to notice the roll call of leading ornaments of this body of persons. Christine Lagarde, current president of the European Central Bank: suspect of complicity in fraud and malversation of public funds

---

20 Philippe Van Parijs, 'Justifying Europe', *After the Storm*, p. 260; *Linguistic Justice for Europe and for the World*, Oxford 2011, passim.

21 See Adrian Favell, *Eurostars and Eurocities: Free Movement and Mobility in an Integrating Europe*, Oxford 2008, p. x.

in covering for the crook Bernard Tapie, improperly paid €404 million by Crédit Lyonnais under Chirac in 2008, when she was minister of economy in France; in due course, discharged by the state in 2016 for mere 'negligence' with no penalty in view of her 'personality' and 'international reputation' as by that time head of the International Monetary Fund—where her predecessor Dominique Strauss-Kahn had had to resign on charges of sexual assault and attempted rape, and his predecessor Rodrigo Rato had been imprisoned on charges of embezzlement. Ursula von der Leyen, current president of the European Commission: charged in 2015 with plagiarism of 43 per cent in her doctorate of 1990—some pages over 70 per cent. The university commission that absolved her of no more than 20 per cent errors, headed by an old acquaintance from the alumni association at the institution, was heavily criticized in the media, but after the fall of two previous ministers in Merkel's government, zu Guttenberg and Schavan on charges of plagiarism, exhaustion had set in and she was allowed to keep her doctorate.

Von der Leyen's predecessor, Jean-Claude Juncker of Luxembourg: survived repeated exposure of his involvement in the tax evasion and money-laundering for which his country is famous. Her vice-president and high representative for foreign and security affairs, the Spaniard Josep Borrell: forced this year to resign as president of the European University in Florence for concealing the annual salary of €300,000 he had been receiving since 2010 from a Spanish energy company. Michel Barnier, EU commissioner in charge of negotiations with Britain over Brexit: showered with 'donations' amounting to over 300,000 francs—more than seven times the total received by his seven rivals—when running as a Gaullist candidate for the Haute-Savoie in the legislative elections of 1993, before these were ruled illegal and he redirected his political ambitions from

France to Brussels. Olaf Scholz: finance minister and vice-chancellor of Germany, hoping to succeed Merkel this year: caught in the headlights of the media after appointing—a first in the BRD—the co-CEO of Goldman Sachs in Germany and Austria, Jörg Kukies, as his deputy for Financial Market and European Policy, only to have to admit that he knew Kukies had been on intimate terms with Marcus Braun, fraudster-boss of the now bankrupt Wirecard company (assets once valued at $25 billion) in the largest financial scandal in the history of post-war Germany. Scholz's chances of surviving parliamentary investigation intact: slim.

Tawdry episodes of this kind, routine at the top levels of the EU establishment, should not be generalized to the whole European political class, in many strata of which they would be eschewed or redundant, let alone to expatriates living abroad without official positions.[22] What unites this force is not so much the prebends its representatives extract from office as the interests and passions invested by it in the European project as such. In the UK, the mass demonstrations and media outcry over Brexit—in scale more impressive than any counterpart on the continent, not out of a greater depth of conviction but simple proximity of danger—are a good gauge of the degree of commitment of the same layer to the development of a united

22 For the best sociological study of the latter, based on a sample working in Amsterdam, Brussels and London, see Favell's sympathetic but clear-eyed study which concludes: 'Those who have really turned European mobility into a design for life are the exception', in part because 'the high tide of liberalism in the 1990s that swept a whole generation of free movers around Europe, in search of new opportunities and experiences against a European backdrop, has subsided'; but also because 'as soon as intra-EU mobility passes some threshold—which may be 5 per cent or lower—the value associated with being a pioneer drops sharply. If it's no longer original, and people are crowding in as foreigners to the international cities, then host societies are very quickly going to react against it', making expatriate projects 'a rather lonely path to take': *Eurostars and Eurocities*, pp. 221, 229–30.

Europe. Identification with the cause of the Union need involve no immediate material stake in it, even if in the case, say, of university lecturers, employers may be dependent on Brussels for funding of one kind of research or another. Where Europe is concerned, there is rarely a contradiction between—sufficiently mediate—self-interest and genuine idealism.

Of necessity, the premise of both is the passivity of the population below the line of the political class and its adherents. Has the course of events since the global financial crisis of 2008 seriously shaken this? With the exception of Britain, it would be difficult to hold that in any sustained or consequential way it has. Of the populist revolts in Southern Europe, Syriza—a fully establishment party once Tsipras signed on to the conditions of the Troika—gained less than a quarter of the vote in the European elections of 2019, before being routed at the polls in Greece shortly afterwards. In Italy, the Five Star Movement scored just 17 per cent in the European elections, before joining its hitherto execrated adversary the Democrats in a coalition regime in Rome. In Spain, Podemos took 10 per cent in the European polls, before joining the Socialist Party in an unsteady minority government in Madrid. Of the populist revolts on the right, Marine Le Pen's re-named Rassemblement National achieved less than one-quarter of the vote in France, Salvini's Lega just over one-third in Italy. To the East, the parties led by Kaczyński and Orbán are still in a class by themselves, capturing respectively 43 and 53 per cent of participants in the European elections, before each lost the mayoralty of their capital city to mainstream liberal opponents; Law and Justice also falling short of a majority in parliament, though it narrowly retained the presidency.

Viewed soberly: nowhere do prospects look particularly favourable to populist forces in Europe. Where they remain outsiders in the political system, the risk they represent to it tends to strengthen the status quo. Where they enter the political system, as either supports or partners of the establishment, they tend to lose their identity at European level and become assimilated to the dominant consensus. The fears on which they play, while often radical in form, easily become conservative in effect where issues of identity or immigration arise. Overarching them is the reality that the centrist bloc of opinion encompassing moderate conservatives, temperate liberals, cautious social-democrats and self-satisfied greens—acronymically in Brussels, the EPP, RE, S&D, and Greens/EFA—is much larger than its opponents on right or left, and remains overwhelmingly dominant in the Union. In the spread-eagled, distended space of Europe, control of the media landscape and ample funding from the Commission make this force as fully capable, in Michael Mann's terms, of outflanking symptoms of disgruntlement from below as its homologues in India, China or America. It would take another, altogether more seismic 2008 to shake these political coordinates apart.

VI

Are we now living through something like this? Not according to today's Gentz. Van Middelaar has consistently taken a dual view of the post-war history of Europe. On the one hand, each step forward has been the product of forces external to the Community and its successor. From the Schuman Plan to the victories of Lecourt, integration was preceded and accompanied by the attentions, and often initiatives, of the United States. So too when Giscard founded the European Council, the impulse came from the breakdown of Bretton Woods and the diminution of American interest in the Old World during the seventies. Maastricht and the arrival of monetary union came as a reaction to the collapse of Soviet control of Eastern Europe and the reunification of Germany. The global financial crisis of 2008 triggered the Fiscal Compact and European Stability Mechanism. The Covid-19 pandemic of 2020 has forced through a Next Generation Europe package of €750 billion, to be raised by the Commission borrowing on the strength of mutualized bonds, hitherto forbidden by Northern members of the Union and hailed as a breakthrough by van Middelaar.[23] At maturities extending beyond 2028, over half of this—€390 billion—is to be distributed as grants rather than loans to member states in need. Given the scale of the likely economic contraction in the eurozone—some 7 per cent of its GDP in 2020 or in the region of €1.3 trillion—the support package is modest enough. Under pressure it can no doubt be increased. Plain, however, is that once again the momentum behind 'ever closer union' is not self-generated, but exogenous.

Does this matter? For both admirers and adversaries of the direction of Union politics since Maastricht, the answer appears essentially negative. In surveying the ongoing scene, it is striking that such disparate figures as the complaisant van Middelaar and critical Bickerton, the sceptical Majone and starry-eyed Fabbrini, converge in description and overlap in prescription.[24] For this spectrum of writers, power has tended to pass from the

23 Merkel 'broke the last two taboos of German monetary thinking: collective debt and outright grants. For just this once. But in Paris and Berlin they know that whoever crosses this bridge once can do it more often: the precedent is set.' For van Middelaar, in the pandemic the currency union has gained the strength which it failed to acquire in the euro crisis of 2012: 'Hoe de vorige crisis doorwerkt in het nu', *NRC Handelsblad*, 21 August 2020.

24 See, respectively, van Middelaar, ibid.; Bickerton et al., 'The New Intergovernmentalism: European Integration in the Post-Maastricht Era', *Journal of Common Market Studies* 4, 2015, pp. 703–22; Majone, 'The European Union Post-Brexit: Static or Dynamic Integration?', *European Law Journal*, August 2017, pp. 9–27; Sergio Fabbrini, *Europe's Future*, Cambridge 2020.

supranational instances of the Union that nourished dreams of federalism to more inter-governmental instances, concentrated at the top in the European Council, where member states have proved perfectly capable of defending their national interests when conflict arises, and will go on doing so; and relayed below in versions of informal coordination and pursuit of consensus in areas such as diplomacy, security or migration.

Common to this range of opinion is rejection of any idea that the future of the Union lies in a federalist super-state, accompanied by belief in a powerful forward motion nevertheless still at work in the EU. The Covid-19 relief package is not a prodrome of the United States of Europe to which Kohl looked forward on the morrow of Maastricht. Nor has it resolved the tensions and incongruities of the Union, which for Majone require its conversion into a true confederation along Swiss lines, if limited to foreign and security policy. For Fabbrini the solution lies in the division of the EU into a single economic community covering the whole of continental Europe and a separate political union (not a state) of federal character, grouping only those countries prepared to accept a common currency, fiscal authority, budgetary policy, security and military system, border control and immigration policy, if retaining domestic versions of some of these attributes. Majone admits his proposal is not currently feasible, while Fabbrini puts his hopes—shades of van Middelaar—in a 'coup', along the lines of the American founders, to bring his own into being. Bickerton, by contrast, simply registers the paradox of further integration without significant supranational advance, while van Middelaar concedes that Macron's announcement of France's return to planning, followed by Germany, sets the course for a new European dirigisme to which even the Netherlands will have to adapt.

What these differing prospects—each is convinced that the ideas of Monnet and Hallstein, Delors or Kohl, are dead—overlook is the cumulative direction and impact of successive advances towards closer union, which are not in any simple way under the control of the powers steering the European Council. From the beginning there have always been significant forces, entrenched in the Commission and the Court of Justice, latterly in the Central Bank and the Parliament, with another agenda, committed to federal union of the continent. They have never achieved their goal. But nor, since the defeat of the European Defence Community in 1954, has incremental progress towards it ever been either stopped or reversed. Is it credible that it has now reached its uttermost limit?

It does not take a great deal of imagination to wonder how faithful van Middelaar and others who have generally agreed with him—Ankersmit might be a case in point—would remain to their traditional preferences if geopolitical conditions change. In 2018, observing the way the United States and China were each wrenching themselves apart from the world order that took shape after the Cold War ended, van Middelaar asked himself what place Europe might occupy in the ensuing disorder. His answer was quite modest. 'The EU is an experiment in multilateralism on a continental scale', he wrote, 'born to break power politics, but not to make power politics.'[25] In that faint note of strategic resignation, might there lie the germ of some structural flexibility to come, as steps towards yet closer union inch forward, to meet mounting challenges from the superpowers of America and Asia? Or is the current formula of the Union—dilute sovereignty

25 'Europa moet puzzelen om te overleven', *NRC Handelsblad*, 28 December 2018.

without meaningful democracy, compulsory unanimity without participant equality, cult of free markets without care of free trade—likely all the same to last indefinitely?

INDEX OF NAMES

INDEX OF AUTHORITIES